£30-00

D0585716

NEW CAMBRIDGE SHAKESPEARE
STUDIES AND SUPPLEMENTARY TEXTS
General editor: Philip Brockbank

Shakespeare and *Sir Thomas More*
Essays on the play and its Shakespearian interest

The play of *Sir Thomas More* has come down to us on twenty-two leaves of manuscript, including a vellum wrapper inscribed 'The Booke of Sir Thomas Moore'. Seven hands have been identified (including that of Henry Tilney, whose comments are made as Master of Revels, concerned with censorship and conditions of licensing) and there are six additions to the original text. A degree of consensus has attributed the first form of the text to Anthony Munday and Henry Chettle and to the years 1593–4; but some have proposed other initiating authors, and other dates from 1586 to 1603. Attention has focused most closely on the possibility, first aired by Percy Simpson, that the three leaves of Addition IIC in Hand D (148 lines) are Shakespeare's autograph composition.

In 1923 A.W. Pollard edited a collection of essays whose main effect was, through a study of palaeographical evidence, to strengthen the Shakespearian claims to Hand D. The present volume grew out of a seminar held during the April 1983 meeting of the Shakespeare Association of America at Ashland, Oregon. While most of the contributions originated on that occasion, there were appropriate additions to this new book on *Sir Thomas More* over the next three years, including fresh commissions and further research. The range of topics is much wider than that of the 1923 collection, taking in the problems presented by the play as a whole, considering its authorship and revision, structure, occasion and staging.

The book provides the most comprehensive examination to date of the problems of the manuscript, drawing on fresh bibliographical and textual analyses. Some scepticism and dissent persist, but the terms of controversy are realigned and the stature of the play re-established, making it appear more than ever likely that Shakespeare contributed to its revision.

NEW CAMBRIDGE SHAKESPEARE
STUDIES AND SUPPLEMENTARY TEXTS
General editor: Philip Brockbank

Titles in this series

Peter W. M. Blayney, *The Texts of 'King Lear' and their Origins*
Volume 1: *Nicholas Okes and the First Quarto*
Eliot Slater, *The Problem of 'The Reign of King Edward III': A Statistical Approach*

Shakespeare and *Sir Thomas More*

Essays on the play and its Shakespearian interest

Edited by
T. H. HOWARD-HILL
University of South Carolina

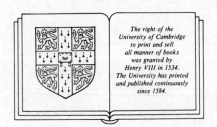

The right of the
University of Cambridge
to print and sell
all manner of books
was granted by
Henry VIII in 1534.
The University has printed
and published continuously
since 1584.

CAMBRIDGE UNIVERSITY PRESS
CAMBRIDGE
NEW YORK   NEW ROCHELLE   MELBOURNE   SYDNEY

Published by the Press Syndicate of the University of Cambridge
The Pitt Building, Trumpington Street, Cambridge CB2 1RP
32 East 57th Street, New York, NY 10022, USA
10 Stamford Road, Oakleigh, Melbourne 3166, Australia

First published 1989

Printed in Great Britain at the University Press, Cambridge

British Library cataloguing in publication data

Shakespeare and Sir Thomas More: essays on the play and its Shakespearian interest. –
(The New Cambidge Shakespeare studies are supplementary texts).
1. Drama in English. Sir Thomas More – Critical studies
1. Howard-Hill, T.H. (Trevor Howard)
822′.3

Library of Congress cataloguing in publication data

Shakespeare and Sir Thomas More: essays on the play and its Shakespearian interest / edited by
T.H. Howard-Hill.
p.   cm – (New Cambridge Shakespeare studies and supplementary texts)
Includes index.
Contents: 1. 'Voice and Credyt'/G. Harold Metz – 2. The occasion of the Book of Sir Thomas
More/William B. Long – 3. The Book of Sir Thomas More/Scott McMillin – 4. The Book of
Sir Thomas More/Giorgio Melchiori – 5. The date and auspices of the additions to Sir Thomas
More/Gary Taylor – 6. Henry Chettle and the original text of Sir Thomas More/John Jowett –
7. Webster or Shakespeare?/Charles R. Forker – 8. Sir Thomas More and the Shakespeare
Canon/John W. Velz.
ISBN 0-521-34658-4
1. Sir Thomas More (Drama) 2. More, Thomas, Sir, Saint,
1478–1535, in fiction, drama, poetry, etc.   1. Howard-Hill, T. H. (Trevor Howard)   11. Series.
PR2868.A2H6 1989
822.′.3 – dc 19   88–29927   CIP

ISBN 0 521 34658 4

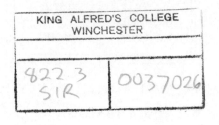

Contents

Preface

For many years so much of the general interest in *The Book of Sir Thomas More* centred on the possibility that the manuscript preserved a passage in Shakespeare's handwriting that its value as evidence of the practices of the Elizabethan theatre was, to an extent, neglected. It is true that no-one can address the authorship question of Addition IIc without first coming to a pretty sound understanding of the characteristics of the manuscript of which it is part, but there has been a certain tendency in the work of some scholars to accommodate the play's date and auspices to what they conceived to be the fact of Shakespeare's authorship of a part of the play. The passage of sixty years after the publication of *Shakespeare's Hand in 'The Play of Sir Thomas More'*; *Papers by Alfred W. Pollard, W.W. Greg, E. Maunde Thompson, J. Dover Wilson & R.W. Chambers* (Cambridge, 1923), which aimed 'to strengthen the evidence of the existence ... of three pages written by Shakespeare in his own hand as part of the play' (Pollard's 'Preface'), and a small flow of scholarly articles on different problems of the *More* manuscript suggested that it would be valuable to discover what consensus could be reached by modern scholars knowledgeable in the theatrical history of the last years of Elizabethan reign and in other areas of expertise impinging on the play's study. Consequently, the Shakespeare Association of America agreed to my proposal to discuss the *More* manuscript and its problems at a textual seminar during its annual meeting at Ashland, Oregon, in April, 1983.

Invigorated by the success of their discussions, some members of the seminar decided to gather together a collection of essays which, using the 1923 Pollard volume as a starting-point, would represent the best judgements of modern scholars writing with the benefit of more recent investigations of the manuscript. Contributors were charged to pursue their investigations as their own judgements commended but they were not required to cut their cloth to a common pattern. Most of the present essays originated in the seminar, but all were substantially revised in the light of conclusions reached there and research on the manuscript continued in the ensuing three years, notably by Giorgio Melchiori. Other essays were commissioned to attend to features of the play not examined earlier; this accounts for the difference between the dates of the seminar and publication of these essays.

Unless specifically noted to the contrary, quotations of the manuscript are from W. W. Greg's *The Book of Sir Thomas More* (Malone Society Reprints, 1911; repr. with a supplement by Harold Jenkins, 1961), corrected from an independent examination of the manuscript by Peter W.M. Blayney. I have distinguished the lines after the first lacuna by an asterisk, and those after the second by an obelus. Occasionally, the old spelling title of the manuscript is used when it is desirable to distinguish the manuscript from the play it contains. Following Greg, scene numbers are cited in roman minuscules, the Additions in roman capitals. However, the conventional designations of recto and verso sides of leaves have replaced Greg's 'a' and 'b'. Because I have checked all quotations of the text of *More* against my annotated copy of Greg, misprints there should be laid to my charge. Quotations preserve manuscript deletions and the like only where the deletions are significant for the argument, and for ease of printing I have lowered suspensions silently, expanded brevigraphs with italics, and omitted the carets which indicate uncertain readings in Greg's edition. The line numbering is also that of the MSR edition. Also, I should draw attention to G. Harold Metz's annotated bibliogaphy of *More* scholarship in his *Four Plays Ascribed to Shakespeare* (New York, 1982) which, together with his fresh survey of scholarshiip printed in this volume, supplies the place of a bibliography.

Finally, I am most pleased to acknowledge, besides the happy co-operation of the contributors, the indispensable labours of my graduate assistant, Carmen Rivera, who supervised the preparation of the text by computer, and much else. I and the collaborators in this volume are greatly indebted to the Press's reader; his detailed comments have been most beneficial.

Abbreviations

Add./s.	Addition/s
Bald	R.C. Bald, '*The Booke of Sir Thomas Moore* and its problems', *Shakespeare Survey*, 2 (1949), 44–65
Chillington	Carol Chillington, 'Playwrights at work; Henslowe's, not Shakespeare's, *Book of Sir Thomas More*', ELR, 10 (1980), 439–79
EETS	*Early English Text Society*
ELN	*English Language Notes*
ELR	*English Literary Renaissance*
fol./s.	folio/s
Greg	W.W. Greg, ed. *The Book of Sir Thomas More*. Malone Society Reprints (Oxford, 1911). Repr. with 'Supplement to the Introduction' by Harold Jenkins, 1961
JEGP	*Journal of English and Germanic Philology*
MLN	*Modern Language Notes*
MLQ	*Modern Language Quarterly*
MLR	*Modern Language Review*
MP	*Modern Philology*
MSR	Malone Society Reprints
NQ	*Notes and Queries*
PBSA	*Papers of the Bibliographical Society of America*
PMLA	*Publications of the Modern Language Association of America*
RES	*Review of English Studies*
SB	*Studies in Bibliography*
Shakespeare's Hand	*Shakespeare's Hand in the Play of Sir Thomas More*, ed. by A.W. Pollard (Cambridge, 1923)
ShS	*Shakespeare Survey*
SJW	*Jahrbuch der deutschen Shakespeare-Gesellschaft West* (Heidelberg)
SNL	*Shakespeare Newsletter*
SP	*Studies in Philology*
SQ	*Shakespeare Quarterly*
SStud	*Shakespeare Studies*
TLS	*The Times Literary Supplement*

Introduction

T. H. HOWARD-HILL

The collection of essays on *Shakespeare's Hand in the Play of Sir Thomas More* edited by A.W. Pollard in 1923 and W.W. Greg's Malone Society edition of 1911 provide the essential points of focus for all subsequent work on *The Book of Sir Thomas More* (B.L. Harleian MS 7368), particularly the present collection which takes the 1923 volume as its model. Nevertheless, the large extent of work since undertaken on the play and the Elizabethan theatre ensures the significant difference of the two collections. Modern scholarship can draw upon Greg's *Dramatic Documents of the Elizabethan Playhouses* (1931), R.A. Foakes and R.T. Rickert's new edition of Henslowe's diary (1968), the Harbage-Schoenbaum *Annals of English Drama, 975–1700* (1964), besides fresh reconsiderations of the manuscript in Harold Jenkins' Supplement to Greg's *MSR* edition (1961) and R.C. Bald's 'The "Shakespearian" Additions in *The Booke of Sir Thomas Moore* Addition II,c', (*ShS*, 2 (1949)), to name but two examples, as well as the literature comprehensively surveyed in G. Harold Metz's essay here. The design of Pollard's collection was quite narrow, being directed to examine the question of Shakespeare's presence in the manuscript play, as the writer of Hand D in Addition IIc, and the initial plan would seem to have been only to attend to that part of the question which profitably could be settled from study of the manuscript by bibliographical and (mainly) palaeographical methods. We learn from Pollard's introductory essay that the historian R.W. Chambers's influential essay on 'The Expression of Ideas – Particularly Political Ideas – in the Three Pages and in Shakespeare' was contributed 'as the result of a chance conversation' (p. 31). Consequently, many other crucial issues related to the play as a whole were treated in a quite cursory fashion or omitted altogether. The essays in the present volume illustrate how difficult it is to examine even a problem so apparently well-defined as the identity of Hand D without implicating such matters as, for instance, the construction of the play, the organization of the theatrical company for which it was written, or the role of the censor, about which little or nothing was written in 1923.

However, the dating of the manuscript was crucial for Pollard's collaborators if Shakespeare was to be connected with it in any way. After making the good point that a play which introduced a London riot must have been written when the playwrights would not 'have run a risk of being hung for their share in it' (p. 22), Pollard settled on composition and preparation for performance 'late in 1593 or early 1594' (p. 28), an acceptable conclusion as W.B. Long confirms in his essay here (p. 54). He commented how 'remarkable' it was that composition in 1593

I

'enables us to fit everything in': Shakespeare as the author of the Jack Cade scenes in
2 Henry VI and of Addition IIc of *More*, the young Dekker's ''prentice' work in
Addition IV (fol. 13ᵛ), the earlier handwriting of Munday's *John a Kent and John a
Cumber*, the scouring of Moor Ditch in 1594, the occurrence of the actor Thomas
Goodale's name in the plot of *The Seven Deadly Sins* and in *More*, and the last known
mention of Ogle the wigmaker in *More*. (It is even more remarkable that the status
of most of this evidence for the date of composition is challenged in the present
volume: see p. 4 below). Pollard did not conceive of the possibility that the
composition of the Original Text, as Greg distinguished it in his 1911 edition, and
of the Additions could be separated, and Greg, writing on *The Handwritings of the
Manuscript*, noted 'how persistently different lines of argument point to 1597 as
the *terminus ad quem* alike for the original draft and for the additions' (p. 56). Pollard
had thought that if a date as late as 1599 could be entertained for *More*, it would be
'an obstacle to Shakespeare's authorship so great as to be almost fatal' (p. 31). It is a
measure of the movement of scholarship since 1923 that two of the contributors
here can plausibly suggest that the revisions were made later than 1599 and that
Shakespeare was involved in the revision at that late date.

Pollard and his fellows made up a 'little company of upholders of Shakespeare's
authorship of the "three pages"' (p. 31), being joined in a 'cause', as Pollard termed
it, that more than anti-Stratfordians or Oxfordians were disposed to oppose. The
contributors to the present volume write in a different context, for none of them
believes that the case for Shakespeare's presence in the *More* manuscript is less
strong than that which could be made to deny it or to identify another playwright as
the scribe of Addition IIc. This is not to say that anyone can claim that the
identification of Hand D as Shakespeare's can be made with the rigour which might
satisfy an expert in forensic documents in a court of law where life-and-death issues
might be at stake. That consideration is irrelevant to scholarly enquiry in any event.
The hypothesis of Shakespeare's authorship and hand in the 147 or 148 lines of
Addition II, supported as it is by separate but convergent lines of enquiry
conducted by scholars of pre-eminent skill and authority (notably those of the 1923
collection) cannot be met by simple denial or doubts as to its adequacy. An
alternative hypothesis must be suggested, but none adequate to challenge that of
Shakespearian authorship has been offered.

However, even though the Shakespeare question was not a primary issue of
concern in this volume, Charles Forker's essay on 'Webster or Shakespeare? Style,
Idiom, Vocabulary and Spelling in the Additions to *More*' has achieved results of
double significance for the authorship question. Shortly before this volume was
commissioned Dr Carol Chillington mounted a substantial attack against the
proposition of Shakespeare's participation in the revision of *More* in her
'Playwrights at Work: Henslowe's, not Shakespeare's, *Book of Sir Thomas More*'
(*ELR*, 10 (1980)). She argued, with the support of a gap in an entry for payment to
Chettle and Heywood in Henslowe's *Diary* (fol. 119) and the assumption that *More*
was written after Essex's rebellion in 1601, that Webster – who had been associated

with Munday and the other identified revisers, Chettle, Dekker and Heywood – rather than Shakespeare was their partner in the revision. Her case was impeded – or perhaps facilitated – in that no scrap of Webster's handwriting exists for comparison with Addition IIc, and the argument was made largely on stylistic grounds within the general framework of a possibility derived from theatrical history. Webster is perhaps the only playwright of the period capable of composing the passage (though Heywood is sometimes suggested as a possible author). Forker has shown that the probability that Webster composed the 147 lines is infinitesimal. Moreover, although he is properly cautious not to claim what is not his object to demonstrate, he has also garnered significant details to support the existing consensus that Addition IIc was composed by Shakespeare. Readers of Forker's essay must agree with Giorgio Melchiori (see his note 38) that the evidence for Shakespeare's authorship is stronger now than it was before.

Forker's approach to the authorship question – also illustrated in this volume by John Jowett's analysis of Chettle's presence in the Original Text – uses principally those elements of an author's language which most readers would agree are the more significant determiners of 'style', at least, so far as it might be recognized by the sensitive critic. In the interval since the Pollard symposium a number of studies have examined elements of style which are unlikely to have been influenced by the requirements of genre or, as with the selection of vocabulary for instance, the subject of the work. In stylistic studies generally, aided by the capability of computers to handle large arrays of information and perform complex statistical calculations in a short time, efforts have been made to move beyond dependence on elements of language selected intuitively, to the substratum of language almost below the author's conscious selection. Treated with the appropriate statistical rigour, such details would provide more objective grounds for the determination of authorship. This tendency achieved its apogee for *More* studies with the publication of Thomas Merriam's 'The Authorship of *Sir Thomas More*' (*ALLC Bulletin*, 10, 1982), an earlier version of which preceded Chillington's attribution of Addition IIc to Webster. Merriam acknowledged that 'The 147 lines in Hand D are insufficient for identification alone' (p. 3), employing the tests he applied to the play. Nevertheless, he concluded that 'about 90% of the play was composed by Shakespeare, including material in Hands S, C, and D'. The use of 32 statistical tests revealed that the 'stylometric characteristics' of the manuscript were those of *Lear*, *Hamlet*, *Julius Caesar* and *Titus Andronicus*, works which span twelve years. Merriam's conclusions, so greatly at odds with the findings of earlier scholars who had used other and a greater variety of evidence to agree (in general) that *More* was substantially Munday's, with the probable collaboration of Chettle, may be set aside for the moment until he explains fully his methods and the character of his tests. Nevertheless, the publication within a short time of each other of two studies which challenged in strikingly different ways the consensus on the matter of Shakespeare's involvement in *More* inevitably directed particular attention to a scholarly issue which the contributors to this volume intended to treat mainly in a larger context.

The discrepancy of the results of stylistic studies and critical judgement tends to bring only the first into disrepute, for whereas critical evaluations of the merits of a composition depend ultimately on critical taste and experience, the 'scientific' methods of stylometrists are descredited when stylometrists disagree on particular issues or their methods are not understood by critics.

Notwithstanding the reluctance of many scholars to accept the result of stylometric studies when they do not accord with their own critical appreciations of texts, there is a particular need for objective conclusions in a case as contentious as *More*, especially when, as it turns out, many of the details used to establish probabilities (almost to the point of certainty in some instances) become capable of alternative constructions. In particular, the status of most of the considerations accommodated by Pollard's 1593–4 date of composition and revision (mentioned above on p. 2) has been affected by subsequent discoveries. Most notably, I.A. Shapiro discovered that the date on the last leaf of Munday's *John a Kent*, which had been bound apparently quite early with *More*, another Munday manuscript, did not read '1596' as Pollard and Greg believed in 1923, but 1590.[1] To the extent that the dating of that manuscript bears on the dating of *More*, the six years' difference is important. W.B. Long in this present collection identifies the hand of the inscription as that of the book-keeper (Hand C in *More*) who made theatrical markings in both manuscripts; he suggests that 'Decembris 1590' dates the acquisition of the manuscript by Strange's men whose employee C was. However far the association of the two Munday manuscripts and the Strange's men book-keeper may be taken,[2] Pollard's alternative suggestion in 1923 (p. 10) that the date records when some private purchaser acquired it from the players cannot be given credence.

Furthermore, in 1949 R.C. Bald drew attention to the fact that the scouring of Moor Ditch was authorized again in February, 1603, and so removed the significance of the reference to its condition at Add. iv, 215–16 as an argument for the early date of the revision.[3] Again, Thomas Goodale, whose name added in Addition v supported an early date for the revision, was alive in 1599, a fact established after the publication of *Shakespeare's Hand*.[4]

Given the altered status of facts once firmly established as the details mentioned above, it is natural that the claims of more recent stylometric studies to resolve inconclusive issues should be urged more forcibly in recent studies of *More*. Gary Taylor, for instance, mentioning work by D.J. Lake and MacD.P. Jackson, reinforces previous stylometric analyses with evidence of his own. His 'colloquialism-in-verse' test places the composition of Addition iic amongst Shakespeare's works written around 1603, a date which additional arguments dispose him to suggest for the revision as a whole.[5] The confluence of the results of these independent and, to an extent, objective analyses constitutes a substantial argument for the later and therefore separate date of composition of the Additions which comprise the revision of the Original Text. The stylistic evidence is not easy to ignore: if Shakespeare indeed wrote Addition iic after 1600, then it would be most difficult to believe that the other Additions were not written on the same occasion.[6]

Despite Taylor's insistence that the dating of the Original Text and the revision constitute two separable issues, some contributors to this volume have not distinguished the two, and there is significant disagreement on the dating of the revisions. Theatrical history cannot be indifferent to resolution of the matter. If Melchiori is correct in his view, the *More* manuscript provides good witness – somewhat complicated by the number of hands involved and the consequential condition of the manuscript – to a process that was probably quite common in the period, particularly when on account of its subject and theme a play script was likely to incur especially close official scrutiny. By having the company anticipate the censor's foreseeable objection to the Original Text, Melchiori effectively assigns Chettle and the other contributors the role of modern 'play doctors', (without the benefit of a try-out in Philadelphia). In his reconstruction of the sequence through which the play achieved its present form, Melchiori assumes that early revision was necessary on account of structural weaknesses and was desirable as well to adapt the collaborators' design to what the Master of the Revels was likely to approve for performance. The product of the revision was a play structured on sound principles, with suitable accommodation to the characteristics of the company (for instance, addition of a clown's part), but the revisers' success was nullified by the force of Tilney's admonition to 'leave out the insurrection wholly and the cause thereof and begin with Sir Thomas More at the mayor's sessions'. 'Under such conditions', Melchiori concludes, 'it is hardly possible that the author–revisers set to work again in order to comply with Tilney's injunction: it would have meant contradicting the very principles on and for which the play had been written, both on the formal and on the ideological level' (p. 92). On the other hand, Gary Taylor – whose particular charge herein was to determine the dating of the Additions – reaches a contrary conclusion. The unstated assumption is that the Original Text was abandoned either in the face of Tilney's objections to it (his influence in *More* is restricted to the Original Text alone) or, as Long suggested, when the plague brought about the closing of the theatres.[7] Almost ten years later, when political circumstances were propitious for plays reviving suitably doctored treatments of Tudor worthies, the old play was recalled by one of the collaborators, presumably Chettle, who alone shared in the Original Text and Additions alike, and was prepared for a revival by an experienced consortium of theatrical odd-job men.

There is little possibility that the competing claims of the two datings for the revision of *More* could be moderated here within the space of a brief introduction, even if that were my charge. Different points will weigh more heavily for different readers. It would be reassuring, for example, to have documentary evidence that *More*, if revised in 1603, was performed, because the proposition that the play was written and revised on two separate occasions, each time failing to reach performance is not easy to accept. It is possible to wonder, too, in the light of Melchiori's conjectural reconstruction of the evolution of the play, whether a play

as theatrically imperfect as he has shown the Original Text to be, would ever have
been submitted to the censor, reserving the perfecting revisions until the revival.
(The old view that the play was censored and immediately revised to accommodate
Tilney's injunctions but abandoned when it was found impossible to do so is no
longer possible to support: Melchiori has shown that the revision is complete, and
successful.) To different effect R.C. Bald noticed that the use of the term
'Lombards' in Addition iib, 82, 104 in place of the identification of the aliens as
Flemish or French in the Original Text, being consistent with Tilney's substitution
of 'Lombard' in scene iii for 'straunger' (l. 364) and 'ffrencheman' (l. 368), implies
that the Additions were written after the Original Text was submitted to the
censor.[8] Indeed, Taylor concludes that 'Such evidence makes it impossible to
assume or assert that the play and the additions to it date from the same moment in
time' (p. 112).

Scott McMillin, in suggesting that Shakespeare's contribution to the play in the
form of Addition iic was made early on as part of the preparation for the stage,
offers a possible compromise between those who see the Additions as part of the
original composition or divided from it by several years. McMillin entertains the
possibility that some revisions were made at a separate and therefore later stage, but
the exact date is not crucial to his argument. (He concludes that *More* was revived by
the Admiral's men after 1600.) In his view Shakespeare wrote Add. iic 'before
Tilney censored the play and before the revisions had been performed on the
apprentices and the Clown' (p. 59). No other conclusion explains why Hand
D was not aware of Tilney's objections to the designation of the aliens as
'strangers', why he did not know that the unruly apprentices had been removed
from the play in the revisions, and that a clown had been introduced. Hand D's
work on *More*, therefore, 'belonged to the original composition of the play'. It is an
index of the complexity of the *More* problem – and possibly of the insufficiency of
evidence good enough to bring issues to closure – that however plausible and well
supported a case may be, opposing arguments rear themselves immediately. For
instance, McMillin's conclusion alters the old question of why Shakespeare ignored
Tilney's objections to 'strangers' to the complementary question: why, when
Tilney received the Original Text with Addition iic inserted in it did the censor
ignore Hand D's seven references to 'strangers' and to 'France' and 'Flanders'
(l. 127)?[9] The insufficiency of determinative knowledge that created the *More* problem
in the first place enables opposing opinions to be held on such matters as the dating
of the Additions.

Most of what can be known about *More* has a physical basis in the manuscript.
Scholars have sought unremittingly in B.L. Harl. MS. 7368 for physical evidence
that might bear on questions of method and intention in the evolution of *The Booke
of Sir Thomas Moore* to the play of *More* ever since Greg established the first
authoritatively edited text. Peter W.M. Blayney, besides offering new readings and
identifications of ink and handwriting, added the 148th line in Hand D's
contribution to the play, the speech-prefix 'all.' in the top left-hand corner of fol. 9ᵛ

of Add. IIc. But after seventy years' intensive scrutiny by a large variety of accomplished students, it cannot be expected that the manuscript has much more to yield. Much recent attention has focused on the watermarks of the Additions, which are apparently different from those of the leaves comprising the Original Text.[10] (Such study has not been facilitated by the perspex which shrouds the manuscript leaves and renders it impossible to make b-radiographs of the watermarks.) Scot McMillin, reporting on his examination of the manuscript with G.R. Proudfoot (p. 60), states that, although the watermarks of the Additions are of the common 'pot' variety, they are different in shape: the Additions therefore may have come from different sources, at different times.[11] Potentially of more value for understanding of the process by which *More* reached its present form is Melchiori's observation that the book-keeper (C) transcribed the speeches later pasted on the lower part of the cancelled fol. 11^v (Addition III) and 14^r (Add. v) on two halves of a single original leaf. He infers that 'the two monologues must have been written practically simultaneously by different authors at a fairly late stage of the revision' (p. 89). Further, since Shakespeare has sometimes been identified as the author of the monologue on fol. 11^v, a view argued more recently by J.M. Nosworthy and supported by Harold Jenkins in 1961,[12] if he did indeed write Add. IIc, 'then all the revisions must have been effected within a very narrow period'. This new observation and its implications invite close examination by readers of these essays.

The narrow focus of the Pollard symposium and, in after years, the continuing interest in the Shakespearian association, overshadowed recognition of the value of *The Booke of Sir Thomas Moore* as testimony to the methods by which dramatic manuscripts were prepared for performance. Of course, whether *More* was performed remains an open question in the lack of explicit record. Nevertheless, performance was intended and so many hands were not involved in the manuscript lightly. Renewed attention to the physical characteristics of the manuscript, together with determination to examine *More* in the context of theatrical rather than literary history are responsible for significant achievements in the present volume. It is unquestionably important to understand the activities of Munday, the book-keeper and the other revisers, within the constraints of the theatrical conditions illuminated here by Scott McMillin, in relation to Munday's 'plot' for the play, the fundamental design which was enhanced collaboratively by all those who worked on the play. (What is refreshing in these essays is the sense that *More* is a play, often misprised, which repays the scholarly effort given to its elucidation.) Giorgio Melchiori's synopsis of the development of the play through its stages (pp. 83–92) interprets the physical evidence of the manuscript with complete mastery of its intricacies, informed by sensitive understanding of the collaborators' common purpose for the play as a worthy spectacle of the Elizabethan stage. It is not a reconstruction likely to be significantly modified by future scholarship.

Nevertheless, the collaborators laboured under the constraints of their medium. Scott McMillin earlier showed that *The Booke of Sir Thomas Moore* 'is a coherent theatrical document' representing 'a play written and revised for actual production' (p. 57). Here he demonstrates that the play was designed for an unusually large company of players, having an exceptionally large number of speaking parts; further, *More* contains one of the longest principal parts in Elizabethan drama. This evidence independently confirms the early opinion that *More* was originally written for Strange's men and Edward Alleyn in the 1590s. Other evidence (for instance, the introduction in the additions of a clown's role, with significant terminology; and reduction of the cast size) points to the revival of the play by the Admiral's men shortly after 1600. McMillin's conclusions are, (with the exception of the date of Hand D's participation), consistent with Taylor's conclusion that *More* was revived when there was fresh interest in plays based on early Tudor history, in the early seventeenth century. McMillin gives important support for the theory of later revision of the abandoned original text, but his essay is even more significant for the solution of a problem – not even perceived in Pollard's 1923 symposium – that can scarcely be resolved by other (e.g. historical or bibliographical) methods, through the analysis of the play's theatrical characteristics.[13]

The balance of arguments presented in the present volume, most readers will agree, tips the balance further in favour of Shakespeare as the author and hand of Addition IIc, and, through the agreement of arguments made by McMillin and Taylor, for the first time establishes a respectable case for the revision of *More* after 1600. As to whether Shakespeare's contribution was earlier or later, there are strong arguments on either side: the point that he did not know the Original Text tells against his participation in the late revision when the Original Text must have been available to him, but the stylistic evidence which links Addition IIc with plays of his middle period tells against him as collaborator in the early text. This volume did not aim to arrive at certainty for every point at issue but rather, by drawing upon the extensive scholarship on *More* published since the 1923 symposium, to approach a possible consensus with the aid of new evidence and fresh arguments. Readers will decide themselves from their own perusal of the following essays the extent to which this aim has been achieved.

NOTES

1 'The Significance of a Date', *ShS*, 8 (1955), 100–5.
2 See Taylor below, p. 108.
3 '*The Booke of Sir Thomas More* and its Problems', *ShS*, 2 (1949), 52. Giorgi Melchiori argued in a fuller version of his essay in this collection that the reference at ll. 215–16 would have been more appropriate a couple of years before Moor Ditch was cleansed in 1595.
4 Taylor, p. 104.
5 See pp. 120ff. below – The value of such a stylometric test does not depend on the prior assumption of Shakespeare's authorship. It would not be possible to locate the 147 lines within the span of Shakespeare's literary activity unless the passage had characteristics (from common authorship) which made the comparison possible. On the other hand, it is true, it is possible to argue that the stylistic characteristics used to place Addition IIc within the range of characteristics evidenced by Shakespearian plays may be shared by Shakespeare and other authors; therefore the

apparent fit at such a relatively late point in the Shakespeare spectrum could be used to argue that he did not compose Addition IIc. Furthermore, it remains troubling that the extent of Add. IIc is not so large as to permit complete confidence in the statistical results of stylometric tests: see notes 68 and 70 of Metz's essay following.

6 Taylor cites borrowings in Chettle's *Hoffman* which indicate that he was 'influenced by one of the additions to *Sir Thomas More*' (p. 119), an observation that leads to the conclusion that the additions were written during the later peiod.

7 Long indeed believes that the play was left unfinished (p. 48).

8 Bald, p. 60. It does not appear necessary to extend the Lombards in Add. IIb to cover the dating of all the Additions. Melchiori's position could be maintained despite Bald's observation, since Add. IIb was written out by Hand C, i.e. the book-keeper. Because the Addition is necessarily a copy of earlier text, it might equally well have been transcribed (for whatever reason), alone of the revisions submitted to Tilney, incorporating Tilney's amendments.

9 McMillin does, however, endorse objections to Greg's proposal in 1911 that the revisions were written before Tilney saw the play, based on the fact that there is no explicit sign of Tilney's reading amongst the Additions (p. 70).

10 Michael L. Hays, 'Watermarks in the Manuscript of *Sir Thomas More* and a possible Collation', *ShQ*, 26 (1973), 67.

11 Giorgio Melchiori argued in a fuller version of his essay here that Munday owned a mixed stock of paper which he distributed to the authors of the additions. McMillin's observation, of course, facilitates his detachment of Hand D from the work of the other revisers, whereas Melchiori's argument is that the difference of the watermarks in the Original Text and Additions does not oblige a conclusion that the two were separated by any significant stretch of time.

12 'Shakespeare and *Sir Thomas More*', *RES*, n.s. 6 (1955), 12–25; 'Supplement', p. xxxviii.

13 A late date for the revisions would not seem to jeopardize the value of Melchiori's reconstruction of the stages through which the play evolved.

I

'Voice and credyt': the scholars and *Sir Thomas More*

G. HAROLD METZ

Sir Thomas More is a dramatic biography of the sometime Lord Chancellor of England. It is one of a relatively small group of such plays, the most noteworthy others being *Sir John Oldcastle* (1599), *Thomas Lord Cromwell* (1600) and *Sir Thomas Wyatt* (1604). These plays are episodic and loosely organized, the only elements tending to structural unity being the personality and selected events in the careers of the protagonists. There are three main actions in *More*: the Ill May Day rising of 1517 and More's efforts to pacify the insurrectionists; More's domestic life offering an opportunity to show his social skills, his kindness and generosity to people of a lower social standing and his love of fun; and his service as a Privy Councillor and Lord Chancellor concentrated mainly though not exclusively on his fall from power and his eventual execution. Certain elements of what may be called his public career are intermingled with the other two sequences. Some of the most important events in More's life are omitted entirely or barely noticed, possibly as a concession to theatrical limitations. There is, for example, no mention of his literary activities, not even an allusion to *Utopia*, the most widely admired book to have its origin in England in the early sixteenth century, nor is much made of his enduring friendship with Erasmus, which was well known throughout Europe, and produced *Encomium Moriae* with the pun on More's name. The effort to depict More's character and personality, an important and theatrically effective part of the play is, if viewed as serious biography, less than satisfactory. *More* is briskly dramatic in the insurrection sequence, warmly human in the domestic scenes, and sympathetically admiring of More's unwavering adherence to principle throughout the concluding movement. The playwrights managed to meet the inherent structural challenge of a decline in tension in the middle section and to rebuild the tempo leading to More's execution. Most scholars consider *More* theatrically the most successful of the biographical history plays. Despite these attributes it would probably have settled long ago to the level of a curiosity, largely because of its exhibition of the workings of the censor, were it not for its association with Shakespeare. The suggestion that a three-page segment of the play was composed by him and is in his holograph was first put forth by Richard Simpson in a brief article asking 'Are there any Extant MSS. in Shakespeare's Handwriting?' His response was that the manuscript entitled *The Booke of Sir Thomas Moore* contained passages 'in his writing'.[1] Thus was set on foot a debate that has endured for more than a century and engaged the participation of some of the most eminent Shakespearean scholars. It was particularly intense during the early decades of this century, then it subsided somewhat but it is still continuing and even shows signs of reinvigoration.

The earliest surviving record of the existence of the manuscript is in a note made by Thomas Hearne, an Oxford antiquary, on 17 January 1728. He records in his diary-like book of comments that John Murray of London, a book collector and perhaps a book dealer, had on 12 October 1727 lent him a 'thin folio paper MS . . . entitled *The Booke of Sir Thomas Moore*' which he read. He adds that it is 'in many places strangely scored & in others so altered that 'tis hard to make some things out'.[2] The exact transcription of the title and the brief but accurate description of the state of the manuscript leave little doubt that it is the one we now know as Harley 7368. Probably Edward Harley, second Earl of Oxford who knew Murray, obtained it from him and it was among the vast collection of his papers that was acquired in 1753 by what is now the British Library.

PUBLICATION

The play was first published in 1844 in an edition prepared for the Shakespeare Society by Alexander Dyce. Based on a meticulous transcription from the original manuscript, it preserves a number of readings now lost as a consequence of the subsequent deterioration of the manuscript. However Dyce's text, though scholarly and valuable but not totally error-free, conflates the original version and the additions which were written to replace deleted passages, leaving it vulnerable to the censure that it represents neither the original nor the revision.[3] A.F. Hopkinson printed for private circulation in 1902 an edition that is a modern spelling version of Dyce's text.[4] C.F. Tucker Brooke included a similar slightly altered reprint of Dyce in his *Shakespeare Apocrypha* (1908).[5] John Farmer brought out a photographic facsimile in Tudor Facsimile Texts (1910) which is the only such facsimile ever issued that reproduces the entire manuscript.[6] Like Dyce's transcription it is invaluable in that it preserves readings since lost. Sir Walter Greg published the Malone Society Reprint of the play in type facsimile in 1911 that is a model of editorial scholarship.[7] The bibliographical precision with which the text was prepared makes it unlikely that it will be replaced and it remains in print to this day. All subsequent scholarship is deeply indebted to the Farmer and Greg facsimiles. The manuscript, though fragile, is now adequately protected and available for study by qualified scholars in the British Library. John Shirley (1938) and Herbert Farjeon (1953) printed the complete text of the play based on Greg's edition.[8] Harold Jenkins published a full text in an edition of the *Complete Works of Shakespeare* by C.J. Sisson (1954) based on a fresh collation of the manuscript with Dyce's and Greg's texts, which produced a few new readings.[9] Jenkins's objective was to generate as far as possible the revised version of the play incorporating the revisions and additions. He realized that it is not within the realm of feasibility to arrive at a definitive revised text 'because the revision was never brought to finality'. Nevertheless he has given us as sound a 'final' text as is possible and the only one of its kind that we have.

Excerpts from *More* have been frequently reprinted, limited, with only occasional exceptions, to those portions believed to have been composed by Shakespeare: the insurrection scene and More's soliloquy on the potential vicissitudes of high office. Of these the most notable are those of Sir Edward Maunde Thompson, Greg, R.C. Bald, John Munro, Thomas Clayton, P.J. Croft and G. Blakemore Evans.[10] Photographic facsimiles of selected pages of the manuscript, or of portions of such pages, have also been reproduced, chiefly limited to fols. 8^r, 8^v and 9^r containing the 147 lines thought by most Shakespearian scholars to be in Shakespeare's autograph. Thompson reproduces the three pages in his monograph on *Shakespeare's Handwriting*. The 1961 issue of Greg's MSR edition prints facsimiles of portions of fols. 6^r, 7^r, 7^v, 9^r, 13^v and 22^r (different pages were reproduced in the 1911 issue). *Shakespeare Survey* presents the three pages with Bald's transcription of Addition IIc. Croft provides fol. 9^r. Samuel Schoenbaum reproduces 9^r in *William Shakespeare A Documentary Life* and all three pages in *William Shakespeare Records and Images*, in both cases along with the single word 'all' from fol. 9^v. Anthony Petti presents portions of fols. 9 and 13 and Evans reproduces the three pages.[11] There are numerous others.

THE MANUSCRIPT

The manuscript comprises a total of 22 leaves of which the first two are the original vellum wrapper, a double leaf extracted from a fifteenth century Latin breviary, on one page of which is inscribed '*The Booke of Sir Thomas Moore*', in ornamental italic letters. Thirteen of the leaves contain most of the original text of the play, but there are two lacunae, one probably representing the loss of two leaves (after fol. 5) and the other possibly the loss of one leaf (after fol. 11). The remaining leaves contain additions to the play, some of which represent replacements for the text on the lost leaves, while others constitute revisions or expansions of, or insertions into, the extant original text. Alterations and deletions are marked in the original version, some of which are minor, some substantial, and not all of the additions and revisions are properly integrated into the text.

THE PENMEN

Early in the study of *More* it was recognized that several hands were discernible in the manuscript. After some scholarly debate it was generally accepted that there are seven. In addition to that of Edmund Tilney, the Master of the Revels and stage censor who signed the most extensive and important of his notes, there are six hands evident in the text itself. These are not identified in the manuscript and Greg in his edition designated them S (for Scribe, the writer of the Original Text), A, B, C, D and E. Except for some alterations, minor in extent, in the original by B and C the latter five hands are found only in the additions, from which S and Tilney are completely absent. There are six additions numbered I to VI. The designations of both the hands and the additions are in the sequence in which they first appear in the manuscript.

Much of the early scholarship is concentrated on the identification of the penmen represented by the various hands. In the Introduction to his Malone Society reprint Greg describes each hand in some detail (pp. vii–x). He considers S a scribe, merely a copyist, and has nothing to suggest as to his identity, nor as to those of Hands A, B, or C. Of Hand D he says: 'It is this hand which has been thought to be Shakespeare's' (p. ix). Of Hand E he says: 'A comparison with MS. Addit. 30262, fol. 66b, at the British Museum [a receipt by Dekker], and with Henslowe's *Diary*, fols. 101 and 114, at Dulwich College [respectively, another Dekker receipt and an acknowledgement of a debt], suggests that this hand may be Thomas Dekker's. There is at least a strong resemblance between the two' (p. ix).

Upon the publication (in 1912) by Farmer of a Tudor Texts photographic facsimile of the signed manuscript of Anthony Munday's *John a Kent and John a Cumber* Greg recognized the writing as the same as Hand S in *More*. Since Munday was an established playwright it was no longer tenable to regard him as a mere copyist. He must have been at least part author of the original play of which he was probably assigned to prepare a fair copy for submission to Tilney.[12] Greg identified Hand C with equal confidence as that of a playhouse scribe and reviser when he found it in the playhouse plot of *2 Seven Deadly Sins* (a Strange's play) and in the partially preserved plot of *2 Fortune's Tennis* (an Admiral's play).[13] In his contribution ('The Handwritings of the Manuscript') to the 1923 symposium[14] Greg suggests that Hand B should be compared with the manuscript of *The Captives* which, he says, is presumably in the writing of Thomas Heywood. 'There is a considerable resemblance both in the writing and the spelling, but there are also differences which make it impossible to venture on an identification' (p. 44, n. 1). Meanwhile Thompson, the most eminent palaeographer of his time who had studied English manuscripts of the Tudor era for decades, published (1916) his comprehensive examination of the writing in Hand D compared to the six signatures which constitute the only surviving examples of Shakespeare's handwriting. He determined on the basis of a general similarity and of specific resemblances in the formation of certain letters, including the now famous 'spurred *a*', which occurs in both Shakespeare's signatures and in the manuscript of the play, that Hand D is Shakespeare (pp. 53–4), a conclusion he confirmed in his even more detailed study in *Shakespeare's Hand* (pp. 57–112).

Four years later Greg set forth a balanced and thoughtful survey of the critical discussion to 1927 of the arguments for and against the recognition of Hand D as Shakespeare's.[15] He reviews all the evidence and argument centring around Thompson's determination and finds that the advocates for the negative have weakened a few of Thompson's points, particularly in regard to specific letter formations, and that some of his contentions are 'somewhat reduced in force, though by no means disposed of' (p. 199). He doubts that 'the available data are extensive enough to make complete proof possible' and concludes by advancing 'the following propositions', the last 'of a somewhat challenging nature':

1. The palaeographical case for the hands of S[hakespeare] and D being the same is stronger than any that can be made out for their being different.
2. The hand of S is more nearly paralleled in D than in any other dramatic document known to us.
3. Setting S aside, it can be shown the D was not written by any dramatist of whose hand we have adequate knowledge.
4. On purely palaeographical grounds there is less reason to suppose that all six signatures were written by the same hand than there is, granting this identity, to suppose that the hand of the signatures also wrote the addition to *More*.

These propositions incline the balance of probability, he thinks, in favour of identification of Shakespeare as the writer of Hand D (p. 200).

In the same year (1927) Samuel Tannenbaum published a study in which he re-examined evidence for identification of the various hands in the play.[16] His most important contribution in this book is the conclusive identification of Hand A as that of Henry Chettle based on a detailed analysis of the handwriting in the play and comparison with the facsimiles of Chettle's calligraphy included in Greg's *English Literary Autographs*.[17] Tannenbaum (in the same book) also supports the identification of S as Munday primarily by comparison with *John a Kent*; of B as Heywood on the findings of Alexander Judson and Greg, but without Greg's reservations; and E as Dekker on Greg's determination supported by Thompson and E.H.C. Oliphant.[18] However he also put forth a hypothesis that Hand C is that of Thomas Kyd. He believes that Kyd is part author, transcriber, editor and stage manager, thus accounting for his reviser's role in the manuscript. He reiterates the position he had taken in his first book on Shakespearian penmanship that D could not possibly be Shakespeare. He offers no other candidate.[19] Responses to the opinions in his books, (which while important, are manifestly of uneven value), by R.B. McKerrow, Charles Sisson, Greg[20] and others were unanimous in accepting Tannenbaum's identification of Chettle as Hand A, and agreed in rejecting his arguments in favour of Kyd as C, and against Shakespeare as D. Initial reactions to his fairly persuasive case for Heywood as B were mixed, Greg's being reserved, even though he had made the original suggestion, Sisson's being positive ('it is reasonably certain to my mind'), and Baldwin's almost neutral ('Dr. Tannenbaum's arguments seem plausible'). Robert Adger Law, four years later, expressed scepticism on the basis of disparities between B's and Heywood's chirography in *The Captives* and *The Escapes of Jupiter*. He cites differences in spelling, in capitalization, in punctuation and in general writing style, supported also by literary evidence, showing that the case for Heywood as Hand B is not proved.[21] Nosworthy, building on a discussion of Heywood's hand by Arthur Brown in his Malone Society reprint of *The Captives* (1953), demonstrates a series of differences in letter formation, capitalization and spelling between B's and Heywood's handwriting, presumably the differences to which Greg had alluded earlier. To Nosworthy these are sufficient to support a judgement that 'Tannenbaum's identification is, on the whole, unsatisfactory'. However he acknowledges that 'perhaps thirty years' separates the two plays, with attendant probable changes in calligraphy, and that 'nothing very positive seems to emerge' by way of identification if B is not Heywood.[22] Surveying these opinions Jenkins notes that both Heywood's hand, which is notoriously difficult to read as he himself acknowledged,[23] and Hand B, are not only equally bad but bad in the same way; and that some spelling and other similarities support the identification. He concludes, 'I cannot regard the identification as improbable; but the matter is undecided'. In a retrospective summary of the discussions on the identification of the six hands to 1961 Jenkins notes that they 'are now assigned as follows, with [following Pollard] varying degrees of confidence.

S	Anthony Munday	C	a playhouse book-keeper
A	Henry Chettle	D	William Shakespeare
B	Thomas Heywood	E	Thomas Dekker'[24]

Acceptance of these identifications of the penmen a quarter of a century after Jenkins's succinct summation, while more general, has not become universal. The association of Hands S, A and E with, respectively, Munday, Chettle and Dekker is so manifest palaeographically that there has been virtually no dissent. Tannenbaum rejected the recognition of C as an Admiral's book-keeper and nominated Kyd, but the evidence he adduced is defective and his identification has not won any support. Greg's determination is unshaken. In regard to Hand B, while the majority of critics accept it as Heywood's, a few judicious scholars, perhaps recalling Greg's reservations, have remained unconvinced. As to Hand D, most students of the play believe it is Shakespeare's but a few do not. Those not inclined to accept it place primary emphasis on the insufficiency of authentic Shakespearean handwriting with which to make a comparison. By contrast, in the case of Munday we have an entire play – *John a Kent* – and the preliminaries to a devotional book – *The Heaven of the Mind* – both of which are signed by him and are undoubtedly holograph. It is regrettable that we are not so fortunate in the case of Shakespeare. However, the inadequacy of the control is ineluctable and does in fact constitute a substantial problem to be faced in a palaeographic investigation. This circumstance is the reason Thompson, as Greg noted in his 1927 re-examination, felt constrained to search for minute bits of support and thus overextended some aspects of his argument. All who have studied the matter, including the qualified palaeographers and those of us who wish we were, regret the lack but we must work with what we have. Authenticated Shakespearean handwriting is beyond question small in quantity, but it is not negligible. To deny the identification because of a paucity of control exemplars is a refusal to face the problem. Greg supplies an aphorism: 'though certainty may be unattainable, speculation is not therefore idle' (*Shakespeare's Hand*, p. 50).

Negative arguments offered, other than the shortage of Shakespearean calligraphy, are simple denial that the two hands share identifiable characteristics, contention that the general impressions of the two hands are divergent, a letter by letter refutation of Thompson's analysis of characteristic letter formations and a showing that the spellings of Addition IIc are not Shakespearean.[25] Paul Ramsey, building on R.A. Huber's inconclusive finding, provides the most telling summation for the negative: 'the paleographical case is slightly negative ... the orthographical case is slightly for the identification ... *scilens* and *straing* remain striking evidence; the literary argument at least somewhat against the identification; the metrical evidence inconclusive; the rhythmical evidence against, but based on a very limited sample. To add that up, I would, if I had to make a decision, lean on my first and continuing literary and personal impression and say, "D is not Shakespeare." ' But he concludes: 'Yet I certainly would not claim that D is, beyond reasonable doubt, not Shakespeare'. Sisson provides an effective response for the affirmative: 'my own experience suggests the improbability of the discovery of evidence against the significance of two crucial parallels, the spelling *scilens*, and the "spurred *a*". During some forty years of continuous reading of a wide variety of contemporary manuscripts, amounting perhaps to half a million sheets, with these two forms constantly in mind, I have found no other instances'.[26] In the penultimate decade of the twentieth century, more than a century after Richard Simpson's brief paper, the question rests incompletely resolved. A majority of Shakespearians, including many of the most eminent, believe D is Shakespeare's hand; but a significant minority, including some respected students of the play, deny it or conclude that there is insufficient evidence to arrive at a decision.

AUTHORSHIP

The question of authorship, though closely related to that of the identification of the penmen, is not exactly the same, in the sense that it is not coterminous. If agreement were achieved as to the identity of the writers of Hands S, A, B, C, D and E, there would still remain problems of authorship because C is not a playwright.[27] The lines in his hand, more numerous than any except those in Hand S, were composed largely if not exclusively by others.

The original text of *More*, to the extent it has survived, is throughout in Hand S which has been conclusively proved to be the handwriting of Munday. Because of this some commentators decide that he is also the sole author of the first version especially in view of his earlier activities in the drama. That Munday is at least a part-author seems beyond cavil but there are some indications that, in his preparation of the fair copy of *More*, he was working from foul papers that included contributions by other dramatists in addition to his own. The most significant of these indications is the meaningless word *fashis* (l. †1847, p. 61) where the sense undoubtedly requires *fashion*. Greg drew attention to this in his Malone Society edition and explained it as a misreading of *fashiõ*. 'This is quite an easy mistake, for the two [endings] resemble one another closely in some hands, but it is a mistake of which it is almost impossible to suppose that an author would be guilty in copying his own work' (p. xvi). [28] Perhaps of equal significance is the presence of duplicate endings to the play (ll. †1956–64, pp. 64–5; and ll. †1965–86, p. 65). It is scarcely conceivable that the original author would have transcribed into his fair copy his own two endings as they presumably stood in his foul papers, the first of which he would probably have previously rejected. The fair copy appears to represent a scribal transmission of original work not his own. After he (Munday) had written out both endings in succession either he or someone else noticed the duplication and, rather than recopy the page, the first ending was scored out. Peter W.M. Blayney in his penetrating re-examination of the manuscript finds an additional nine instances in which Munday seems to have erred in transcribing from his copy, some parts of which he thinks 'may have been altered in rough, and that Munday has misunderstood deletion marks'. [29] There is thus presumptively sufficient evidence that Munday was copying from a draft which included material other than his own, and in the process he made transcription mistakes. Consequently he is unlikely to be the sole author of the original play. If this is so the question arises as to who the other playwright or playwrights were. Oliphant addressed himself to this question, conducting his 'examination . . . on purely literary grounds – verse-structure, habit of thought, use of words, and so on'. He perceived 'that three different styles were discernible in the original version of the play'. The first style is 'somewhat old-fashioned', the second is 'much jerkier and less regular' and the third 'much finer and more impressive verse than either of the others'. [30] He assigns these sections of the original draft to, respectively, Munday, B and A, on the assumption that if Munday did have collaborators in the original they are to be found among the authors of the additions. Some, at least, of the additions are believed to be revisions of the individual playwrights' own originals. He also thinks that Dekker had participated because he would not have taken part in the revision if he had not been one of the original authors. However, Dekker's contribution does not seem to be in the fair copy and probably was deleted while still in draft form. Oliphant also makes the interesting observation of C that 'this man's hand is identifiable, on the score of style, with that first of one and then of another of the writers of other portions of the play'. Jenkins finds nothing improbable in the suggestion that Chettle (Hand A) may have collaborated with Munday on the original text 'since Chettle was a close friend of Munday at least from 1592 . . . but the case is by no means clear, and the opposite view has also been expressed' by Greg (pp. xvi–xvii) and Tannenbaum (*Booke*, p. 83). [31] However Greg by 1923 appears to have become more receptive to the idea that the original text was a collaboration (*Shakespeare's Hand*, pp. 47–8). Bald inclines towards acceptance of Oliphant's hypothesis: 'It would seem, then, that Munday, Chettle, and B (Heywood?) first collaborated on the play; Dekker may also have done so, or may have come in later as a reviser'. [32] Nosworthy, finding that 'there is ample evidence, both bibliographical and stylistic, that he [Munday] was not the sole author', searches for indications of possible collaborators in

Henslowe's *Diary*. In entries ranging in date from 1597 to 1602 he finds Munday and Chettle working together, sometimes with other dramatists, on five plays; and Munday and Dekker, again with others, on four. He eliminates as collaborators, B who is 'unidentified', C because he is a 'professional scribe', and D 'since Shakespeare's *locus standi* has yet to be ascertained', and concludes that Munday's associates in the original draft of *More* were Chettle and Dekker.[33] A.C. Partridge analyses the use of contractions and the spelling, grammar, punctuation and vocabulary of each of the playwrights, then tests Oliphant's proposition in the light of his investigations. This process, he finds, tends to support Oliphant: 'The above analyses, if they prove anything at all, serve to confirm the triple authorship of *Sir Thomas More* by Munday, Heywood(?) and Chettle, on the lines indicated by Oliphant, and largely accepted by Greg'.[34] The evidence thus marshalled seems to lead to the conclusion that Munday was only one of the authors of the original draft.

It is clear, and generally accepted, that Chettle is the author of all that is in his writing (Hand A, Add. I, pp. 66–8, More in melancholy), and possibly, though not certainly, nothing else. It is also widely acknowledged that C is not a playwright nor a contributor of any significant number of original lines. He makes minor adjustments at several points in the text, including the original, as a book-keeper would do, his most important alteration being to delete three of D's lines which he apparently did not understand and to insert a banal half-line of his own (ll. 235–7 of Add. II, p. 77). He is, for example, in one unquestionable instance merely a copyist when he transcribes a brief passage written in Hand B (Add. VI, ll. 68–73, p. 93) into its proper place in Add. V (ll. 2–7, p. 89), inserting only one additional unnecessary word, apparently to regularize the metre.[35] Hand E was determined early by Greg to be Dekker. Only thirty-one lines of Add. IV are in Dekker's hand. These are at the end of the second segment of the More–Faulkner scene (ll. 212–42, pp. 87–8). The preceding lines 1 to 211 of Add. IV are in Hand C. But Dekker inserted three words ('I am ipse') added to line 193 (identified by Tannenbaum but not previously noted by Greg), manifestly showing the author emending his own text although it is written by C. Most scholars now accept Dekker as the author of all 242 lines of Add. IV. The remaining two hands, B and D, present much more challenging problems of authorship.

Hand B (Heywood) is found in two separate places in the ms. He writes the first portion of the three part Add. II and all, except for the opening stage direction, of Add. VI. Add. IIa (ll. 1–64, pp. 69–71) shows the insurrection approaching a climax. In Add. IIb (ll. 66–122, pp. 71–2, l. 65 is doubtful) the Lord Mayor and members of the Privy Council discuss corrective measures, and More proposes to appease 'wth a calm breath this flux of discontent' (l. 107, p. 72). IIb is written in Hand C. Add. IIc comprises the famous lines in Hand D (ll. 123–273, pp. 73–8) in which More persuades the rioters to lay by their weapons and sue for clemency. B is clearly part-author as well as the penman of IIa since he can be seen making insertions and changes *currente calamo*. The revision is a relatively unimaginative reworking of original lines 412–52 (pp. 14–16) undertaken apparently for the purpose of adding some eighteen comic lines to the part of Rafe Betts. B also inserts other such lines in the margins of the original MS. (e.g., ll. *638–41 and *647–58, pp. 22–3). Almost all of the forty-one lines of the early text are carried over to Add. IIa by Heywood with only a few incidental alterations. By means of these changes and additions he created the role of the Clown, as pointed out by Giorgio Melchiori.

Add. IIb is continuous both physically and in dramatic action to both IIa and IIc. Although they are distinct, Greg sees the 'three different scribes working however in conjunction' (p. 69n.). If IIb, in the hand of the playhouse reviser, could be taken to have authorial affinity to one of the other two parts of Add. II, then it is at least a possibility that in IIb C is copying the work of B. (It is apparent that IIb is not the work of D.) There are a few minor indications in IIb which seem consistent with Heywood's original lines in Add. IIa and in Add. VI. This would lend some support to such an assignment and there seems to be no stylistic disparity to prohibit it. Add. VI (pp. 91–3), all composed by B, is an original continuation of the players' scene intended to show More's shrewdness and generosity. Its literary qualities point to Heywood. In sum, then, Heywood is part-author as well as the penman of Add. IIa and sole author of Add. VI. He may also have been the author of Add. IIb. Another explanation for the phenomena observed in IIb, suggested by Professor Melchiori, is that C is transcribing Munday's original, heavily 'corrected' possibly by B.

A year after Richard Simpson answered his own question by identifying as Shakespeare's three parts of *More* – the insurrection scene, More's soliloquy on the risks of royal service, and the Faulkner sequence – James Spedding responded. A reading of the three passages in Dyce's edition and an examination of the manuscript convinced him that the handwriting of the insurrection scene is Shakespeare's and that he is not only the penman but also the author. His grounds for agreement with Simpson's determination in the case of this one scene are that the handwriting 'answers to all we know about Shakespeare's' and that the corrections which 'occur are not like corrections of mistakes made in copying, but like alterations introduced in the course of composition'. However he disagrees on the other two scenes because they are in another hand, and he calls for a palaeographical analysis.[36] Hopkinson reverts in part to Simpson's position, concluding that Simpson's three segments are all in Shakespeare's hand, that he is the author of the insurrection scene, of More's soliloquy and of the Faulkner–Erasmus sequence but not the part of Add. IV that is in Dekker's hand.[37] Frederick Furnivall denies Shakespeare's participation as penman or playwright.[38] Brooke assigns to Shakespeare the scenes of the Lord Mayor's conference on the riot, More's pacification of the insurrectionists and his soliloquy, the Faulkner–Erasmus sequence and the brief segment in which the Lord Mayor's visit to Chelsea is announced.[39] All of these attributions either are said to be or are presumably founded on studies of the handwritings and the text.

In the Malone Society edition Greg imposed some order on the early scholarly speculations in regard to authorship. With bibliographical precision he limited the participation of Hand D to fols. 8^r, 8^v and 9^r, setting aside the suggested alternate assignments, including Add. III, which had earlier been put forth largely as a consequence of a failure to discriminate Hand C from Hand D. Greg adds that Hand D's lines, which have 'undoubted literary merit', are possibly in Shakespeare's hand but he cannot 'regard them with the admiration they have aroused in some critics' (p. xiii).

In *Shakespeare's Hand in the Play of Sir Thomas More*, A.W. Pollard brought together a noteworthy pride of scholars 'to strengthen the evidence of the existence (in the Harleian MS. 7368 at the British Museum) of three pages written by Shakespeare in his own hand as part of the play of *Sir Thomas More*' (p. v). The contributors, in addition to Pollard himself, are Greg, Thompson, Dover Wilson and R.W. Chambers. Greg's 'The Handwritings of the Manuscript', his first comprehensive statement on the subject in twelve years, canvasses the literature on Hands S, A, B, C and E (Hand D being Thompson's province). Greg's examination of the evidence, adduced by himself and others, is, in its approach, chiefly though not exclusively palaeographic. He concludes that S is part-author of the original play and A, D and E composed the portions of the Additions that are in their hands. C is only a copyist. B in Addition IIa is transcribing, but in Add. VI 'he is making an addition to a scene originally written by himself' (p. 46). Thompson confines himself to the calligraphic question and does not offer opinions on authorship. Dover Wilson compares letter formations and spellings exhibited in Add. IIc of the manuscript with misprints and related bibliographic evidence in fifteen good Shakespearean quarto texts, demonstrating that the forms in *More* could have led to misprints such as are present in the quartos. He sets forth an impressive array of bibliographic detail to show what took place, but his most notable contribution is finding two rare spellings in the manuscript and in Shakespearean quartos that occur virtually nowhere else – *straing* for *strange* and *scilens* for *silence*. The latter spelling is of prime importance since it is found in only three other plays: *Q 2 Henry IV* where, as a character's name, it is printed eighteen times, and once each in the apocryphal *The Puritan* and John Mason's *The Turk*.[40] R.W. Chambers discusses the expression of ideas – particularly political ideas – in the three pages of Add. IIc and in Shakespeare. There is a remarkable concurrence in conceptions of social structure, the evils of civil unrest and the sympathetic portrayal of the common people between the insurrection scene and a number of Shakesperian plays – *2 Henry VI* (the Cade scenes), *Julius Caesar*, *Troilus and Cressida* and *Coriolanus* especially, but found in less explicit or less comprehensive form in others of the canon – for example, *Richard II*, *Hamlet* and *The Winter's Tale*. Chambers emphasizes that while the ideas so expressed, which in themselves are indicative of the authorship of the 147 lines, are important, they are less so than the linkages of underlying thought which they reveal. Though sometimes clothed in completely different expressions, the same ideas and even the specific sequences of thought are identifiable in canonical plays. He supports his contention that Add. IIc contains characteristic Shakespearian ideas with striking examples.[41] Pollard's contribution, in addition to integrating the four essays by his colleagues, is a discussion of the date of composition which will be noticed later.

The significance of this collection of studies lies in its synergism. The confluence of the disparate findings of literary, palaeographic, bibliographic, imagistic and, what has sometimes been called 'psychological', disciplines, all of which individually tend to support the Shakespearian authorship of Addition IIc and which collectively present a reinforcing argument, established *Shakespeare's Hand* as a peak in the history of the scholarship of the play equal to that of Greg's Malone Society edition. A thoughtful and conservative critic, Samuel Schoenbaum, says in summary: 'The varieties of evidence presented in the Pollard collection . . . converge upon a single destination; all roads lead to Shakespeare'.[42]

Greg's 1927 propositions, quoted above, are confined to the palaeographic question of the identity of the penman of Hand D, but they nevertheless indirectly bear on the question of authorship. It is notable that he does not restate his earlier reservations about Shakespeare's authorship of Add. IIc. By the time he arrived at his ultimate statement of the canon in 1955 Greg, in a note, says simply: 'In the present discussion it will be assumed that the three pages are in Shakespeare's autograph', and that 'most English students now accept the Shakespearian authorship of the three additional pages'.[43]

The most effective and most persistent of the opponents of the Shakespearian authorship of Add. IIc during the critical ferment of the twenties and early thirties were Tannenbaum and L.L. Schücking, both of whom had established reputations as Shakespearian scholars. Tannenbaum's attack in a stream of books and articles (see notes 16, 19, and 20), while directed primarily against the palaeographic identification of Hand D as Shakespeare's, also seeks to deny the Shakespearian authorship of the 147 lines. He argues tenaciously, but the combination of his insistence that whatever he presents as evidence be accepted without question, of his immoderate style of debate, the waywardness of some aspects of his rationale inextricably mingled with sound scholarship, and his unwillingness to credit the most palpably valid elements of his opponents' case – plus his inability to nominate any other dramatist as D[44] – induces a reluctance on the part of more balanced scholars to accept his argument against the Shakespearian authorship of the Addition. In contrast to this, witness the universal assent, even from those he regards as opponents, to his perceptive recognition of Hand A as Chettle's. Schücking's case against Shakespeare's participation in *More*, stated and restated in his three articles (n. 25), is grounded on literary considerations. He finds no trace in Add. IIc of Shakespeare's clear conception of his play nor of his insight into human motives, and the appeal to the mob's reason in *More* compares poorly to, for example, Antony's rabble-rousing speech in *Julius Caesar*. The implied threat in More's speech is clearly not Shakespearian. Taking a hint from Pollard, and quoting a passage from his Introduction,[45] Schücking decides that assigning IIc to Heywood rather than Shakespeare is nearer to the mark. He thinks that the sentimentality in More's crucial speech is typically Heywood and he supports this conjecture with verbal parallels between *More* and some of Heywood's plays. The fact that the hand in which IIc is written is not Heywood's 'should not cause us to abandon the idea of his possible authorship . . . the final judgment must needs be that Shakespeare's authorship of the "147 lines" is more than doubtful'.[46] Tannenbaum and Schücking were worthy disputants who incisively tested the hypothesis that Shakespeare is the author of Add. IIc. However, observers who adopted a neutral posture towards the debate concluded that, in Schoenbaum's words, 'in neither instance was the opposition damaging'.[47]

R.W. Chambers had touched on the imagery in the three pages but his primary interest lay elsewhere so it was Caroline Spurgeon who first systematically analysed it.[48] She had been studying the canonical plays for a number of years, identifying and cataloguing the images to define characteristic Shakespearian patterns. She undertakes to add to the previous examinations of Add. IIc 'a detailed study and comparison of the imagery in this fragment with that in the known work of Shakespeare'. Twelve images are identified and examples from acknowledged plays compared to those in the three pages. Spurgeon points out that recurring Shakespearian images do not involve repetition: 'certain ideas or pictures [are] to be found again and again in varied form and with different applications' (p. 260). Of the twelve images in the 147 lines, all are paralleled in Shakespeare's known plays, seven of which express a particular application that recurs many times in Shakespeare and three others have identifiable peculiarities. All fall into image categories established by study of the canon. In conclusion she asks: 'Is it too much to claim that the cumulative evidence they offer forms one more link in the gradually strengthening chain of proof which is leading some of us to believe that the fragment was written by Shakespeare?' (p. 270). Karl Wentersdorf adds an image from More's speech on insurrection to those previously described: the unnatural savagery of pagans.[49] He finds it at two places in the addition especially in the phrases 'momtanish inhumanyty' (l. 263, p. 78) – the inhuman cruelty of the infidel Mohammedans (the Turks) – and in ten plays of the canon, three of which specifically mention Turks. William Matchett cites parallels of words and ideas between *The Merchant of Venice* and Add. IIc which he considers to be associational links between the two plays and which constitute 'yet another of the many arguments confirming that Shakespeare was its author'.[50]

In reflecting on the years of debate regarding the authorship of the 147 lines Dover Wilson summed up the situation in 1956 in his typically thought-provoking manner: 'We shall probably never be able to prove that Shakespeare wrote the Three Pages in *Sir Thomas More*. But a case, which in Greg's words rests on "the convergence of a number of independent lines of argument . . . and not on any one alone", can never be *dis*proved and is bound to win acceptance from an ever-widening circle of scholars'.[51] His appraisal has proved to be prophetic.

Add. III is the 21 line soliloquy by the Chancellor on his rise to power, his relationship to his father, whom he now outranks, and on the risks of eminence in government under Henry VIII. The addition is written in Hand C but it must have been composed by one of the playwrights. Simpson, Hopkinson and Brooke considered it Shakespeare's but Spedding and Greg did not because they made a palaeographic distinction between Hands C and D. Sir Edmund Chambers and Bald seem to have been studying Add. III from a literary viewpoint at about the same time and arrived at conclusions that are remarkably similar. Chambers asks:

> If Shakespeare wrote Addition II(c), is it not possible that he also wrote Addition III, although it is in C's hand? . . . My attention was first called to the passage by the parallel in the first line to *Oth.* I.iii.322 . . . But the whole is at least as good as anything in Addition II(c). The vocabulary is consistent with Shakespeare's. The coupling of words, especially of the English 'smooth' with the Latin 'dexter' is like him. Even the pun [on More's name] in the fourteenth line is characteristic.

He supports his point on the agreement in vocabulary with thirteen examples from ten accepted plays. Bald says that the internal evidence of verbal parallels, echoes and a few identical phrases, from eight canonical plays is sufficient to establish Shakespeare's authorship. All have the genuine Shakespearian ring.[52] H.W. Crundell called attention to two characteristically Shakespearian ideas which are intertwined in Add. III: the 'law of children' – More's relations with his father – and 'corruption of the blood', a criminal law conception regarding such crimes as treason. He cites *Julius Caesar*, III.i.36–42 and the 'treason of Goneril', apparently II.iv.152–68. In a response, R.W. Chambers endorses Crundell's twin points and accepts the assignment of Add. III to Shakespeare, adding that any such finding 'might be regarded as subsidiary evidence that Shakespeare had a hand in the play as a whole' and that his claim as 'the author of the "147 lines" . . . would therefore be strengthened'.[53] Nosworthy critically examines the evidence presented to support Shakespeare's authorship of the soliloquy, especially the lexical parallels and the thought content, in the light of accepted work of Shakespeare and decides that 'Addition III . . . is demonstrably Shakespearian in tone, style, thought, and dramatic function. It bears no clear resemblance to the style of any other dramatist of the period and, on grounds of quality, seems beyond the scope of most. Its relationship to the canonical works turns out to be closely parallel, on all counts, with that established for the three pages of Addition II.'[54] Munro in his edition cites an unpublished letter of 11 February 1882 from S.A. Abbott to Furnivall in which Abbott finds likenesses between Shakespeare's work and Add. III. Munro disagrees. 'These 21 lines', he says, 'from their style, have been thought possibly or probably Shakespeare's in origin', but a comparison to a similar passage in *Thomas Lord Cromwell* inclines him to think that they are 'the work of an author concerned with *Cromwell*, and that this excludes Shakespeare'.[55]

G. Blakemore Evans brings into focus current scholarly thinking on the authorship of both Additions IIc and III in his introduction to the reprint of the two additions. Both 'are now generally accepted as the work of Shakespeare . . . The evidence advanced to connect Shakespeare with the two passages commonly attributed to him is significantly of various kinds'. He lists the painstaking handwriting analyses, 'the surprisingly large number of uncommon spelling links'

24

to Shakespearian quarto and folio texts, R.W. Chambers's 'expression of ideas', metrical and vocabulary studies. 'The real strength of the case for Shakespeare's authorship of these two passages rests, then, not on any single piece or kind of evidence but on the quite remarkable manner in which several independent lines of approach support and reinforce one another in pointing to a single conclusion – the "hand" of Shakespeare.'[56]

DATE

The problem of the date of composition of *More* is manifestly two-fold. To be established are both the date of the initial draft and the date of the revisions. Most students have either assumed or have stated without much discussion that the additions probably were written shortly after the original. Greg clearly assumes this to be so (pp. xix–xx), and so does Pollard (pp. 20–31). Collins, in the conclusion to the first substantial argument for a late date, locates both the original text and the additions in the same year. Shapiro sets the date of the additions in 1593 possibly two years after the original. Wentersdorf dates the original in 1592 and the additions two years later. Blayney thinks both were written in 1592.[57]

For the original date of composition almost every year has been suggested from 1586 (proposed by Simpson) to 1605 (by Schücking).[58] The stage of development of Munday's handwriting as exhibited in the manuscript is of prime value in establishing a date for the early draft. In the brief paper in which he identified Hand S as Munday's, Greg compares it with the penmanship in the manuscript *John a Kent* and the handwritten preliminaries to Munday's *Heaven of the Mind*, both of which are holograph, signed and dated. Greg concludes that these three exemplars show differences sufficiently significant to demonstrate a development in Munday's writing. The hand in *More* has forms related to both the other texts and therefore it must have been written between them, after *John a Kent* and before *Heaven*. He interpreted the date in *John a Kent* as 1596, which is a misreading, and that in *Heaven* as 1602, which it patently is. On the basis of this evidence Greg suggests a date of composition of 1598–1600. He concludes the note with other equally hastily formed opinions which he was later to abandon. Shortly thereafter Thompson reviewed the same evidence and pointed out that the date of 1596 for *John a Kent* was only a downward limit, that it may have been written as early as 1590, that Munday's writing in *More* 'lies much closer chronologically' to *John a Kent* and that an appropriate date for the collaborative play would be 1592–3. Greg in the 1923 symposium conditionally accepts Thompson's suggestion for the date of original composition, saying that 'should *John a Kent* prove to be before 1596, as it well may, a correspondingly earlier date must be assigned to *More*' (p. 51). In a later list of manuscript plays he notes, as to date, merely '*c.* 1593?'.[59]

Sir Edmund Chambers in *William Shakespeare* is ambivalent about the alternatives of an early or late date of composition. He lists a number of verse features such as double endings and extra mid-line syllables and notes that their incidence 'for what it is worth, does not suggest the earliest Shakespeare' (I, 509, n. 2). After a review of 'the clues to date' he says 'If Shakespeare wrote the Addition, these facts would perhaps fit best with a date in 1592–3', but that date 'would be rather early' for Dekker's and Heywood's participation. He thinks Schücking's date is ruled out by the palaeographical evidence, and concludes that 'the date, or dates, must remain undetermined' (I, 513).[60]

The date appended to *John a Kent* was closely examined in facsimile by Shapiro who provisionally determined that it read 1590 rather than 1595 or 1596. This was verified by staff members at the Huntington Library by a close examination of the manuscript and Shapiro prints a convincing photograph of the date. On the basis of Thompson's opinion that Munday's writing in *More* is close to the date of *John a Kent* and a reference to that play in a Martinist tract of September 1589, Shapiro concludes that Munday's original version of *More* 'would have to be dated not later than 1591 and . . . possibly earlier', and that the revision may have occurred 'about 1593, when Lord Strange's men, who then included Shakespeare [and the writer of Hand C], were temporarily associated with the Admiral's company'.[61] Jenkins also emphasizes the contemporaneous presence of Shakespeare and Hand C and decides that the additions would have to have been written before the reconstitution of the companies in 1594. 'The dates which best fit the evidence seem to be *c.* 1590–3 for the original composition and *c.* 1594–5 for the revision.' On the same grounds Wentersdorf settles on dates of 1592 when 'the original play must have been written for Edward Alleyn and the Strange's men', and the late spring of 1594 when 'the manuscript of *More* was hastily revised by Shakespeare and the dramatists working for Henslowe'. Blayney prosecutes a study of the style and vocabulary of four of Chettle's writings: *Piers Plainnes seauen yeres Prentiship* (1595), *Englands Mourning Garment* (1603), *The Tragedy of Hoffman* (printed 1631, but probably written much earlier), and *Kind-Harts Dreame* (1592). *Kind-Harts Dreame* shows more echoes of *More*. This evidence affords an opportunity to date Add. IIC with rather unusual precision: 'a fairly certain date for the Shakespeare addition of October/November 1592'. Blayney concludes that the composition of *More* began in the 'early months' of 1592, was submitted in June to Tilney who returned it in August with notes of his objections to 'prison-breaking, street brawls, and general trouble with prentices' . . . 'the necessary revision is made . . . [and] the MS is re-submitted', only to have Tilney object 'to the "Ill May Day" episode as a whole'. Although further revisions are planned the continuing unrest in London over aliens caused the effort to be abandoned. Some of the details of Blayney's case, though plausible, do not by their nature lend themselves to conclusive proof. However the evidence showing common vocabulary and usage between *Kind-Harts Dreame* and Add. IIC appears sound.[62]

Evans finds two main points favouring an early date for both sections of the play. The first is the palaeographic evidence from Munday's handwriting supported by Shapiro's reading of the date in *John a Kent*. The other is the association of Hands C and D in the same ms. The most likely time, he says, 'for an association [of Hand C] with D would have been prior to, or very shortly after, the official formation of the

Lord Chamberlain's Men (Shakespeare's company) in 1594'. Most critics prefer 'a date between 1590 and 1593 for the original play and of 1594 or 1595 for the revisions'.[63]

In 1912 Schücking suggested a late date of composition (1605) primarily by reference to the dates of other plays, especially *Thomas Lord Cromwell*, with which he thinks *More* has affinities but his proposal received little notice or support. Oliphant, on the basis of a comparison with the known dates of Munday's other dramatic writings, says '"More" should date not earlier than 1598–9'. G.B. Harrison applied an internal stop test to 41 lines of Addition IIc and compared his counts to the frequency of the same type of metrical phenomena in the plays which R.W. Chambers cited in his contribution to *Shakespeare's Hand*. The incidence of internal stops in the 41 lines of the addition is comparable to that of *Julius Caesar* and *Troilus and Cressida* and consequently 'it seems difficult, then, on internal evidence to place the More Speech before *Julius Caesar*; indeed, if the rhythmical tests, which are usually applied to date Shakespeare's plays, count for anything, it is later. It is still more difficult to believe that Shakespeare could have written it between 1595 and 1597'. Immediately thereafter Pollard applied the same test, using Harrison's method, to two speeches in Act IV of *The Merchant of Venice*, comprising together 37 lines, and found a slightly higher incidence of internal stops in *MV* than Harrison found in *More*, which leads him to conclude that 'I cannot myself see any difficulty in Shakespeare having written this speech of More about the same date as the *Merchant*, that is, 1594–5.'[64]

Collins notes that 'no serious study has been made of the emotional disturbances arising from the conditions of the time' which would account for the severity of Tilney's strictures. He calls attention to astrologically alarming events, the political conditions that led to the Essex rebellion, economic and sociological troubles such as the throng of loose and masterless men about the city. He decides that, in view of these circumstances which certainly would have worried Tilney, 'a date about 1601 has much to commend it'. In support he cites Harrison's internal stop test and comments by Sir Edmund Chambers. In consultation with Harrison he decides on this chronology: Dekker, Heywood and Munday wrote the play for the Admiral's men in 1601. Their prompter began preparation of the script for production, but the company decided not to proceed with it and returned it to the authors who then offered it to the Chamberlain's. Shakespeare touched up one scene and the play was submitted to Tilney who required such drastic alterations that it was never acted.[65] Bald finds it hard to ignore Harrison's evidence and decides that 'his general contention for a date *c.* 1600 rather than *c.* 1595 on metrical grounds is well founded'. He also cites Collins's argument that the best explanation for Tilney's refusal to permit the insurrection scenes to be played lies in the Essex rebellion. In late 1600 the Fortune was being built and the Admiral's men were on tour so it would be natural for Henslowe's dramatists to offer their new play to the Chamberlain's company. 'According to this hypothesis . . .' Bald says, '*Sir Thomas More* was begun in the latter part of 1600' (pp. 51–4).

Nosworthy studies the vocabulary characteristics of Addition IIc, finding that there are a few unique words but, more usefully, that there are a number of uncommon words which also occur in canonical plays. He finds 26 such words in plays ranging from *2 Henry VI* to *The Tempest*. Although 'such usages cannot be cited as absolute proof of anything . . . it may legitimately be claimed that the vocabulary of the three pages is entirely characteristic of Shakespeare's verbal habits for, roughly, the period 1598–1602'. He adds that *Henry V* is 'on a purely mathematical basis . . . the most relevant play' which would suggest a date of 1599, but because of R.W. Chambers's showing of the affinity between *More* and *Troilus and Cressida*, even though the latter 'is but slenderly represented in the lexical tabulation', he settles on a date of 1601–2.[66] Partridge prefaces a study of the play with a 'statement of what is already known, accepted or conjectured' about it. Probably it was 'written between 1593 and 1598, though some critics have argued for a date as late as 1600'. He analyses the contractions, grammatical forms, spelling and punctuation of the Shakespearian addition and finds relationships to the canonical middle plays. In his 'Conclusions' he tells us that 'the original play was probably written between 1593 and 1597, and the revisions, at any rate Dekker's and Shakespeare's, between 1598 and 1601. In either case the later dates are to be preferred'. Matchett determines a later date as a result of the relationship he has defined between *More* and *MV*. He makes a fairly convincing case that the two plays share significant imagery and lexical preferences, but his case for the priority of *MV* is weak. However, on the basis of an assumption that the canonical play is the earlier he tells us that he is 'naturally prepared to argue that the *More* fragment must have been written after the writing of *The Merchant of Venice*, which is to say at the 1600 end of the usual dating spectrum'.[67] Jackson presents indices of selected colloquial forms in all the plays of the canon based on earlier counts by Frederick Waller, and shows that their use by Shakespeare increases steadily, with only a few aberrations, from the earliest to the latest plays. There is a notable shift to more frequent use of such forms around 1600, *Twelfth Night*, for example, showing a three-fold increase compared to *As You Like It*. The frequency of these colloquial forms 'unequivocally associates Hand D of *Sir Thomas More* with the post-1600 Shakespeare plays . . . everything points to composition no earlier than 1600'. Jackson thinks that Shakespeare's addition is most unlikely to have been written before 1600 and that 'he might well have written it several years later'. He offers no opinion regarding the date of composition of the original version.[68]

Thus we have two primary schools of scholarly thinking in regard to the date of composition of the two elements of *More*. Those who favour an early date for the original and a date for the revisions of a year or two thereafter are in the mainstream of criticism in company with some of the most eminent students of the play. The alternative line of thought, possibly shaped by the spectacular failure of the Essex rebellion,[69] sets the original date of composition at about the turn of the century and, again, with the additions composed soon after. There is a third conception, not so much separate from the other two but rather in the nature of a synthesis, latterly represented by the thinking of Lake, Taylor and McMillin (the last two in papers in this collection) that posits an early date for the original version and a post-1600 date for the additions. Pollard hinted at it in *Shakespeare's Hand* when he noted 'the further possibility . . . that the play was drafted at one of the early dates and rewritten with additions at one of the later ones' (p. 21). Sir Edmund Chambers thinks 'it is just possible that *Sir Thomas More* was laid aside when Tilney sent it back, and taken up later by new writers, with different literary notions from Munday's, in the hope that the political cloud had blown by and that Tilney might now be persuaded to allow the main original structure to stand'. He does not say how much time he assumes between the two efforts, but it appears he was thinking of at least a few years. Lake has little doubt 'that the original play . . . belongs to the early 1590s'. He then examines the Shakespeare and Dekker additions, finding the Shakespearean style 'unmistakeably mature' based on indices of frequency of feminine endings, alexandrines and half lines in the range found in *The Merry Wives of Windsor, Hamlet, Measure for Measure, Macbeth* and *Antony and Cleopatra*. Dekker's use of colloquialisms in *More* as compared to his plays written after 1600 seems to show that his addition was written shortly before *Satiromastix* and *2 Honest Whore*, both dated by Fredson Bowers 1605–7. Neither Shakespeare's nor Dekker's additions, according to Lake, were written 'earlier than 1600. They may well be several years later than that'.[70] Perhaps further studies will settle the issue of the date of composition but at this time Collins's comment of a half-century ago remains valid: 'In spite of all this spade work, no satisfactory conjectural date has been forthcoming. There are a number of difficulties which have to be considered, and no date proposed so far has eliminated all of them'.[71]

SOURCES

Unlike the problems of the identification of the hands, of authorship, and of the two dates of composition, which have received considerable critical attention, the problem of the sources of *More* has been largely neglected. In the history of the scholarship only two studies of significance have been published, one by Marie Schütt in 1933, the other by Vittorio Gabrieli in 1986. Dyce offered no comment on sources in the brief Preface to his edition, but under the heading 'Illustrations of the Earlier Scenes of the Play' he reprinted a substantial segment of Hall's *Chronicle*, recounting the incidents leading up to Ill May Day 1517, the riot itself and the aftermath, concluding with the King's pardon of the insurrectionists. Dyce also printed a ballad entitled *The Story of Ill May-Day in the time of King Henry VIII., and why it was so Called, and how Queen Catherine begged the lives of Two Thousand London Apprentices* covering the same events. In his commentary notes, he provides additional 'illustrations', drawn from Hall's *Chronicle*, from Roper's and Cresacre More's *Lives* and from *Lusty Juventus*. Hall is cited three times, once in paraphrase, Roper six times, Cresacre More three times and *Lusty Juventus* once. Most of these, except for *Lusty Juventus*, are anecdotal. In a short paragraph headed 'Sources of Plot' Hopkinson notes that for the earlier scenes the playwrights' source was Hall, for later scenes Hall, Stow or Holinshed, and, for More's execution, Foxe. They also had access to Roper's *Life* and drew on the 'stories and traditions of More . . . current at the time'. Brooke in *The Shakespeare Apocrypha* identifies Hall as the 'main source of the drama', says that the story of More's life and death was 'common property' and announces that he has found the source of the incidents of 'the fight in Pannier Alley' and of the long-haired ruffian in Foxe. Greg does not discuss sources in the Introduction to his edition except to notice the borrowings from *Lusty Juventus* and *The Disobedient Child*.[72] Subsequent to the Malone Society reprint little attention had been paid to sources, the typical observation being that Hall provided the historical facts. In *Shakespeare's Hand* Pollard mentions only Foxe as a source (p. 2) although a curious negative comment in a discussion of date may indicate his ideas of other sources: 'There is no mention of anti-alien riots [of 1586] in Holinshed or Stow' (p. 25). The subject of sources does not come up in Sir Edmund Chambers's *William Shakespeare*.

In her essay Schütt observes at the outset that the possible sources for a play on More during the latter part of the sixteenth century are many and varied. She categorizes them as Protestant, therefore unsympathetic to More; Catholic, in which he is the saint and martyr; and the oral tradition in which he is a man of spirit, wit and humour. The five biographies of More of the sixteenth and early seventeenth centuries are listed and briefly described: those of Roper, Harpsfield, Stapleton, Ro: Ba: and Cresacre More. It is clear that she considers the *Lives* collectively as the major, though not the only, source. The play is reviewed scene by scene, and in all but four cases, she determines the source. The insurrection sequence and the council scene are derived from Hall and the long-haired ruffian incident from Foxe. Hall also supplies some minor elements in the concluding Tower and execution scenes. The major portion of the play comes from one or other of the biographies supplemented from the oral tradition with which the playwrights were no doubt familiar – Brooke's 'common property'. The four incidents for which Schütt does not suggest a source are the play-within-a-play, except, of course, More's participation which derives from Roper, the presentation of the 'Articles' to the Council for signature, Fisher at the Tower and the scene of More's serving men. In conclusion she says: 'Zusammenfassend kann man sagen, dass Halls Chronik und Ro. Ba.s Biographie als Hauptquellen anzunehmen sind, dass aber die Verfasser einzelne Zuge auch aus anderweitiger Tradition schöpften'.[73]

Critics who have expressed views on the sources of *More* since Schütt have generally avoided direct comment on her essay, perhaps due to caution about the prominence given in her study to the perceived contribution from Ro: Ba:'s *Life*, which is late and derivative. R.W. Chambers finds Hall's *Chronicle* the most important source, mentions Roper and Stapleton's *Lives* and 'London tradition', but not Ro: Ba:. 'Hall's *Chronicle* was directly followed and was a main source for the first part of the play', Jenkins tells us in the introduction to his edition. He also cites as sources 'the lively tradition of anecdote', Foxe and *Lusty Juventus* but declares that 'any direct relation between the biographies and the play is most unlikely'. Most commentators who do discuss sources, though not in any detail, mention Hall, Foxe, the *Lives*, *Lusty Juventus* and the oral tradition, occasionally noting other less likely possibilities such as Erasmus's letter to Ulrich von Hutten. Sources of minor elements in the play such as the urinal jest (ll. †1751–5, p. 58), which first appeared in print in Sir John Harington's *The Metamorphosis of Ajax* (1596), are even more rarely noticed.[74]

Parallel to what may be considered the orthodox view of the sources of *More* – Hall as the principal source, with Roper's *Life*, the other biographies, Foxe and the orally transmitted stories secondary – there has been an alternate conception that the primary source is Roper with the others subsidiary. Schütt implies this by saying that one of the 'Hauptquellen' is Ro: Ba:'s *Life* which ultimately derives from Roper through Harpsfield and Stapleton. Irving Ribner, after describing the three part structure of the play, says 'For all of their material the authors seem to have gone mainly to Roper's life of More, although some use must also have been made of John Foxe's *Acts and Monuments*, from whence came the anecdote of the long-haired servant, which Foxe attributes to Thomas Cromwell, but which our authors decided to give to More'.[75] In an essay on the structure and meaning of the play Judith Doolin Spikes finds that 'many, perhaps most, of the virtues of the play are those of its principal source, William Roper's *Life*'. In a note she adds 'The authorities agree that Roper's *Life* is the principal source . . . [but] the playwrights had read John Foxe's *Acts and Monuments* . . . also . . . Hall's *Chronicle*'. She sums up: 'the correspondences between the play and Roper's *Life* are so numerous and so close that its status as the principal source cannot be doubted, even though use of it may well have been at second or third hand' presumably as incorporated into subsequent *Lives*. She also raises a question concerning the manner in which it came into the playwrights' hands.[76] Michael Anderegg, one of the most knowledgeable scholars on Morean biography, undertook, in answer to Spikes's question, to 'suggest a possible way that a manuscript of Roper's (or Harpsfield's) biography could have come to the attention of at least one of the playwrights involved in the composition of *Sir Thomas More*'. He recalls that a copy of Harpsfield's *Life* was found in the study of Thomas More, the Chancellor's grandson, when he was arrested by Richard Topcliffe at Cambridge on 13 April 1582, according to a note written in the manuscript itself now in the Emmanuel College Library. Topcliffe, well-known as a recusant hunter, was a superior of Munday's whom he employed 'to guard and take bonds of recusants'. Anderegg conjectures that under circumstances similar to those in which the Harpsfield *Life* was found, Munday may have come upon a manuscript copy of Roper's and 'might have seen in it the germ of a play'. He believes that 'the early lives of More are very much in the background of *Sir Thomas More*'.[77] Among those who have studied the problem of the play's sources it has become habitual to assume that the playwrights borrowed Foxe's anecdote of the long-haired ruffian and substituted More for Cromwell as the protagonist in the play's version of the story. In *Shakespeare's Hand* Pollard says that it is 'rather unhappily transferred to More'[78] and almost all later commentators have followed Pollard's lead. Another explanation appears possible. That the playwrights were *au courant* with the Morean anecdotal tradition is generally accepted. Perhaps they knew a form of the story with More as the principal rather than Cromwell. One of the collaborators may have read Foxe's version in *Acts and Monuments* and decided to use it in the 'domestic' sequence of the play except that he restored More as the hero in accord with the version transmitted orally. This explanation is admittedly speculative but no more so than Pollard's assertion for which he has no superior warrant. I believe it is even possible that Foxe knew the oral tradition of the anecdote with More as the central figure and adapted it to his purposes in his eulogistic presentation of Thomas Cromwell whom he greatly admired, calling him 'a continual nourisher of peace'.[79]

Gabrieli studies the potential sources of *More* which he classifies as 'historical, biographical, dramatic and literary'. Of the first category he determines that 'Hall's *Union* was the ultimate authority on the May Day events in London'. However since Hall's book was 'quite rare', he thinks that 'Munday . . . appears to have used it in the less grandiloquent version it assumed in Holinshed's *Chronicles*' in the enlarged reprint of 1586–7. He supports his finding by reference to passages in the play that are closer to Holinshed's adaptation of Hall than to Hall's original text: 'Where Hall and Holinshed differ, the wording in *STM* is always closer to the latter.' Of the biographical sources Roper's *Life* is regarded as seminal, but Gabrieli concludes that the playwrights used Harpsfield's (based in part on Roper) which was not printed until 1932 but during the sixteenth century circulated widely in manuscript, of which eight copies are still extant. He rejects Schütt's contention that Ro: Ba:'s *Life* is one of the 'Hauptquellen' of the play, accepts Foxe as the source of the Jack Faulkner incident and identifies Stapleton's *Vita* as a minor source. *2 Henry VI*, *Richard III*, *Troilus and Cressida*, *Julius Caesar*, *King Lear* and *Coriolanus* are cited as dramatic sources or analogues, generally for scenes involving the common people. Literary sources – all minor – include More's *English Works*, Erasmus and Polydore Vergil. The portion of Gabrieli's essay devoted to the sources is the most thoughtful and illuminating we have. In the only other source study F.P. Wilson traces the metaphor of humanity preying on itself, which occurs in More's address to the rioters, to John Poynet's *Short Treatise of Politic Power* (1556) who cites Theodoretus, one of the Church Fathers.[80]

TILNEY IN THE MANUSCRIPT

The manuscript *Booke of Sir Thomas Moore* is one of only a small number of play manuscripts surviving from the Elizabethan era which show the censor actually at work on a script. The censorship responsibility was assigned to the Master of the Revels who was under the general direction of the Lord Chamberlain of the royal household. The surviving records do not clearly establish that the review and 'reformation' of plays prior to performance was a duty of the Master of the Revels when Edmund Tilney was appointed the first regular incumbent in that office in 1579. However, in a special commission issued 24 December 1581 which arose out of a rivalry between the London corporation and the Privy Council for control of the stage, including plays, actors, playwrights and playing places, the responsibility was clearly assigned to the Master. The patent setting forth the commission provides in part that Tilney is authorized 'or all suche showes, plaies, plaiers and playmakers, together with their playing places, to order and reforme, auctorise and put downe, as shalbe thought meete or vnmeete vnto himselfe or his said deputie'.[81]

Tilney wrote an explicit charge at the head of fol. 3ʳ of *The Booke of Sir Thomas Moore* which leaves no doubt either of his authority to censor plays submitted to him or of the kind of play content that concerned the government. It reads: ' <Leaue out>| ye insur <rection>| wholy &| ye Cause ther off & | <b>egin wt Sr Tho:|Moore att ye mayors sessions|wt a reportt afterwards|off his good servic'|don being' Shriue off London|vppon a mutiny Agaynst ye|Lumbards only by A shortt|reportt & nott otherwise|att your own perrilles|E Tyllney' (p. 1). The two most important subjects considered inappropriate for playhouse entertainment were political topics, including criticism of court personages, and matters of religion. Playwrights, then as now, tended to be, at minimum, irreverent, and the targets of their gibes, then as now, were the very persons and things the serious segments of society were sensitive about. Tilney could not in conscience encourage the sympathetic treatment of sedition on stage and consequently ordered the spectacle of civil disorder to be reduced to a neutral report. As to controversial religious topics, the dramatists of *More* successfully avoid them completely.

The precise relationship between the censor and the *Booke of Sir Thomas Moore* poses another scholarly puzzle. Greg identified Tilney's hand at several places in the play in addition to the note on fol. 3ʳ. He made several marks of disapproval, and comments 'Mend yis' opposite line 320 (p. 12) and 'all altr' at line †1256 (p. 42), but Greg says (p. xiv) that his hand does not seem to occur in any of the revisions. The *Booke* has been examined at first hand by a number of students of the play and all concur in this determination although it is recognized that some of the marks in the additions are not sufficiently distinctive to be identifiable. Before Greg's Malone Society reprint some scholars believed that the additions had been written in response to Tilney's strictures (e.g. Simpson, Ward and Brooke),[82] but Greg's explanation has proved so cogent that no later critic accepts the earlier hypothesis. He sums up his discussion with the assertion that no 'notice whatever [has] been taken of the censor's orders' (p. xiv).

A variety of solutions have been proposed to the problem of determining in what form the play was submitted to Tilney for his review, what the process was, and if possible, what the date was. Before Greg's edition scholars decided, without much analysis, that the authors submitted to Tilney the original fair copy in Munday's hand. Greg's determination led him to conclude that 'every indication in the manuscript points to its having been submitted for license in its present form' (p. xiv), that is, the original text plus the revisions and additions as the manuscript now stands. Sir Edmund Chambers objects. Greg's argument, he says, 'obliges us to suppose that the play was sent to Tilney in a most untidy and in places almost unintelligible condition; in a variety of hands; with long passages only marked for deletion by marginal lines; with Addition I fitted into the wrong scene; with Addition VI so fitted in as to break the continuity of Sc. ix, and still containing a draft of part of Addition V'. He thinks the script 'was laid aside when Tilney sent it back, and taken up later by new writers' who composed the additions.[83] Some critics who have written since Chambers have accepted Greg's view that the additions do not respond to Tilney's strictures but have elected to follow one or another version of Chambers's conjecture as to the sequence of events. The weakness in this theory is that it does not offer a satisfactory explanation for Tilney's absence from the additions. Sir Edmund's reason for rejecting Greg's hypothesis is that it is unreasonable to assume that Tilney would review an untidy script. But the censor may have accepted it even though the manuscript was not easy to read. Wentersdorf points out that we know next to nothing about Tilney's relationship with the players and that he might have raised no objection to reviewing a messy manuscript, especially if, as Wentersdorf speculates, the company proffered an additional fee. Greg notes that those who argue that Tilney accepted the *Booke* for allowance in its chaotic state can point to the late play *The Launching of the Mary* which was reviewed and allowed by Sir Henry Herbert in a state of 'extreme untidiness'.[84]

While most scholars settle for either Greg's or Chambers's theory, a few have attempted to devise an explanation for all aspects of the case. Bald analysed the conflicting suggestions of Greg and Chambers and noted that in Add. IIb the aliens are 'Lombards' rather than French, Dutch or strangers. This may mean that the playwrights had learned that Tilney did not object to the foreigners being Lombards, perhaps because Lombardy had virtually become enemy (i.e. Spanish) territory. This leads Bald to

surmise that the play was submitted to Tilney not once, but twice; the first time he made only a few minor deletions in the early scenes, but altered the references to the aliens' nationality, and confined his attention mainly to the scenes on the missing leaves . . . [and he] insisted on seeing that his instructions had been observed in the revisions . . . When the play was re-submitted, Tilney proved, perhaps owing to recent political developments, even more rigorous than he had been on the first occasion, and the actors, in spite of the fact that they had gone so far as to cast the play, decided that it was useless to attempt any further revision.

Bald acknowledges that his solution is 'almost all pure conjecture' but thinks it 'more satisfactory' than Chambers's (pp. 50–1, and n. 11). Dover Wilson describes the problem and tells us that the play as it stands is in the process of being drastically overhauled. 'In some way . . . the instructions of the censor must be related to the disorderly condition of the "booke"'. This he calls 'the chief puzzle of the manuscript' but, uncharacteristically, he has no solution to offer. In his review of the scholarship to 1961 Jenkins says 'Tilney's censorship of the play – or rather the relation between his censorship and the revisions – remains an enigma'. He does not subscribe to Greg's conjecture and cannot believe that the additions followed shortly after the original text because 'Munday's hand is absent from them'. Furthermore the additions 'bear no mark recognizable as Tilney's and there is no reason to think he read them. It seems clear to me that the confusions of the present manuscript are due to alterations begun and not perfected'. Bald's hypothesis 'involves supposing that the play was submitted to the censor (on the second occasion) unfinished and chaotic, and it leaves the other additions entirely out of account. I therefore incline to the alternative, tentatively suggested by Sir Edmund Chambers, that what Tilney read was the original version of the play'.[85] Blayney finds 'two distinct biasses in the censorship, first against prentice riots and prison breaking, second against anti-alien trouble'. He suggests the following time-table and history of the manuscript: Early months of 1592 to June – the play is drafted and Munday prepares a fair copy which is submitted to Tilney; he censors the references to prison breaking, street brawls and prentice troubles, and returns the manuscript in August; revisions are made and the play resubmitted in November; Tilney now objects 'to the "Ill May Day" episode as a whole' and returns the manuscript in January 1593; revisions are planned but an outbreak of plague closes the theatres in February and the play is abandoned. Blayney's solution involves two submissions for allowances and two stages of revision of which the second was planned but not carried out.[86] Chillington believes that some time in 1601–2 Tilney saw the original draft of the play which was returned with the admonition of fol. 3^r. His hand is not in the additions 'because he had not seen them'. The playwrights did not take Tilney's orders literally and began a revision which would make some concession to his requirements, but they did not think it necessary to abandon completely the presentation of Ill May Day. To obtain a licence they relied on their ability to negotiate with Tilney via 'back-alley communications with the Revels Office' to gain his acceptance of a partial recasting of the script. But Elizabeth's death and an onset of plague closed the playhouses and caused the collaborators to abandon the play.[87] Another explanation conjectures that Tilney's review of *More* and the changes attributable to literary and theatrical considerations took place at the same time, that the company interested in the play arranged for revisions, working from the foul papers, after the fair copy had been sent to the Master of the Revels but before it was returned to them. This hypothesis obviates the necessity to explain why Tilney would accept a confused copy for review and accounts for his absence from the additions – he never saw them.[88] All of these explanations from Greg's onward are, of course, speculative since there is no external evidence and the only thing approaching 'hard' internal evidence is the absence of Tilney's hand from the revisions which, in itself, is nothing more than an aspect of the problem.

EARLY STAGE HISTORY

The early stage history, like almost everything else about *More*, is subject to controversy. Most scholars who have studied the play have formed the opinion that it was not acted in Elizabethan times. This judgement is based on the interpretation of two kinds of evidence. First, it is thought that the opposition of the Master of the Revels expressed in his note on folio 3^r is conclusive. His admonition is so sweeping that the play could not be presented in anything like its original form, that in fact, if his requirements had been met, the script would have been unplayable. Second, the state of *More* is so disjointed and incoherent that in the condition in which we have it, it is unfit for the stage, suggesting that it was abandoned before it could be adequately prepared for performance. Of course even if we accept that the manuscript as it is could not have been used as a promptbook that does not prove that a promptbook was not prepared from it. Nevertheless, on these grounds Greg decided that 'it is evident throughout that the manuscript has not been finally revised for presentation . . . [so it was] laid aside and the play never came on the boards' (p. xv). An overwhelming majority of critics from Greg down to several participants in this symposium have expressed like sentiments.

There are some bits of evidence that the play was cast. On fol. 13*^{r} (Add. v, l. 2, p. 89) opposite a stage direction 'Enter A Messenger to moore' there is a well-known note that reads 'Mess T Goodal,' preceded by a cross within a circle. Thomas Goodale's name also appears in the playhouse plot of *2 Seven Deadly Sins* (1592), a play which probably belonged to Lord Strange's men, the predecessor company to the Lord Chamberlain's. Greg, in his notes to the transcription of the Ill May Day scenes reprinted in *Shakespeare's Hand* (pp. 202, 208 and 209), points out that in two separate entry directions in the additions (in Hand C), no entry is provided for Sherwin, although he was in the original text, and two of his lines have been reassigned to other speakers. He says that 'this attempt to get rid of a minor but still important character can only be due to difficulties of casting and corroborates the evidence afforded by the occurrence of Goodall's name (fol. 13*^{r}) that the parts were actually assigned'. W.J. Lawrence interpreted the Goodale note and the preceding cross as a prompt warning and found four others in the ms. 'Either these are prompter's warnings or they are meaningless' and he adds 'The inference is that the whole play as we have it, *plus* the lacunae, formed a prompt copy'.[89] Greg responded by questioning the validity of Lawrence's designating two of the marginal notations as prompt warnings, but adds 'It certainly seems probable that the preparations for performance had reached a fairly advanced stage'. However 'the work of incorporating the alterations was never completed and this is an even more formidable objection to supposing that the play was actually performed'.[90] Muriel St Clare Byrne, who addressed herself primarily to another aspect of Lawrence's original item, the date of composition, briefly comments on his prompt copy hypothesis: 'His contention that this play was acted – contrary as it is to the opinion hitherto more generally held – is certainly a satisfying one'.[91] In the summation of his case Lawrence adds two stage directions that mention properties in support of his theory that the manuscript is a promptbook but modifies his contention in regard to prompt warnings to 'one sheet has an unmistakable prompt warning, and . . . on a few others there are possible warnings'.[92] Similarly there are two morsels of evidence from other playwrights which may indicate that they knew the play. C.R. Baskervill finds a series of elements common to Jonson's *Bartholomew Fair* and *More* and, since the latter was not in print in 1614, he thinks Jonson knew it in performance. These include the censure of the victim, not the cutpurse; the rebuke of the censurer; the downfall of the overconfident man; the manner of the discovery of the loss; the moral brought home to the censurer; a reference to a judge while on the bench losing 'a fair pouch of velvete'; a play-within-a-play (in *Bartholomew Fair* it is a puppet show) and in each case a list of shows by title; and the delay in starting the play followed by some jesting about the performance. He also finds close similarities, both general and specific, between pairs of characters from the two plays, e.g. Suresbie – Overdo, both justices, and Faulkner – Waspe, both ruffians. S.R. Golding quotes some lines from *The Death of Robert, Earl of Huntingdon* which link Lady Vanity and long-haired ruffians. This can only refer to *More*. 'The reference' he adds 'seems to imply that "More" had recently been performed on the stage, since an allusion of this kind would have been unintelligible to the audience, if the play had only existed in manuscript or if the production of "More" had ante-dated that of "The Death" by several years. If, therefore, my interpretation of the passage quoted is correct, there are adequate reasons for the belief that "Sir Thomas More" was acted towards the close of 1597'.[93]

In his 1961 retrospective review of prior scholarship Jenkins says the evidence adduced for and against performance is inconclusive. He cannot hold with Lawrence that the 'much scored and altered manuscript . . . can . . . have served as a promptbook' but the annotations by C indicate that the manuscript 'passed through the hands of a book-keeper who had the preparation of a promptbook in mind'. Because the manuscript could not itself serve as a promptbook does not mean that one was not made (pp. xliii–xliv). McMillin studies *More* as a theatrical rather than a literary document. He believes that the principal purpose of some of the revisions is to facilitate casting and points out that Add. VI (p. 93) includes, in a section of dialogue between Luggins and the Vice, two speech prefixes at lines 61 and 66 that read 'clo' (clown) instead of Vice as would have been expected. This shows that the playwright knew that the actor who would play the part of the clown in *More* would double as the Vice in *The Marriage of Wit and Wisdom*. Thus 'the revisers attended to the specific casting of the play as they worked'. He also concludes that although from a literary point of view the manuscript may not be completely satisfactory 'the action has been made coherent, the revisions have been fitted into place with the possible exception of folio 6, speech prefixes and dialogue have been brought into good condition, but entrance and exit directions have been left in an uncorrected state'. Relatively little remains to be done to facilitate preparation of a promptbook. He decides that *More*, 'despite its apparent disorder, is a coherent theatrical document'.[94] It is probable that the casting of the parts had proceeded a considerable way towards completion and that producing a prompt-book, while perhaps not an easy task, would not, in Jenkins's words, 'be beyond an experienced playhouse book-keeper such as we take this annotator [C] to have been'. While sufficient evidence has been adduced to constitute a challenge to the orthodox theory that the play was not acted at the time it was written, the matter is not settled.

NOTES

1 Richard Simpson, 'Are there any Extant MSS. in Shakespeare's Handwriting?' *NQ*, 183 (July 1871), 1–3.

2 Thomas Hearne, *Remarks and Collections*, Vol. 9. Ed. by H.E. Salter for the Oxford Historical Society. (Oxford, 1914), pp. 392–3.

3 Alexander Dyce, ed., *Sir Thomas More, A Play; Now First Printed*. (For the Shakespeare Society. London, 1844). Fleay calls the text muddled, 'neither the original version nor the altered, but a farrago of the two' in *A Biographical Chronicle of the English Drama*. (2 vols. London, 1891. Rpt. New York, 1969), II, 312.

4 A.F. Hopkinson, ed., *Sir Thomas More*. (Privately printed. London, 1902. Rpt., with introduction revised, 1915). Citations are to the 1915 issue.

5 C.F. Tucker Brooke, ed., *The Shakespeare Apocrypha*, (Oxford, 1908. Rpt. 1967). He collated the original ms. with Dyce's transcription and made some minor corrections to Dyce's text but also made some errors of his own.

6 John S. Farmer, ed., *The Book of Sir Thomas Moore*. Tudor Facsimile Texts, no. 65. (Edinburgh and London, 1910. Rpt. New York, 1970).

7 W.W. Greg, ed., *The Book of Sir Thomas More*. Malone Society Reprints. (Oxford, 1911. Rpt. with 'Supplement to the Introduction' by Harold Jenkins, 1961). Line and page citations in this chapter, unless otherwise noted, refer to Greg's edition.

8 John Shirley, ed., *Sir Thomas More: An Anonymous Play of the Sixteenth Century Ascribed in Part to Shakespeare*. (Canterbury, n.d. [?1938]). Herbert Farjeon, ed., *The Complete Works of William Shakespeare*. 4 vols. (London; New York, 1953), *Sir Thomas More*, vol. III.

9 Harold Jenkins, ed., *Sir Thomas More* in *Complete Works*. Ed. by C.J. Sisson. (London, 1954), pp. 1235–66. The most recent edition of *Sir Thomas More* is that of Vittorio Gabrieli and Giorgio Melchiori (Bari, 1981) in the 'Biblioteca Italiana di Testi' series. The text is modernized and the *apparatus criticus* is in Italian. For those fortunate enough to have a modicum of Italian this edition will prove valuable.

10 Edward Maunde Thompson, *Shakespeare's Handwriting*. (Oxford, 1916), pp. 32–7. W.W. Greg, ed., Section VI, 'Ill May Day. Scenes from the Play of Sir Thomas More'; and Section VII, 'Special Transcript of the Three Pages' in *Shakespeare's Hand in the Play of Sir Thomas More*. Ed. by Alfred W. Pollard. (Cambridge, 1923. Rpt. 1967), R.C. Bald, "*The Booke of Sir Thomas More* and its Problems," *ShS*, 2 (1949), 44–65. John Munro, ed., *The London Shakespeare*. (London, New York, 1957), 6 vols. *Sir Thomas More*, vol. 4, pp. 1255–78. Thomas Clayton, ed., *The 'Shakespearean' Additions in the Booke of Sir Thomas Moore: Some Aids to Scholarly and Critical Shakespearean Studies*. Shakespeare Studies Monograph Series 1, ed. by J. Leeds Barroll. (Dubuque, Iowa, 1969). P.J. Croft, ed., *Autograph Poetry in the English Language*. (London, 1973), vol. 1, no. 23. G. Blakemore Evans, ed., 'Sir Thomas More' in *The Riverside Shakespeare*. (Boston, 1974), pp. 1683–1700.

11 Thompson, *Shakespeare's Handwriting*, plates 1–3 following p. 32. Greg, following p. xlvi. Bald, 'Booke', plates XIII–xv following p. 48. Croft, *Autograph Poetry*, 1, no. 23. S. Schoenbaum, *William Shakespeare; A Documentary Life*. (New York, 1975), plate 118, p. 159; *William Shakespeare; Records and Images*. (New York, 1981), plates 52–4, pp. 113–15. Anthony G. Petti, *English Literary Hands from Chaucer to Dryden*. (Cambridge, Mass., 1977), pp. 87, 91, 95 and 111. Evans, ed., pp. 1698–1700.

12 W.W. Greg, 'Autograph Plays by Anthony Munday', *MLR*, 8 (1913): 89–90; *Shakespeare's Hand*, p. 48. See also E.M. Thompson, 'The Autograph Manuscripts of Anthony Munday', *Transactions of the Bibliographical Society*, XIV (October 1915–March 1917), 325–53.

13 W.W. Greg, ed., *Elizabethan Stage Abridgements: The Battle of Alcazar & Orlando Furioso*. Malone Society Reprints. (Oxford, 1922. Rpt. 1964), pp. 22–3. *Dramatic Documents from the Elizabethan Playhouses*. 2 vols. (Oxford, 1931. Rpt. 1969); 'Commentary,' pp. 105–22; 130–7; 'Reproductions & Transcripts,' II, IV.

14 *Shakespeare's Hand in the Play of Sir Thomas More*, pp. 41–56.

15 W.W. Greg, 'Shakespeare's Hand Once More'. *TLS*, 24 November and 1 December 1927, pp. 871, 908. (Rpt. *W.W. Greg: Collected Papers*. Ed. by J.C. Maxwell. (Oxford, 1966), pp. 192–200). Page citations in the text refer to the *Collected Papers*.

16 Samuel A. Tannenbaum, *The Booke of Sir Thomas Moore; A Bibliotic Study*. (New York, 1927).

17 W.W. Greg, ed., *English Literary Autographs 1550–1650*. 3 parts. (Oxford, 1925–32. Rpt. Nendeln, 1968), plate VII.

18 Alexander C. Judson, ed., *The Captives*. For the Elizabethan Club. (New Haven, 1921). W.W. Greg, 'The Escapes of Jupiter; An Autograph Play of Thomas Heywood's', *Anglica* (*Palaestra*, vol. 148, 1925), 211–43. (Rpt. *Collected Papers*, pp. 156–83). Thompson, 'Autograph MSS.', pp. 334, 352–3. E.H.C. Oliphant, '*Sir Thomas More*', *JEGP*, 18 (1919), 226–35.

19 Tannenbaum, *Booke*, pp. 69–78; 89–93. See also Samuel A. Tannenbaum, *Problems in Shakespeare's Penmanship*. (New York, 1927. Rpt. New York, 1966), pp. 179–211.

20 R.B. McKerrow, Rev. of Tannenbaum's *The Booke of Sir Thomas More*, *RES*, 4 (1928), 237–41. Charles Sisson, Rev. of *Problems in Shakespeare's Penmanship* and of *Booke*, *MLR*, 23 (1928), 231–4. Greg, Rev. of Tannenbaum's *Booke*, *Library*, 9 (1928), 202–11. T.W. Baldwin, Rev. of Tannenbaum's *Booke*, *MLN*, 43 (1928), 327–32. Tannenbaum replied to the criticisms of the reviewers in *Shakespeare and Sir Thomas Moore*, (New York, 1929) and *An Object Lesson in Shakespearian Research*, (New York, 1931).

21 Robert Adger Law, 'Is Heywood's Hand in *Sir Thomas More?*' *Texas Studies in English*, 11 (1931), 24–31.

22 J.M. Nosworthy, 'Hand B in *Sir Thomas More*', *Library*, 5 no. 11 (1956), 47–50.

23 Heywood appended an errata list to the end of his *Exemplary Lives and Memorable Acts of Nine the Worthy Women of the World* (1640), 'Excusing the Compositor, who received this Coppy in a difficult and unacquainted hand'. Most of the palaeographic students of *More* comment unfavourably on Heywood's writing, using such terms as 'ill-formed' (Greg, *Shakespeare's Hand*, (p. 42), 'atrocious' (Tannenbaum, *Booke*, p. 56), 'ungainly' (Nosworthy, 'Hand B', p. 47) and 'abominable' (Petti, *English Literary Hands*, p. 55).

24 Jenkins, in Greg, p. xxxiv. For Pollard's phrase see *Shakespeare's Hand*, p. 1.

25 For example, Albert Feuillerat, *The Composition of Shakespeare's Plays: Authorship, Chronology*. (New Haven, 1953), pp. 48–9 n. L.L. Schücking, 'Shakespeare and *Sir Thomas More*', *RES*, 1 (1925), 40–59. His view is reiterated in 'Über Einige Probleme der Neueren und Neuesten Shakespeare-Forschung,' *Germanish-Romanische Monatsschrift*, 33 (1951–2), 208–28. See also his earlier 'Das Datum des Pseudo-Shakespeareschen *Sir Thomas Moore*', *Englische Studien*, 46 (1912–13), 228–51. Tannenbaum, *Shakspere's Penmanship*, pp. 179–211. Ralph H. Lane, 'Shakespearean Spelling.' *SNL*, 8 no. 4 (September 1958), 28.

26 Paul Ramsey, 'Shakespeare and *Sir Thomas More* Revisited: or, A Mounty on the Trail,' *PBSA*, 70 (1976), 333–46. R.A. Huber, 'On Looking over Shakespeare's "Secretarie"', *Stratford Papers on Shakespeare, 1960*. Ed. by B.A.W. Jackson. (Toronto, 1961), pp. 53–70. C.J. Sisson, 'Postscript', pp. 70–7. Munro, ed., *The London Shakespeare*, p. 1259, lists a dozen earlier critics who have been sceptical of the identification of D with Shakespeare, 'nearly all of them, it is true, before the full force of the cumulative evidence was manifest'.

27 Greg, pp. xvii–xviii; confirmed by Jenkins, p. xxxv, and generally accepted.

28 Efforts by a few scholars to explain away the error have not proved persuasive. MacDonald Jackson, while acknowledging the mistake, seeks to excuse it: 'It seems to me no less difficult to imagine a copyist of Munday's intelligence misreading a manuscript so absurdly, than to imagine that the author himself made such a mistake.' Yet Munday did misread his original and it is

inherently more likely that he was copying someone else's work rather than his own. Richard Beebe offers examples of penslips in *John a Kent and John a Cumber* and in *More* in an effort to prove that *fashis* 'is not necessarily a copyist's error' but he fails to prove his point. I.A. Shapiro does not discuss the *fashis* question but asserts that *More* 'was conceived, as well as written, wholly by Anthony Munday'. MacD.P. Jackson, 'Anthony Mundy and *Sir Thomas More*', *NQ*, 208 (1963), 96. Richard Beebe, '*Fashis* in *The Booke of Sir Thomas More*', *NQ*, 216 (1971), 452–3. I.A. Shapiro, 'Shakespeare and Munday', *ShS*, 14 (1961), 25–33.

29 Peter W.M. Blayney, '*The Booke of Sir Thomas Moore* Re-Examined', *SP*, 69 (1972), 167–91. For a different interpretation of this evidence see Professor Melchiori's essay in this volume.

30 E.H.C. Oliphant, '*Sir Thomas More*', pp. 228–9. The first style he discovered in lines 1–†877 (pp. 1–30); the second in two places, lines †878–†1157 (pp. 30–9) and †1603–†1987 (pp. 53–65); the third in lines †1158–†1602 (pp. 39–53).

31 Harold Jenkins, *The Life and Work of Henry Chettle*. (London, 1934), pp. 59–71. In his Supplement to the Introduction to Greg's edition, Jenkins maintains his position (pp. xxxviii–xxxix). John Jowett, in his essay in this collection, employs a sequence of ten separate tests affording a comparison of Chettle's and Munday's stylistic, lexical and image preferences. Parallels of vocabulary, thought and feeling between *More* and Chettle's *Hoffman* are also investigated. Jowett presents a convincing case for the presence of Chettle in six scenes, and possibly a seventh scene, of the original text, amounting to approximately one-third of the early version of *More*.

32 Bald, '*Booke*,' p. 47.

33 J.M. Nosworthy, 'Shakespeare and *Sir Thomas More*', *RES*, n.s. 6 (1955), 12–25.

34 A.C. Partridge, *Orthography in Shakespeare and Elizabethan Drama: A Study of Colloquial Contractions, Elision, Prosody and Punctuation*. (London; Lincoln, 1964); Ch. 7, 'The Manuscript Play *Sir Thomas More*: List of Contractions in dramatic use by 1600', pp. 43–66; Appendix 4, 'The Hands in *Sir Thomas More*', pp. 169–71.

35 No name has been successfully attached to C. Tannenbaum, as we have seen, nominated Kyd; Acheson suggested Peele (Arthur Acheson, *Shakespeare, Chapman and Sir Thomas More*, (London, 1931), pp. 265–73); and Bald asks: 'was C himself Goodal? It is just possible' (p. 60 n. 10).

36 James Spedding, 'Shakespeare's Handwriting', *NQ*, 184 (1872), 227–8.

37 Hopkinson, ed., *Sir Thomas More*, p. xxviii.

38 Frederick Furnivall, Introduction to the *Leopold Shakespeare*. (London, 1877), p. cii.

39 Brooke, ed., *Shakespeare Apocrypha*, p. xlix.

40 F.P. Wilson, *Shakespeare and the New Bibliography*. Rev. and ed. by Helen Gardner. (Oxford, 1970), p. 111, n. 1*.

41 R.W. Chambers reworked his essay three or four times as a lecture and for publication and printed his definitive version in *Man's Unconquerable Mind*. (London, 1939. Rpt. New York, 1967), pp. 204–49. As part of this version he provides a summary of the critical dialogue on *More* to the date of his book (pp. 227–48). The literature on the play includes numerous scattered notes, comments and references, particularly in the columns of the *TLS*, as well as such more extensive bodies of discussion as Thompson's, Greg's and Tannenbaum's books and articles, to which the latter part of Chambers's essay is a useful guide. Bald's analogous summation to 1948, and Jenkins's to 1961 (Greg, pp. xxxiii–xlvi) are similarly helpful.

42 S. Schoenbaum, *Internal Evidence and Elizabethan Dramatic Authorship*. (Evanston, 1966), p. 106. Schoenbaum repeated this view in his *Shakespeare's Lives*, (Oxford; New York, 1970), p. 696; in *Documentary Life*, p. 158; and in *Records and Images*, pp. 111–12.

43 W.W. Greg, *The Shakespeare First Folio*. (Oxford, 1955, Rpt. 1969), p. 99. He also says that 'the masterly statement of the case by R.W. Chambers in his essay on "Shakespeare and the Play of More" in *Man's Unconquerable Mind* . . . comes as near to formal proof as its nature allows, and is likely to be held conclusive by anyone capable of judging evidence'.

44 In *Booke* Tannenbaum admits that the 'differences between Shakspere acknowledged auto-graphs and the three pages of *More* are not of a nature to prove that he could not possibly have been the author and the writer of the revision in the insurrection scene' (p. 70). Later (p. 77) he notes that we have either no samples or, at best, inadequate specimens of the calligraphy of no fewer than eleven notable contemporary playwrights but he does not suggest that any of them is D.

45 Schücking, 'Shakespeare and *Sir Thomas More*', p. 57. Pollard says (p. 14): 'If these three pages were not Shakespeare's work the dramatist to whom on the ground of style and temper I would most readily assign them (despite a difficulty about the date) would be Thomas Heywood. But Heywood is definitely ruled out by his handwriting, that is to say, that if Sir Edward [Maunde Thompson] was right, even to this limited extent, Shakespeare survives a test which excludes Heywood, and not only Heywood but all the other dramatists of whose handwriting specimens are known to exist.' Schücking omits without warning Pollard's parenthesis and ends his quote at 'Thomas Heywood' thus leaving out the comment that Heywood's handwriting rules him out, substantially changing Pollard's meaning.

46 R.W. Chambers, in *Man's Unconquerable Mind*, pp. 230–9, debates Schücking's attack on his original essay in the course of which he effectively erases Schücking's championship of Heywood as the author of Add. iic.

47 *Internal Evidence*, p. 107.

48 Caroline F.E. Spurgeon, 'Imagery in the *Sir Thomas More* Fragment', *RES*, 6 no. 23 (1930), 257–70.

49 Karl P. Wentersdorf, 'Linkages of Thought and Imagery in Shakespeare and *More*', *MLQ*, 34 (1973), 384–505. In regard to the variant *momtanish* (= *mahometanish*) see Wentersdorf's note on 'A Crux in the Putative Shakespearian Addition to *Sir Thomas More*', *ELN*, 10 (1972), 8–10.

50 William H. Matchett, 'Shylock, Iago, and *Sir Thomas More*; with Some Further Discussion of Shakespeare's Imagination', *PMLA*, 92 (1977), 217–30. The phrase quoted occurs on p. 221. J.H.P. Pafford draws attention to 'another grain to add to the evidence' in the Shakespearian use of the word *dung* in Add. iic, ll. 134–5 ('The Play of *Sir Thomas More*', *NQ*, 226 (1981), 145).

51 J. Dover Wilson, 'The New Way with Shakespeare's Texts; An Introduction for Lay Readers. iii. In Sight of Shakespeare's Manuscripts', *ShS*, 9 (1956), 69–80. Greg's comment is quoted from his 1927 review of the palaeographic case in *Collected Papers*, p. 200.

52 E.K. Chambers, *William Shakespeare*, i, 514–15. R.C. Bald, 'Addition iii of *Sir Thomas More*', *RES*, 7 (1931), 67–9. See also H.W. Crundell, 'Shakespeare and *Sir Thomas More*', *London Mercury*, 25 (1931–2), 288–9.

53 H.W. Crundell, 'Shakespeare and the Play of More', *TLS*, 20 May 1939, pp. 297–8. R.W. Chambers, 'Shakespeare and More', *TLS*, 3 June 1939, p. 327.

54 Nosworthy, 'Shakespeare and *Sir Thomas More*', pp. 17–24.

55 Munro, ed., *London Shakespeare*, pp. 1255, 1256 and 1260.

56 Evans, ed., *Riverside Shakespeare*, pp. 1683–5. Recently (in *ELR*, 10 no. 3 (1980), 439–79) Carol A. Chillington put forth John Webster as the author of Add. iic. As a beginner in writing plays, he may have been collaborating under Henslowe's aegis with Chettle, Munday, Dekker and Heywood, which Shakespeare would not have done on the date she has selected for *More* – 1601. Forker and Taylor discuss her conjecture in their essays in this collection. Melchiori offers a solution to the textually tangled opening passage of Add. iic (pp. 73–5, ll. 123–61), and sets forth a clean reconstruction of the twice-emended lines. 'Hand D in *Sir Thomas More*: An Essay in Misinterpretation,' *ShS*, 38 (1985), 101–14.

57 D.C. Collins, 'On the Date of *Sir Thomas More*', *RES*, 10 no. 40 (1934), 401–11, p. 410. I.A. Shapiro, 'The Significance of a Date', *ShS*, 8 (1955), 100–5, 102. Karl P. Wentersdorf, 'The Date of the Additions in *Sir Thomas More*', *SJW* (1965), 305–25, pp. 324–5. Blayney, '*The Book of Sir Thomas More* Re-Examined', p. 190. Other scholars have expressed similar opinions regarding the relative dating.

58 Simpson, 'Are there any Extant MSS. in Shakespeare's Handwriting?', p. 2. Schücking, 'Das Datum', pp. 249–51. Other suggestions are Dyce: 'about 1590 or perhaps a little earlier'; Fleay: '1595–6'; Hopkinson: '1595–6'; Brooke: 'The two dates proposed by Simpson and Fleay respectively may safely be accepted.' These suggested dates are based on topical references, except for Dyce's. He offers no explanation.

59 Greg, 'Autograph Plays', pp. 89–90. Thompson, 'Autograph Manuscripts', pp. 327–34. W.W. Greg, *The Editorial Problem in Shakespeare A Survey of the Foundations of the Text*. 3rd edition. (Oxford, 1954), p. 23, n. 1. Pollard thinks that the insurrection sequence is a topical allusion to the apprentice riots of the mid-nineties and he assigns a date of 1593–5 (*Shakespeare's Hand*, pp. 22–31).

60 Chambers cites Dekker's and Heywood's birthdates which would set their ages at approximately 20 in 1592–3. His view that the date is early for them is, of course, personal. To me it seems possible that young men of 20 could have been the authors of the passages in their hands.

61 Shapiro, 'Date', p. 102.

62 Jenkins, Greg, p. xliii. Wentersdorf, 'Date of the Additions', p. 325. Blayney, '*The Book of Sir Thomas More* Re-Examined', pp. 188–90.

63 Evans, ed., '*Sir Thomas More*', p. 1684.

64 Schücking, 'Datum', pp. 250–1. Oliphant, '*Sir Thomas More*', pp. 232–3. G.B. Harrison. 'The Date of *Sir Thomas More*', *RES*, 1 no. 3 (1925), 337–9. Alfred W. Pollard, 'Verse Tests and the Date of *Sir Thomas More*', *RES*, 1 no. 4 (1925), 441–3. Harrison's note, which has proved to be influential on the thinking of a number of scholars who came after him, employs techniques that are subject to question. He modernized the spelling and punctuation of the test passage so that a comparison to the Globe text could be made. There can of course be no assurance that the Globe editors, who excluded the play from their edition, would have pointed it as Harrison did. Different punctuation, which is perfectly possible, that calls for fewer internal stops would yield different statistical results. It is perhaps worthy of note that of the scholars who in the ensuing discussion refer to Harrison's paper or cite his evidence as support for a late date (Collins, Bald, Ribner, Spikes, Lake, Chillington) none discusses or even mentions Pollard's corrective paper.

65 Collins, 'On the Date of *Sir Thomas More*', pp. 402–4, 410–11.

66 Nosworthy, 'Shakespeare and *Sir Thomas More*', pp. 14–17. What Nosworthy means by the expression 'purely mathematical basis' as applied to *H5* is unclear. In his lexical tabulation it occurs four times, as contrasted to three for the 'slenderly represented' *Tro.* to eight for *Ham.* and seven for *2H4*. Nosworthy is silent about four occurrences in *2H6*, the same as for *H5*. Some further explanation would have been in order.

67 Partridge, *Orthography in Shakespeare*, pp. 43, 57–64. Matchett, 'Shylock, Iago and *Sir Thomas More*', p. 221.

68 MacD.P. Jackson, 'Linguistic Evidence for the Date of Shakespeare's Addition to *Sir Thomas More*', *NQ*, 223 (1978), 154–6. For an additional comment and correction see also Jackson, 'Hand D of *Sir Thomas More*', *NQ*, 226 (1981), 146. For the work on which Jackson bases his case see Frederick O. Waller, 'The Use of Linguistic Criteria in Determining the Copy and Dates for Shakespeare's Plays', *Pacific Coast Studies in Shakespeare*. Ed. by Waldo F. McNeir and Thelma N. Greenfield. (Eugene, 1966). Jackson acknowledges the limitations of his data: 'Obviously the absolute figures are too small to allow of any confident inference' ('Linguistic Evidence', p. 156). In Jackson's table of colloquial forms there is one play that is manifestly anomalous. '*The Taming of the Shrew*', he points out 'is the only early play which exhibits in its orthography anything like the degree of colloquialism evident in the later plays'. It is quite possible that Add. IIc, which Jackson finds to be highly colloquial also, may be just such another statistical aberration, and therefore closer in time to *The Taming of the Shrew* than to the middle plays.

69 Jenkins (Greg, ed., *The Book of Sir Thomas More*, p. xli) says that 'the idea that it [*More*] reflects the Essex rebellion . . . seems to originate in the fascination Essex exerts over the minds of modern scholars. The hypothesis might follow if a suitable date for *More* could first be established; it cannot help to establish one'.

70 Chambers, *William Shakespeare*, I, 511–12. D.J. Lake, 'The Date of the *Sir Thomas More* Additions by Dekker and Shakespeare', *NQ*, 222 (1977), 114–6. Lake, like Jackson (see n. 68), recognizes that his statistics are based on a sample that is less than adequate: 'It may be objected that the shortness of the *More* text – eighty lines, only nine speeches – renders these comparisons a little suspect' (p. 115).

71 Collins, 'On the Date of *Sir Thomas More*', pp. 401–2.

72 Dyce, ed., *Sir Thomas More, A Play*, pp. vii–xxiii, 13, 48–9, 61–3, 67, 88, 89, 93, 97, 98, 99–100. Hopkinson, ed., *Sir Thomas More*, p. xxxv. Brooke, ed., *Shakespeare Apocrypha*, p. liv. Greg, ed., p. xix.

73 Marie Schütt, 'Die Quellen des *Book of Sir Thomas More*', *Englische Studien*, 68 (1933), 209–26. About this study Greg felt constrained to comment: 'A careful inquiry into sources by Marie Schütt . . . produces some curious results' (*First Folio*, p. 99). Precisely what Greg meant is not clear, but perhaps he is alluding at least primarily, to Schütt's hypothesis that Ro: Ba:'s *Life*, which is based almost exclusively on earlier *Lives*, is the principal biographical source of the play. Ro: Ba: says, in his address To the Courteous Reader: 'the most part of this booke is none of my owne; I onely chalenge the ordering and translating. The most of the rest is Stapletons and Harpsfeilds' (*The Lyfe of Syr Thomas More*. Ed. by E.V. Hitchcock and P.E. Hallett. (EETS OS No. 222). London, 1950, p. 14). He appears to have completed his biography early in 1599 (Hitchcock, ed., Introduction, p. xix). It therefore is not possible that it was a source of the original draft of *More* in consideration of the palaeographic evidence, and perhaps it was not a source of the additions.

74 R.W. Chambers, *Thomas More*. (London; New York, 1935. Rpt. Ann Arbor, 1958), pp. 45–6. Jenkins, ed., *Sir Thomas More*, p. 1235. For Erasmus's letter to von Hutten see P.S. Allen, ed. *Opus Epistolarum des. Erasmi Roterdami*. Tom. IV. (Oxford, 1922), No. 999, pp. 12–23; translated by Francis Morgan Nichols, *The Epistles of Erasmus*. Vol. III. (London, 1917. Rpt. New York, 1962), No. 585B, pp. 387–401. For Harington's anecdote see Elizabeth Story Donno, ed. *Sir John Harington's A New Discourse of a Stale Subject, Called the Metamorphosis of Ajax*. (New York; London, 1962), p. 101.

75 Irving Ribner, *The English History Play in the Age of Shakespeare*. (Princeton, 1957. Rev. ed., London, 1965. Rpt. New York, 1979), pp. 212–13. Ribner does not mention Hall's *Chronicle* as one of the sources.

76 Judith Doolin Spikes, '*The Book of Sir Thomas More*: Structure and Meaning', *Moreana* XI, 43–4 (1974), 25–39.

77 Michael A. Anderegg, '*The Book of Sir Thomas More* and its Sources', *Moreana*, XIV, 53 (1977), 57–62. For the note in the Emmanuel copy of Harpsfield's *Life* see E.V. Hitchcock and R.W. Chambers, eds. *The Life and Death of Sr Thomas Moore, knight by Nicholas Harpsfield*. (EETS OS No. 186, London, 1932), pp. xiii, 294–6. A scholarly and, especially for students of the play's sources, very useful essay by Anderegg on the five early biographies of More under the title 'The Tradition of Early More Biography' is in *Essential Articles for the study of Thomas More*. Ed. by R.S. Sylvester and G.P. Marc'hadour. (Hamden, Conn., 1977), pp. 3–25. For a commentary on Anderegg's essay which interprets differently the evidence on Roper as the source of *More* see Metz, 'The Play of *Sir Thomas More*; the Problem of the Primary Source', *Moreana*, XXI, 82 (1984), 41–8.

78 Pollard, *Shakespeare's Hand*, p. 2. Why the transfer should be unhappy is not clear. The handling of the story in the play is anything but unhappy. It is dramatically effective and in the latter part of the scene in Addition IV, where Dekker is rewriting and extending the incident, it is quite lively, possibly theatrically the play's best, other than Addition IIC.

79 See Metz, 'Thomas More, Thomas Cromwell and Jack Faulkner', *NQ*, 230 (1985), 28–30.

80 Vittorio Gabrieli, '*Sir Thomas More*: Sources, Characters, Ideas,' *Moreana*, XXIII, 90 (1986), 17–43. F.P. Wilson, 'Shakespeare's Reading', *ShS*, 3 (1950), 14–21.

81 E.K. Chambers, *The Elizabethan Stage*. 4 vols. (Oxford, 1923. Rpt. 1945), Appendix D, IV: 286. For the development of stage censorship see I: 269–307; 317–28, concisely summarized by Chambers in his *William Shakespeare*, I: 98–105. Greg discusses censorship in the course of describing extant promptbooks in *Dramatic Documents*, 'Commentary', pp. 189–369.

82 Simpson, 'Extant MSS.' p. 1. Adolphus William Ward, *A History of English Dramatic Literature*. Revised ed. (London, 1899), 1, 214. Brooke, ed., *Shakespeare Apocrypha*, pp. xlix–l.

83 Chambers, *William Shakespeare*, 1, 511–12.

84 Wentersdorf, 'Date of the Additions', pp. 311–13. Greg, *Dramatic Documents*, 'Commentary', p. 200.

85 J. Dover Wilson, *ShS* 9, p. 72. Jenkins in Greg, pp. xxxix–xl.

86 Blayney, '*The Book of Sir Thomas More* Re-Examined', pp. 190–1.

87 Chillington, *ELR* 10, pp. 469–76. The passages quoted are in n. 21, p. 471.

88 Metz, 'The Master of the Revels and *The Booke of Sir Thomas Moore*', *SQ*, 33 (1982), 493–5. Professor Jenkins in a private letter questioned my suggestion but added 'the facts about this play are so odd and so seemingly contradictory that hardly anything can be ruled out. 'See also Taylor's observation in this collection (n. 57).

89 W. J. Lawrence, 'Was *Sir Thomas More* Ever Acted?' *TLS*, 1 July 1920, p. 421. Of Lawrence's four additional prompt warnings three are added in the margins by C, the book-keeper, at ll. 410–12 (p. 14), l. *553 (p. 19) and ll. †954–5 (p. 32), the first of which was noted by Greg, and one by Munday at l. *523 (p. 18) in a box concerning which Greg comments: 'the rules round the S.D. may have been added by C'.

90 W. W. Greg, 'Was *Sir Thomas More* ever Acted?', *TLS*, 8 July, 1920, p. 440. There is a further exchange on 15 July, p. 456, and 29 July, p. 488.

91 Muriel St. Clare Byrne, 'The Date of *Sir Thomas More*. Some Further Points', *TLS*, 12 August 1920, pp. 520–1. Lawrence replies 2 September, p. 568.

92 W. J. Lawrence, *Pre-Restoration Stage Studies*. (Cambridge, Mass., 1927. Rpt. New York, 1967), pp. 387–92.

93 C. R. Baskervill, 'Some Parallels to *Bartholomew Fair*', *MP*, 6 (1909), 1–19. S.R. Golding, 'Further Notes on Robert Wilson and *Sir Thomas More*', *NQ*, 155 (1928), 237–40. There is also some lexical connection between *More* and Chettle's *Hoffman* but we need not assume performance to explain the connection. See Taylor's discussion.

94 Scott McMillin, '*The Book of Sir Thomas More*: A Theatrical View', *MP*, 68 (1970), 10–24. For new findings by McMillin and further developed evidence specifically on staging see his essay in this collection.

The occasion of *The Book of Sir Thomas More*

WILLIAM B. LONG

<Leaue out > |yᵉ insur <rection> |wholy & |yᵉ Cause ther off & | <b >egin wᵗ Sʳ Tho: |Moore att yᵉ mayors sessions |wᵗ a reportt afterwards |off his good servic' |don being' Shriue off Londo*n* | vppo*n* a mutiny Agaynst ye Lu*m*bards only by A Short | reportt & nott otherwise |att your own perrilles |E Tyllney (B.L. MS Harley 7368. Reproduced in Greg.)

So wrote Edmond Tilney along the left margin of the first lines of *The Booke of Sir Thomas Moore* – the longest inscription by a censor in a manuscript of a surviving pre-Restoration play. Tilney crossed out six speech-heads to squeeze this in, and he took a remarkable amount of trouble to tell the playwrights how to revise the play to avoid difficulty. He did not forbid production. But in attempting to explain the order of the revisions in the manuscript, W.W. Greg declared that 'only collective insanity' could account for the playwrights' revising the insurrection scenes after this (p. xiv).

Such a restrictive view of governmental influence seems more appropriate for a twentieth-century censor than for the late sixteenth-century Master of the Revels. Many researchers hold the (often unstated) position that the Revels Office was the implacable foe of much that playwrights wished to write and even of dramatic representation in general. Such a conclusion severely limits the investigation of how censorship functioned, and, in this case, of how a different view of censorship might help to untangle some of the intricacies of *The Booke of Sir Thomas Moore*.

The notion that the Revels Office was a stern and unbending instrument of suppression cannot be substantiated. This is not to deny that censorship was a real and powerful force, but surviving instances of Masters working over playbooks show their labours to be both more complex and far more sophisticated than is usually assumed.[1] That Elizabethan-Jacobean-Caroline drama is topical in subject matter, in themes, and in internal references is a commonplace; but that topicality could be used for reasons other than just to interest spectators or to provide matter for the playwrights' pens.

In the early 1590s, the seemingly perpetual Spanish threat and the religious waverings of Henri of Navarre were of paramount importance to the English government. But there were other problems as well, sometimes more immediately disturbing if not of such great consequence. In a society with no standing army and in a city with no metropolitan police force, a large group of unruly citizens could present a formidable threat to the safety of life, limb, and property, if not to the stability of the government itself. The possible problem of a crowd had to do with its size and with its often mercurial temper, and those in turn often were controlled by that elusive element, public opinion. Elizabeth and Burghley were particularly adept in influencing – even in moulding and controlling – this factor. In many facets of governing, Elizabeth chose to be indirect, wisely opting to influence and to point rather than to confront with commands (with the always present possibility, especially in the managing of crowds, of failure).

Homilies and publicly read prayers were often-used methods of policy. (Burghley himself wrote a number of such prayers).[2] On certain occasions and for certain purposes, I believe that plays were another method of influencing public behaviour. The risks could be greater, but so could the rewards. Playwrights and players on occasion found themselves in difficulty for presenting offensive matter; surely it is possible that they could be persuaded to do the opposite. A successful play, perhaps repeated more often than was the wont of Elizabethan repertory companies, might well have had favourable effects. And even if the results were negligible, the government would have lost nothing.

Tilney made major changes to *Sir Thomas More*, as noted by Giorgio Melchiori elsewhere in this volume; scenes and passages found objectionable include 'the prentices' rebellion (scene v, suppressed), violence against public authorities (scenes iv and vi, partly rewritten, partly toned down by the introduction of the clown), street fights among rival gangs (the Paternoster Row fray, suppressed and replaced by scene viii), and possible criticism of royal behaviour (More's speech in scene xiii, reworded by Chettle).' But these do not necessarily argue that Tilney was forbidding the play. On the contrary, I believe they show him making changes and cuts that would allow the play to go on. Proof becomes a matter of interpretation of attitude. It is hardly beyond the realm of possibility that playwrights would construct speeches and scenes that needed toning down or excision even if the play had been written with governmental approval, and Tilney's judgement may very well be reflecting conditions which had changed since the inception of the writing.

It is very important to note that if he were refusing licence, there would have been no reason either for the amount of specific directives here or for the additional directives later in the text. He noted 'Mend Y^{is}' opposite a passage about 'the displeased commons of the Cittie' (fol. 5^r, 316–23) and included for revision another section on the same page (372–85) by carefully placing a vertical line in the left margin. Civil discontent, apparently rather too sharply worded, was the problem here as well. In the passage where More refuses to sign the 'Articles', Tilney wrote in the right margin 'all alter' and drew a vertical line in the left margin indicating that lines †1246–75 are to be changed. He deleted nothing. He did order a revision of 25 percent of the scene. Significantly, he neither cut nor altered More's refusal to sign which is crucial to the whole play.

In none of these passages did Tilney refuse licence or forbid the many potentially dangerous things still in the play; nor was his tone as forbidding as many would hear it. He actually was quite helpful; conditions had worsened since the writing had begun. I take his emphasis on *your own* in 'att your own perrilles' as an indication that he himself was unwilling to take the blame for the playwrights' possible indiscretion. Tilney has attempted to aid the playwrights in making the play serviceable. He even went so far as to indicate the sort of changes that would have to be made throughout areas that need not be rewritten, as his substitution of 'ma*n*' for 'Englishe' and 'Lombard' for 'straunger' and 'ffrencheman' (fol. 5ʳ, 352, 364, and 368). He continued in the text what he had advised in his general admonition at the beginning of the play.

Date is all important, and the history of *More* (B.L. MS. Harley 7368) is inextricably tied to that of Anthony Munday's *John a Kent and John a Cumber*, now in the Huntington Library. The manuscript of *John a Kent* is 'written throughout in the hand of Anthony Munday'[3] and is tied to the *More* manuscript not only by Munday as the principal hand in the *More* manuscript,[4] but also by the fact that both plays were bound by fragments of the same medieval manuscript, thus making it very likely that they were bound at the same time by the same person.[5] In addition, W.W. Greg's identification of the hand that elaborately endorsed the play titles on both wrappers as that of 'Hand C', the playhouse bookkeeper of both plays, offers conclusive proof that the plays were owned at the same time by the company for whom Hand C worked in the early 1590s.[6]

Hand C becomes vital to the study of *More* for two reasons: first, he was instrumental in fair-copying and correctly placing additions in the text; secondly, and more importantly here, he can be seen working as company bookkeeper in *John a Kent* and the plot of *2 Seven Deadly Sins* around 1590. His presence in the same capacity in *More* is a major factor in dating the play. Sir Edward Maunde Thompson's meticulous chronology of Munday's handwriting, noting the changes that occurred between the writing of *John a Kent* and that of *More*, strongly suggests that Munday must have written the basic text of the *More* playbook by 1594.[7] On that basis, Thompson then proposed dates of about 1590 for the composition of *Kent* and of about 1592–3 for that of *More*. I.A. Shapiro's reading of the date on the final leaf of the *Kent* playbook as 'Decembris 1590' rather than the previously accepted '1595' or '1596' provides a most important *terminus ad quem* for the play which may have been written as early as August 1589.[8] With the new dating of *Kent*, Shapiro could refine the date of *More* yet more closely: 'If the experts [Thompson and Greg] are right in their view of the sequence of these two manuscripts and the interval between their writing, Munday must have written *Sir Thomas More* by 1593 at least, and possibly earlier'.[9] Because of the shifting alignment of players during these years, it is somewhat less certain for what group Munday fashioned this play and in which theatre it was performed, but this redating makes *Kent* concurrent with the plot of *2 Seven Deadly Sins* (*c.* 1590) which Greg had assigned to Lord Strange's Men at the Curtain.

Greg's further identification of the writer of the plot as the same person who made the stage markings in the texts and endorsed the titles on the wrappers of the books of *Kent* and *More* as 'Hand C' of the *More* manuscript unites both plays with the plot.[10] Lord Strange died on 16 April 1594,[11] thus necessitating a further reshuffling of the players who were under his patronage. Hand C's fragmentary plot of *2 Fortune's Tennis* (B.L. MS Add. 10449, fol. 4) shows that at least by *c.* 1597–8[12] Hand C had followed Alleyn to the reconstituted Lord Admiral's Men rather than joining those members of Strange's including Burbage and Shakespeare who moved to the new Lord Chamberlain's Men. Chambers connects Hand C with the Admiral's but on other grounds.[13]

Another factor which brings the date, the company, and Hand C together (and upon which neither Greg nor Shapiro comments) is that the date at the end of the *Kent* manuscript has been inscribed by Hand C. He uses the same dark ink that he had used earlier in the manuscript; but far more crucial, the formation of the letters in 'Decembris' can be compared very favourably with those in Hand C's writing in the *2 Seven Deadly Sins* plot. The majuscule *D* of 'Decembris' is almost half missing, but it looks very much as if it were formed by bringing the initial stroke from top to bottom, pulling a loop to the left, then coming to the right for the bottom of the letter, and then up and back across the initial downstroke; similar letters appear in lines 5 (Duke), 14 (Dumb), and 18 (Duke). Matching internal *e*'s occur in lines 3 (being), 4 (sleepe), 10 (sincler); *c*'s in 5 (purceuaunt), 8 (Lechery), and 37 (Lucius); medial *m* occurs in 14 (Dumb), 37 (Damasus); *b* in 3 (being), 9 (back), 20 (bringe); *r* in 3 (Henry), 5 (purceuaunt); 8 (Lechery); *i* in 3 (being), 11 (him), 20 (bringe); final *s* in 7 (Couetousnes), 13 (speakes), 15 (Counsailers). The similarities in letter formation between these in the *Sins* plot and those in the date inscription are very striking; there is no reason not to attribute the dating to Hand C.

What the date signifies is uncertain although it is more likely to be the date of company acquisition rather than of performance or licence. Hand C, as a member of the company in charge of the book and of seeing it through part-copying, rehearsal, licensing, and storage, is the inscriber. The name of the actor Thomas Goodale was one of many to appear in Hand C's *Sins* plot, but his is the only actor's name to find its way into either play, having been carefully noted in Hand C's hand as a messenger in *More* (fol. *13^r), thus more firmly fixing the placing of the two earliest playbooks with Lord Strange's Men at the Curtain, 1590–3.[14] It would seem most likely that *More* was planned as a performance by Strange's Men for the theatrical season of 1592–3.

Many explanations have been offered as to why this playbook, prepared for production and including theatrical markings, was not performed. Most answers centre upon the players' having had difficulties with the censor.[15] I should like to suggest that the explanation rests primarily upon the nature of the original impetus for creating the play and upon the exigencies of time pressing upon the players. Wanting the discovery of a secret notebook (probably in cipher) written by Burghley, by some other Privy Council member, or by Tilney himself which would vindicate my view – a highly unlikely development – evidence for a different interpretation of censorship must necessarily be circumstantial to a considerable degree. But then, so is the evidence for most traditional interpretations. Much depends upon the attitude with which the researcher approaches the material. Instead of the usual hypotheses, I believe that the play as it exists is unfinished and that it originally was commissioned (or at least suggested or approved) by some government official(s) as an aid in dealing with the problem of anti-alien sentiment in particular and with the dangers of civil uproar in general. The play was toned down and modified by Tilney, but not so much as is usually claimed. Subsequently, the play was left unacted because of an unexplained increase in the death rate which closed the theatres for some months and because of the more dangerous nature of the deepening civil disturbances which had occurred since the composition of the play.

Until Sir Henry Herbert's fragmentary records became known,[16] we did not begin to understand the varying, complex, and even erratic ways that censorship was applied. Most commentators assumed that the players and the government were necessarily antipathetic to each other's objectives. This assumption has influenced scholarship both in examining the *More* manuscript bibliographically and in deciding what the play is about. Thus Greg observed 'When the play returned bearing Tilney's remarks, it became clear, as I should have thought it would have been clear to critics from the outset, that it was impossible to comply with the demands of the censor without eviscerating the play in a manner fatal to its success on the stage' (p. xv). This would be true if one supposes that the subject of civil disorder itself would not meet with approval. But Tilney had not forbidden a play on this subject; he merely had made the action less pointed and less likely to inspire instant imitation in the streets. Both thematic and production revisions to comply with Tilney's strictures would have taken more work and, more importantly, more time; but such changes are far from impossible. Following the tacit assumption that the ends of the players and those of the government were necessarily different, Pollard announced that the playwrights were 'blind . . . to the difficulties in their path'; that 'the anti-alien scenes were written for their own sake; they come very near indeed to being a complete play in themselves' but 'of course the miniature anti-alien play was doomed from the start to be censored out of existence'.[17] Dover Wilson, after reviewing numerous other hypotheses concerning 'the chief puzzle of the manuscript', concluded:

In some way or other . . . the instructions of the censor must be related to the disorderly condition of the 'booke' . . . For the play as it comes down to us was clearly in process of being drastically overhauled . . . Yet even had the revisers finished the job, they would have gone no way at all to meet the censor. On the contrary, instead of being left out, the insurrection scene was brilliantly rewritten. We cannot therefore explain the revisions as undertaken in response to Tilney's orders . . . As it stands, the play could not have been acted. Nor do I believe it could have been read – or rather would not have been read – by a dictorial person intent on probing every line to discover whether it concealed dangerous matters of state.[18]

Wilson's image of the censor is indicative of the attitude which impedes much investigation into how dramatic censors functioned, and his explanation of *why* is simplistic in the extreme. Little is said of exactly what they did; yet without thorough investigation, conjectures about why the Masters did things to a play are as meaningless or distorted as what is generally said about Tilney's relationship to the *More* manuscript. Furthermore, this attitude betrays a quite unsophisticated (but unfortunately widely held) assumption that the relationship between the Revels Office and the theatre was perforce an adversarial one, and therefore, that playwrights regularly and necessarily wanted (and tried) to write matter that would not receive 'official' approval.

In large measure, much of the answer to the dilemma of censorship in *More* may be as simple (or as complex) as the figure of Anthony Munday himself. Surely nothing short of loss of sense and memory would have allowed Munday to place himself in a position of ignorance or naiveté concerning the investigative powers and punishing abilities of the government. This is the same man who for years had been (and still was) pursuivant to his 'master' Richard Topcliffe, the notorious recusant-hunter and torturer; Munday, furthermore, proudly signed himself 'Messenger of Her Majesties Chamber'.[19] Tricking unfortunates into Topcliffe's net had not been Munday's only governmental job. John Whitgift, Archbishop of Canterbury, had employed him to write rebuttals to the vexing Martin Marprelate,[20] and Munday had written numerous anti-Catholic pamphlets. Munday seemed too proud of his pursuivant activities and of his carefully assembled respectability for it to be likely that he would have been in favour of participating in a writing scheme which would jeopardize his accomplishments and undermine his apparent agreements with official policies. He was still a Messenger of the Chamber in 1593, the politically troublesome year of *More*; and his future acquisitions of public positions argue strongly for his having continued in this established pattern of adding to his responsibility and respectability. In short, Munday's non-dramatic career had been quite different from what is known of those of other Elizabethan playwrights, and he worked well with volatile materials. He had been a good and faithful servant; he could be trusted to attempt another highly sensitive project.

England in late 1592 and early 1593 was in more than usual difficulties.[21] Particularly troublesome was the steadily increasing anti-alien sentiment.[22] Domestic disorder was always anathema, but the opposition of increasing numbers of small tradesmen and of apprentices to the presence of French and Low Country refugees – the citizens of Protestant allies who were fleeing French and Spanish Catholic persecution – must have been both embarrassing and irritating to the government. An easy, inexpensive, and possibly successful way of relieving the threat of violence if not of remedying the causes of dissatisfaction would have been to commission (or at least to permit) players to demonstrate publicly the consequences of such socially disruptive actions. The subject was fraught with dangers; if the play were to be effective propaganda, it would have to be crafted and/or supervised by someone of proven faithfulness and discretion. Anthony Munday was just such a writer. The theme of *Sir Thomas More* is neither the anti-alien riots (in spite of the extraordinary critical attention that this aspect has received) nor the career and death of More himself,[23] but the unfortunate consequences of disobedience to the rule of the sovereign.

The 'Ill May Day' of 1517 was still a current hobgoblin in the popular mythology. Reporting to Burghley in 1586 of his interrogation of apprentices 'conspiring an insurrection in this cittie against the Frenche and Dutche . . .', William Fleetwood, Recorder of the City of London, believed that he had found 'all things as lyke unto Yll May Day, as could be devised in all manner of cyrcumstances, *mutatis mutandis*; they wanted nothing but execution'.[24] This image of the Ill May Day continued. John Speed, following Richard Grafton, records beside the marginal rubric 'A.D. 1517. / Ill May day. / The English abused by strangers.' this report:

> But the state of *Londons* Trades-men prospered vnder his [Wolsey's] greatness nothing so well, for such was the concourse of strangers, and so much were they borne with, by the superiors, that they abused the English, openly in the markets, kept from a Citizen his owne wife with his plate, yea, and past with a small pennance for killing an Englishman. These first were complained of in a Sermon at Saint *Maries* Spittle, and afterwards assaulted, and much hurt done to their substance and houses, for which riotous offence *Iohn Lincolne* the onely instigator was hanged; and foure hundred men, boyes, and eleuen women led in ropes along the City in their shirts, and halters about their neckes to the Kinges Hall at *Westminster*, where his Maiesty sitting vnder a cloath of estate, pardoned the offenses to the great reioycing of the Londoners.[25]

It is thus almost to be expected that the Ill May Day should have been chosen as the shocking opening of the play. That More appears is part of history, but that his appearances are expanded and his character given added depth is the design of the play. The themes of Elizabethan chronicle plays were regularly developed through significant and often symbolic acts of great men, most of whom come to untimely ends. This play thus begins with More as the stable, wise, and honest public official, adds a series of events which show him also as a warm (and even affable) human being, and climaxes with the death even of such a one who in spite of his host of public and private virtues still must die because he had gone against the will of his sovereign. More's difficulty came not from riot and bloodshed, but, as fitting his nature and position, from a matter of conscience and of interpretation of law.

> MOORE: Subscribe these Articles? stay, let vs pause,
>   our conscience first shall parley with our lawes.   (fol. 17ᵛ, †1238–9)

Critics have been puzzled about why these vague 'Articles' were not made specific. The reason is quite clear; the play is not about Henry's difficulties with Rome, but rather, it is about subjects' obedience to the sovereign's will, regardless of the issue. Thus the play ahistorically but importantly inflattes More's role in achieving domestic tranquillity and in telescoping historical time: the governmental rewards follow each other rapidly and the playwrights greatly shrink the time separating the rebellion (1517) and More's execution (1535). Civil disturbance is a continuing feature of the action of the play, but behind each incident is the ultimate evil of disobeying the monarch. Over and over the idea is stated and implied that opposition to the king is opposition to God: this theme is dramatized in More's almost throwaway acknowledgement after being told that the king has elevated him to the Privy Council (fol. 10ʳ, *543–4), in Lincoln's gallows speech (fol. 10ᵛ, *619–35), in Surrey's comment after More and Bishop Fisher refuse to sign the 'Articles' (fol. 18^r, †1276–8), in Surrey's comment at the end of the play (fol. 22^r, †1983–4), and most explicitly and in most detail in More's address to the rioters (fol. 8^v, 216–18, 220–34). Pollard recognized this emphasis but continued to believe that 'The players forgot that there were subjects which Authority would not allow to be presented on the stage, however judiciously they were handled . . .'.[26] It would be unlikely that the players would forget; it seems totally improbable that Munday would forget or that he would take so foolish a chance.

More must die because he has gone against his sovereign's will. That he is both a good and a great man makes his end the more lamentable; it does not change it. Tilney had no qualms whatsoever about staging the public execution of a man who had been a Privy Councillor and even the Lord Chancellor. All citizens must pay for their mistakes. This example of the great can hardly have been lost on the lesser. And therein, I believe, is the reason for the existence of this unusual play, not because of the 'collective insanity' (Greg, p. xiv) of the playwrights. As Surrey observes in the last speech of the play, 'A very learned woorthie Gentleman |Seales errour with his blood . . .' (fol. 22^r, †1983–4). This is the chief revision in the second ending as if Munday were making the point even more emphatically.

Munday seems to have been in charge of the writing enterprise which because of the pressure of time was probably always a collaboration.[27] Indeed, the need for speed is perhaps the greatest argument in favour of multiple authorship. Munday also may have been the provider of the scenario for the writing of *Sir Thomas More*. Believing Munday to have been a maker and seller of scenarios, I.A. Shapiro provocatively interprets a number of facets of Munday's professional career which emphasize his artistic abilities – among them his being singled out by Francis Meres as 'our best plotter'.[28] Above and beyond Munday's literary and dramatic talents in fashioning scenarios, his familiarity with the intricate realities of government service and the exigencies of current political problems would have added to his particular value in this enterprise. In investigating other features of *More*, Charles R. Forker and Joseph Candido demonstrate that they are well aware of the difficulties attendant upon presenting such materials: 'the tact required to negotiate these treacherous waters is such as to make us wonder that the subject was even attempted'.[29] Anthony Munday was the experienced captain appointed to guide this project.

The theatres had been closed during the summer of 1592. On 23 June, the Privy Council prohibited all plays until Michaelmas. However, Alleyn, touring with Strange's company, was in the provinces at least until 19 December. Henslowe begins his accounts with the receipts for 29 December and continues for twenty-nine weeks through 1 February 1592. Although a new inhibition was issued on 28 January,[30] 'it does not seem to have been for some months that Strange's men made up their minds to travel'.[31] The company apparently played for five days after the issuance of the order. It hardly could have been done in ignorance. Rather, more likely, the decision to attempt playing lay in the players' estimation of how rigorously the ban would be enforced and how long it was likely to last, not in the mere existence of the restriction. Henslowe has no further entries until 27 December 1593, when the Earl of Sussex's men play through 6 Februay 1593–4.[32]

But Henslowe, of course, recorded only receipts for plays at his theatres – in this case the Rose. There is no record of what his son-in-law Alleyn (a servant of the Lord Admiral) was doing in association with Strange's men if they were not at the Rose. Not only did Stange's men not leave London immediately, they waited for over three months. On 6 May 1593, they received a Privy Council licence to play except within seven miles of London or of the Court.[33] Alleyn is specifically mentioned as well as five of Strange's men, all of whom later joined the new Lord Chamberlain's men. Alleyn's being with this company at the time of *More* is all the more intriguing in light of Scott McMillin's showing elsewhere in this volume that the very size of More's role makes it most likely that it was planned for Alleyn.

It would seem that the number of plague deaths was fluctuating at this time and that the players delayed their leaving, hoping for an abatement. Harrison had but one reference (5 April) to the 'plague' from the 28 January prohibition to the time that the players received their licence to travel. But from then until 26 December 1593, when playing resumed, there are seventeen entries.[34] Because of the extreme rarity of weekly plague bills in the sixteenth century, F.P. Wilson has no firm statistics for 1593 as he had for the great infestations of 1603 and 1625.[35] Alleyn and Strange's men were not the only players to chance improved conditions, but apparently the infection worsened; a directive of the City Court of Aldermen dated 12 April 1593 re-emphasizes the need to suppress public 'prophane exercises'. And on 29 April, the Privy Council issued a licence to the Earl of Sussex's players to travel in the provinces – exactly a week before their similar licence to Strange's men.[36]

During these months of waiting, there may well have been some playing, however intermittent. The welfare and activities of a few players hardly could have been of much sustained concern of the Privy Council as a whole. But if public health conditions improved for several weeks, it is not inconceivable that the increasingly desperate players might have appealed to the Master of the Revels to intercede with the Lord Chamberlain for permission to play. Very important directives from the Privy Council often went out over the signatures of only a few of its members; it might have been that the Lord Chamberlain could ease (if only temporarily) a directive of the Council as a whole. In the case of *More*, some sort of special dispensation might not have been impossible if one or more Privy Councillors felt that it might serve a useful purpose.

It looks like *More* was planned for regular production, that the sudden rise in the death rate intervened, but that it was varying in intensity and that either some playing took place or at least that a reasonable possibility of playing existed. The need to do something about the increasing dangers of civil disturbances over the 'strangers' would have added to the hopes of the players and concerned government officials alike. Whether the play was finished before the theatres were closed or shortly thereafter would not alter the playwrights' rush to complete it and the company's to obtain a licence. Far from unexceptionally forbidding production, Tilney's alterations and directives make licencing a strong possibility. Certainly the players have marked their book in anticipation of receiving permission to play.

In the meantime, the anti-alien sentiment was increasing rapidly. If health conditions had allowed, the play might have mitigated an ugly situation. But conditions did not improve, and the players left London. On 5 May 1593, the very day before the dating of the Privy Council licence to Strange's Men, a 'seditious rime' appeared; and the whole issue lurched further toward violence.[37] By the time that public playing was again officially permitted in 1594, the anti-alien troubles had become even more acute. Pollard is more than likely correct in his argument that after 24 July 1595, when five 'unruly youths' were hanged, drawn, and quartered as a result of their part in a civil disturbance over want of food, neither playwrights nor players would have dared to produce a play presenting a London riot, whatever its causes.[38] Nor, of course, would Tilney or any other official be interested in supporting any such play. Even if *More* had had official inspiration and/or sanction late in 1592 or early 1593, the public situation had deteriorated too much to attempt the aid that the play might have given earlier. Certainly any government support would have been withdrawn. The opportunity for amelioration had passed. The race with time had been lost.

The serious nature of the anti-alien problem and its pre-eminent topicality would have placed a premium on speed from the outset, and the added threat of an epidemic forcing a closing of public playing would have added extraordinary time pressures. The assumption of draconian censorship cannot be supported by the recorded actions of the Master in the *More* playbook. His notations are intended to avoid problems, not to forbid production. Tilney's detailed markings, coinciding as they do with the social troubles, with the planning and writing of Anthony Munday, with the workings of Hand C, with the availability of a large company with Edward Alleyn to handle the unusually large role of More, and with the unfortunate interference of the pestilence coalesce to form the 'occasion' of *The Booke of Sir Thomas Moore*.

NOTES

1 Important instances are the anonymous *Second Maiden's Tragedy* (1611) and John Fletcher and Philip Massinger's *Sir John van Olden Barnavelt* (1619) which have been labored over by Sir George Buc.

2 In an area that was sensitive if not secret by nature, written records must always have been few. Nonetheless, for an analysis of Burghley's work with ballads, prayers, and plays to influence and direct 'public opinion' see Conyers Read, 'William Cecil and Elizabethan Public Relations', in *Elizabethan Government and Society: Essays Presented to Sir John Neale*, ed. by S.T. Bindoff, J. Hurstfield, and C.H. Williams (London, 1961), pp. 21–55.

3 Anthony Munday, *John a Kent and John a Cumber*, ed. by Muriel St. Clare Byrne and checked by W.W. Greg, Malone Society Reprints (Oxford, 1923), p. vii.

4 W.W. Greg, 'The Handwritings of the Manuscript' in *Shakespeare's Hand in the Play of 'Sir Thomas More'*, ed. A.W. Pollard (Cambridge, 1923).

5 Byrne, p. vi. In a more detailed investigation, Alfred W. Pollard concurs (*Shakespeare's Hand*, p. 9).

6 Greg, *Shakespeare's Hand*, pp. 55–6. The headings can be compared with the reproductions in the facsimile volume of Greg's *Dramatic Documents from the Elizabethan Playhouses: Stage Plots: Actors' Parts: Prompt Books,* 2 vols. (Oxford, 1931), II (unpaginated).

7 The chronology of Munday's manuscripts was established by Sir Edward Maunde Thompson's minute examinations of the changes in Munday's handwriting. 'The Autograph Manuscripts of Anthony Munday', *Transactions of the Bibliographical Society*, XIV (October, 1915–March 1917), 325–53.

8 'The Significance of a Date', *ShS*, 8 (1955), 100–5. Shapiro thus proved Celeste Turner's conjecture that Munday had written *Kent* about 1590; *Anthony Munday: An Elizabethan Man of Letters* (Berkeley, 1928), p. 106.

9 Shapiro, 'The Significance of a Date', p. 102.

10 Greg, *Dramatic Documents*, I, 225.

11 E.K. Chambers, *The Elizabethan Stage*, 4 vols. (Oxford, 1923), II, 126.

12 Greg, *Dramatic Documents*, I, 131.

13 Chambers, *Elizabethan Stage*, II, 319. Greg gives a fuller account of Hand C in *Dramatic Documents*, I, 45–6.

14 Greg, *Dramatic Documents*, I, 225.

15 A summary of the various explanations as well as an examination of the other problems posed by the play can be found in R.C. Bald's review article '*The Booke of Sir Thomas More* and Its Problems', *Shakespeare Survey*, 2 (1949), 44–55, especially 47–51.

16 See *The Dramatic Records of Sir Henry Herbert, Master of the Revels, 1622–1673*, ed. by Joseph Quincy Adams (New Haven, Conn., 1917).

17 *Shakespeare's Hand*, pp. 3–5.

18 J. Dover Wilson, 'The New Way with Shakespeare's Texts; An Introduction for Lay Readers. III. In Sight of Shakespeare's Manuscripts', *ShS*, 9 (1956), 72.

19 Turner, *Anthony Munday*, p. 76; Chambers, *Elizabethan Stage*, III, 444.

20 Turner, *Anthony Munday*, p. 84.

21 An inclusive summary can be found in J.E. Neale, *Elizabeth I and Her Parliaments, 1584–1601* (New York, 1958), pp. 241–50. For details of Henri's conversion and the repercussions in England and other Protestant countries, see David Buisseret, *Henry IV* (London, 1984), especially Chapter 4, 'The Perilous Leap, 1593–4', pp. 44–55.

22 *Shakespeare's Hand*, pp. 26–9 and pp. 38–40 (quoting Strype's *Brief Annals*, 1731).

23 J. Dover Wilson, 'The New Way with Shakespeare's Texts', p. 71.

24 Quoted by Pollard, *Shakespeare's Hand*, p. 37.

25 *The History of Great Britain* (London, 1614) fol. Xxxxx2ʳ col. 2.

26 *Shakespeare's Hand*, p. 5.

27 Turner conjectures a collaboration, *Anthony Munday*, p. 108, E.H.C. Oliphant claims to have been the first to discern multiple authorship; '*Sir Thomas More*', *JEGP*, 18 (1919),p. 228. His explanation of who wrote what continues on p. 229. Current scholarship on the authorship problem may be found elsewhere in this volume.

28 I.A. Shapiro, 'Shakespeare and Munday', *ShS*, 14 (1961), 25–33.

29 Charles R. Forker and Joseph Candido, 'Wit, Wisdom, and Theatricality in *The Booke of Sir Thomas More*', *Shakespeare Studies*, 13 (1980), 103.

30 Chambers, *Elizabethan Stage*, II, 122–3; R.A. Foakes and R.T. Rickert, eds., *Henslowe's Diary* (Cambridge, 1961), pp. 19–20. Royal proclamations as well as Privy Council orders, however powerful in theory, were difficult to enforce. For a study of the situation during part of Henry VIII's reign, see R.W. Heinze, 'The Enforcement of Royal Proclamations under the Provisions of the Statute of Proclamations, 1539–1547', in *Tudor Men and Institutions: Studies in English Law and Government*, ed. by Arthur J. Slavis (Baton Rouge, 1972), pp. 205–31.

31 Chambers, *Elizabethan Stage*, II, 123.

32 Foakes and Rickert, pp. 20–1.

33 Chambers, *Elizabethan Stage*, II, 123.

34 G.B. Harrison, *An Elizabethan Journal* (New York, 1929), *passim.*

35 *The Plague in Shakespeare's London*, London, 1927.

36 Chambers, *Elizabethan Stage*, IV, 314.

37 *Shakespeare's Hand*, p. 40, and Turner, *Anthony Munday*, p. 112.

38 *Shakespeare's Hand*, pp. 23–4.

3

The Book of Sir Thomas More:
dates and acting companies

SCOTT McMILLIN

The Book of Sir Thomas More can be seen for what it is by setting aside questions of
authorship and pursuing questions of the theatre instead. Persons interested in
authorship, expecting books to be tidy and well made, have allowed the disarray of
The Book of Sir Thomas More to convince them that the manuscript is incoherent.
Persons interested in the theatre know better. They know that what lies behind the
most coherent stage performance is debris of all sorts, including textual debris.
Anyone who walks backstage after a good performance will see the debris at once,
and if he wants to see textual debris he should ask for the original prompt copy, the
one that was used at the beginning of rehearsals. Should the play in question be an
original work, the earliest prompt copy will look rather like *The Book of Sir Thomas
More*. Should the play in question be a work written ten years ago and now revised
for a different acting company, its rehearsal book will look just like *The Book of Sir
Thomas More* although the paper will not be as interesting.

I have elsewhere explained that *The Book of Sir Thomas More* is a coherent
theatrical document, that it represents a play written and revised for actual
production, and that some of the revisions were undertaken not in answer to the
censor's complaints but in answer to problems of casting the parts.[1] To recapitulate
briefly, the original play was an unusually large one, with more than sixty speaking
parts, and some of the revisions were intended to eliminate roles while others were
designed to provide additional time for the actors to change costumes, just when
the doubling pressure became heavy. It is not always grasped in textual studies that
one way to tailor a larger play for a smaller company is to *lengthen* the play at
strategic points. Textual scholars seem to assume that it is the shorter play that
indicates the smaller company, but actors know that changing costumes takes
time and that time is what an extra twenty-five-line speech patched into a scene can
provide.

My purpose now is to relate the theatrical characteristics of *The Book of Sir Thomas
More* to the historical questions of dating the play and identifying the acting
company or companies for which it was written. The theatre is still the focus of my
study, and these questions belong to the discipline of theatre history. Yet I
understand that students of this manuscript continue to find the question of
authorship fascinating, and so I propose to begin with a discussion of one of the
authors, the one known as Hand D. Peter Blayney has recently noticed something

about Hand D which had been forgotten since 1844. On the verso of fol. 9, which everyone since Dyce had been saying was blank, Blayney found one more word written by Hand D: 'all.'[2] Apparently Hand D turned over the page and was beginning to write more dialogue when it came to his attention that his job was over. I propose to begin with a discussion of what Hand D did not know when he was writing his three pages, and it is a pleasure to borrow the first point from Blayney and note that Hand D did not know when to stop.[3]

BEYOND THE GRASP OF HAND D: WHAT HE DID NOT KNOW

Let us look at the plainest matters. When Edmund Tilney wrote his general instructions at the beginning of the manuscript, he was insisting that the Ill May Day uprising be narrated rather than dramatized and that the narration use the word 'Lombards' for the foreigners against whom the uprising was directed. That is what Tilney plainly meant when he said 'Leave out the insurrection wholly', and required it to be replaced with 'a short report' of Sir Thomas More's good service in putting down a mutiny 'against the Lombards only'. He specified 'Lombards' because he disliked the word 'strangers'. There are seventeen instances of the word 'strangers' in the manuscript that Tilney censored, and fourteen of them are in passages marked for deletion. A few lines further on, he replaced 'Frenchman' with 'Lombard'. At one point (l. 364) Tilney even crossed out the offending word and interlined 'Lombard'. Clearly Tilney wanted the foreigners to be called 'Lombards', and the word that was to be eradicated was 'stranger'.

Hand D was oblivious to both of these points. He was dramatizing one of the events Tilney wanted to have narrated (in fact, the event Tilney actually names, for Hand D showed the good service More did in quelling the mutiny), and he used 'strangers' seven times. Indeed, More's clever rhetoric turns on the very word, for in asking the rioters to imagine themselves in another country and suffering mistreatment, he tells them they would be 'strangers' too. We must assume, I suggest, that Hand D never saw Tilney's instructions about reporting the mutiny and calling the foreigners Lombards.

It is also plain that the apprentices who were originally intended to join the mutiny after wounding Sir John Munday in scene v, have been entirely removed in the revisions. Their scene with Munday has been cut, and so has the wounded Munday's report of their behaviour in Addition II. In fact, Munday's role has been entirely eliminated too. These are the cuts which I have suggested were made for purposes of reducing a large play to normal casting, a matter which will be further discussed shortly. For the moment, the point is that Hand D thought that the apprentices were still involved in the uprising. In his scene, the rabble-rousing John Lincoln harps on the injustices done to apprentices. At l. 132 it is the apprentices who are being 'undone' by the customs of the foreigners, and when the Sergeant-at-arms accuses the crowd of being 'simple', they turn on him for calling apprentices simple.

SERGEANT: You are the simplest things that ever stood in such a question.
LINCOLN: How say you now? Prentices simple! down with him!
ALL: Prentices simple! Prentices simple![4]

There is no reason for this emphasis on apprentices after the cuts have been made. Hand D writes with the original apprentice scene in mind.

It is plain that one of the revisers, Hand B, was mainly engaged in building up a Clown's role in the insurrection and that the new role was being created out of one of the two brothers Betts who were paired in the original insurrection scenes. Perhaps calling this plain is a bit disingenuous, for it is plain only after some very close reading. The original intentions can be seen in the opening episode, where l. 63 (by Hand S) makes certain that two brothers Betts are onstage. That Hand B is turning one of the brothers into the Clown's role is apparent at l. 4 of Addition II, where George Betts reacts to the 'Clown' as his 'brother'. This distinction between George Betts and 'Clown' Betts is not apparent to Hand D, who has speeches for only one of the two and calls him simply 'Betts' (when he is not calling him 'other'). Hand C has come along at a later stage to assign some of these speeches to George Betts and some to 'Betts Clown', thus showing knowledge of what Hand B has undertaken as his primary task, but Hand D does not know about this distinction. It is sometimes asserted that Hand D was careless about all the rebels' names, but this is not exactly true. His early lines do resort to 'other' when someone besides the leader, John Lincoln, is speaking, but as the scene progresses, Hand D becomes more specific about the other rebels, and distinguishes among Lincoln, Doll, Sherwin, and Betts. But he does not distinguish between the two Bettses, and given other things he does not know, I think it is reasonable to assume that he did not know that a role for the Clown was being added to the play.

Our examples of what Hand D did not know all point towards his participation in the early composition of the play rather than towards a later stage of revision. He does not know that Tilney wrote on the original manuscript, he does not know that the apprentices have been revised out of the play, he does not know that the Clown has been revised into the play as Betts's brother. These are things professional playwrights have to know about once they have happened, and Hand D has always been recognized as a professional. The conclusion, which seems to me inescapable, is that Hand D wrote his three pages (or more) quite early, before Tilney censored the play and before the revisions had been performed on the apprentices and the Clown.

This is not to say, however, that Hand D wrote all of the original play or that his three folio pages are part of the first draft of the play. As Giorgio Melchiori mentions elsewhere in this volume, Hand S, the writer of nearly all of the original manuscript, sometimes shows signs of being a copyist and sometimes of being an author. He must have written some of the original play himself. That Hand D did not know when to stop and was preparing to continue writing on the verso of fol. 9 suggests that he was aiming to join his contribution to S's writing on fol. 10 and slightly missed the mark. The implication that fol. 10 was already written when

Hand D was doing his piece seems to me correct, but it should not tempt us to assume that D was a later reviser rather than an original author. If we admit the possibility that the original composition of the play involved at least two writers, Hands S and D, we are at the same time admitting the possibility that their contributions would require dovetailing, adjustment, and some rewriting as they worked. Collaboration is normally done that way.

Judging from what Hand D did not know, then, I submit that his work, along with that of Hand S, belonged to the original composition of the play. The phrase 'original composition' does not preclude revisions occurring between the collaborators, but it does intend to set this stage of writing apart from a later stage, in which Hands A, B, C, and E did their work. Unlike Hands S and D, these later writers were concerned about such specific matters of casting as eliminating three apprentices and Sir John Munday from the insurrection, building up a new role for a Clown, and providing patches of additional time at points where costume changes were proving difficult.[5]

THE ORIGINAL VERSION: DATE AND COMPANY

There is, of course, no inherent improbability in the idea that parts of the manuscript were written at different times. The revival of older plays was fundamental to the operation of the repertory companies, and when a company's personnel had changed since the original production, the play would have to be adjusted for the revival. Henslowe's *Diary* shows many examples of playwrights 'mending' or 'altering' older plays. This was a normal part of playhouse business.

Yet in the case of *More*, the usual assumption has been that the writing and revisions belonged to one stage of composition, or at least that all of the Additions were written at one time. A mistake about the paper of the Additions – that the Additional pages all came from the same consignment of paper – has led to the latter idea. It is easier to lay this notion to rest than it is to explain how it arose. Even if the watermarks on the Additional pages were identical, we could not say that the paper came from one consignment, for the very concept of a 'consignment' that passed in one bundle from manufacturer to a stationer's stall is a modern notion that does not recognize the conditions of shipping, shuffled batching, and shelf-life on which the trade was based. At any rate, as Giorgio Melchiori has recently shown, the watermarks on the Additional pages are not identical. They are all of the common 'pot' variety, but the pots are different.[6]

Consequently, we cannot assume from the evidence of the paper that the revisions were carried out at one time, and the fact that Hand D was unaware of changes being made by other revisers suggests either that they were all working together and Hand D did not know what he was doing, or that they were working at different times and Hand D, who knew well enough what he was doing, did not know what the others were doing, because they had not done it yet.

The original version of the play is, from a theatrical point of view, an extraordinary piece of work. The assumption runs through all Hand S's pages, and through Hand D's pages too, that an unusually large company is going to act this play. The opening scenes, through to the first lacuna at l. 472 (fol. 5b), call for twenty-one speaking parts, and a twenty-second role, that of Sir John Munday, is about to appear when the text breaks off. In terms of casting, this is a huge beginning for an Elizabethan play. I have counted the characters in the first 500 lines of every extant play assigned to the years 1580 to 1610 in *The Annals of English Drama*[7] and have found that only 12 texts out of a total of 146 call for twenty or more speaking roles. The original version of *More*, in other words, is in the largest 8% of Elizabethan texts when measured in this way, and if all the speaking roles were counted throughout the plays (*More* has nearly sixty, I have not counted the others), I believe the results would be similar.

This strikes me as evidence for the vexed questions of dating the play and determining the company for which it was written. If one imagines that S and D were closet writers, of course, one might disregard the scale of their play as an example of naiveté. From what little we know about S and D, however, they seem to have been experienced in the practices of the theatre and thoroughly professional in their attitudes (S is thought to be Anthony Munday, for example). If the manuscript of *More* is now recognized as a document intended for real theatrical use (as seems to be the case, judging from the other essays in this volume) and if Hands S and D have a claim on our attention as professional writers for the theatre, then the fact that *More* shares a leading production characteristic with only eleven other plays out of 146 should tempt us to pause over the evidence.

Here are the titles of the other plays with twenty or more speaking roles in the first 500 lines. Also listed are the year under which the title appears in *The Annals of English Drama* and the acting company to which the play is there assigned:

Title	Speaking roles first 500 lines	Date and company in Annals
2 Seven Deadly Sins	20	1585. Queen's, revived 1590. Strange's?
Famous Victories of Henry V	20	1586. Queen's
Friar Bacon and Friar Bungay	20	1589. Queen's
True Tragedy of Richard III	21	1591. Queen's
1 Contention of York & Lancaster	21	1591. Stange's? Pembroke's?
1 Henry VI	21	1592. Strange's
Massacre at Paris	20	1593. Strange's
Taming of the Shrew	20	1594. Sussex's? Chamberlain's?
Downfall of Huntington	23	1598. Admiral's
Sir John Oldcastle	23	1599. Admiral's
1 If You Know Not Me	22	1604. Queen Anne's

Two distinct clusters of large plays are apparent here. The first are associated with the Queen's men between 1585 and 1591. When the Queen's men were formed in 1583, they were instantly the largest professional company to that date in London: twelve leading adult actors, plus boys and hired men.[8] It is not surprising to learn that their plays demand an unusually large number of speaking roles. The other cluster consists of four titles associated with Strange's men in 1591–93: the Quarto version of Shakespeare's *2 Henry VI*, which was published in 1594 as *The First Part of the Contention . . .*; Shakespeare's *1 Henry VI*, which was not published until the Folio of 1623; Marlowe's *Massacre at Paris*, published without date *c.* 1594; and the supposed revival of *2 Seven Deadly Sins*, for which the extant plot is thought to have been written in the early 1590s by Hand C. *The Taming of the Shrew* might also be placed in this cluster, for the Chamberlain's men were constituted in 1594, in part, by actors who go back to Strange's men and are named on the *Sins* plot.[9]

Have we any independent reason to think that *Sir Thomas More* may have originally been written for either the Queen's men or Strange's men? Those interested in questions of authorship will immediately wonder if Anthony Munday can be connected to either of these companies. Unfortunately, we do not know Munday's company relations before he appears in Henslowe's *Diary* as a writer for the Admiral's men after 1594. An earlier play in his handwriting, *John a Kent and John a Cumber*, which carries the date of 1590, was once bound with *The Book of Sir Thomas More*, and there is some reason to connect *John a Kent* with Strange's men when they were associated with Alleyn, but this is not conclusive.[10] Those who accept the argument that Hand D was involved in the original version of *More* will note that Strange's men are thought to have included Shakespeare, author of two of their other large plays. Shakespeare continues to be a contender for the identity of Hand D, as is amply apparent from other contributions to this volume.

There is another outstanding theatrical characteristic of the original *Sir Thomas More* which has not been brought to light before. The leading role is one of the longest in Elizabethan drama, running to more than 800 lines. I have surveyed the same titles from *The Annals of English Drama* to see how many other roles run over 800 lines, using the counts given for Shakespearian plays in Martin Spevack's concordance, those given for some non-Shakespearian plays by T.W. Baldwin, and my own counts in all cases.[11] Of the thousands of roles acted by Elizabethan players, I know of only twenty from the *Annals* lists of public theatre plays, 1580–1610, which run to more than 800 lines. Besides More they are:

Character and play	Lines	Date and company from Annals
Hieronimo, enlarged *Spanish Tragedy* of 1602	1018	1587. Admiral's
Tamburlaine, *2 Tamburlaine*	877	1588. Admiral's
Barabas, *Jew of Malta*	1138	1589. Strange's (by 1592)
Richard III, *Richard III*	1145	1593. Strange's? Pembroke's?

Henry V, *Henry V*	1036	1599. Chamberlain's
Hamlet, *Hamlet*	1507	1601. Chamberlain's
Henry VIII, *When You See Me*	1018	1604. Prince Henry's
Duke, *Measure for Measure*	858	1604. King's
Malevole, *The Malcontent*	over 800	1604. King's and Revels
Iago, *Othello*	1094	1604. King's
Othello, *Othello*	879	1604. King's
Mosca, *Volpone*	over 900	1606. King's
Volpone, *Volpone*	over 800	1606. King's
Vindice, *Revenger's Tragedy*	over 900	1606. King's
Antony, *Antony and Cleopatra*	824	1607. King's
Coriolanus, *Coriolanus*	886	1608 King's
D'Amville, *The Atheist's Tragedy*	over 800	1609. King's?
Subtle, *The Alchemist*	over 900	1610. King's
Face, *The Alchemist*	over 900	1610. King's[12]

There are clusters on this list too. Half of the roles are by Shakespeare, for example. What seems to me more revealing is the clustering by actor, for virtually the entire list can be divided between only two actors, the two who were the giants of their profession, Edward Alleyn and Richard Burbage. Alleyn was known to contempories for his performances as Tamburlaine and Barabas; he must have acted Hieronimo in the earlier version of *The Spanish Tragedy* at his father-in-law's theatre and thus is a likely candidate for playing the role as it was enlarged sometime before 1602; and it was surely his return to the stage after 1600 that prompted the Admiral's men to produce such a star vehicle as *When You See Me You Know Me*. (During the years of Alleyn's first retirement, 1597–1600, the new plays written for the Admiral's men had no role as large as 600 lines; the company's dramaturgy can be charted according to the presence or absence of Alleyn.) Burbage's contemporaries knew his performances as Richard III, Hamlet, Othello, Malevole, and Hieronimo, and it does not take much imagination to give him other large roles which come from the King's men after the turn of the century.

Indeed, for those years of 1580 to 1610, one is hard pressed to name any other actors who are known to played the longest parts. Clearly the King's men had one other, to join Burbage in the Iago–Othello and Mosca–Volpone pairings of 1604–1606, and this was probably John Lowin, who was later remembered for his Volpone. Do we take seriously the gibe at Ben Jonson for having played a poor Hieronimo? If so, we have squeezed out a list of four players who are known to have taken the longest roles – but with due respect to Lowin's talent, and with less than that for Jonson's, the list effectively consists of two names: Alleyn and Burbage.

Thus the two outstanding theatrical characteristics of the original *More* play – the length of its major role and the size of its implied cast – can be placed in contexts of similar characteristics drawn from all of the extant public-theatre plays during the relevant period. The result would seem to be new evidence for dating the original *More* and determining its company. We must remember the limitations of evidence that attend all Elizabethan theatre history. With only about 20% of the plays extant, and with only fragments remaining from other kinds of playhouse documents, we face many blind spots. About Worcester's men in the later 1580s, for example, with whom Alleyn apparently began his career, we know little beyond their capacities for occasional rowdiness. Nevertheless, among the companies for which evidence is available, some discriminations can be made in regard to the original *More* play. The Queen's men, for example, who were one of the companies large enough to undertake casting demands like those of *More*, have left no sign among their nine extant plays of having an actor capable of the largest Elizabethan parts. We may suspect that they had such an actor (Bentley, perhaps, or Knell), but they left no sign. The Chamberlain's–King's men of 1599–1610 (and later, one would assume) obviously had actors capable of the largest roles, but there is no sign that their plays were scaled up to the extraordinary casting scope of *More*.

Where the two contexts of evidence come together is with Strange's men of the early 1590s, the company associated with four of the extraordinarily large plays and the company which at one time or another had both of the great actors with them. The ample resources which Hand S and Hand D expected to have available belong, so far as the evidence shows, only to Strange's men among the adult companies acting in London between 1580 and 1610. Set the plot of *2 Seven Deadly Sins* next to the casting requirements of the original *Sir Thomas More* and the comparison will be obvious. The *Sins* plot calls for thirty-five named roles and twenty-seven unnamed. It records the names, at least in part, of twenty actors, and includes two major roles (Henry VI and Lydgate) for which the actors are not named and which could not have been doubled from the specified twenty (Alleyn, it is assumed, played one of these). It also includes eight lesser roles for which no actor is named, but as these may have been doubled by the named actors, we can only estimate the company at between twenty-two and thirty performers. This is the largest public-theatre company of which we have record in the Elizabethan playhouse, and it is the kind of company that Hand S and Hand D were counting on.[13] There are, of course, other reasons for thinking of Strange's men as the company responsible for the original *More*. Hand C probably wrote the plot of *2 Seven Deadly Sins* for them, they are thought to have staged some of the early history plays by the writer most identified with Hand D, and they flourished at a time when anti-alien demonstrations reached a peak. Other essays in this volume (Melchiori's and Long's, for example) amplify these reasons for considering Strange's men. The theatrical characteristics which we have set forth here allow us to approach the question along an independent avenue. If we think of how large a role More's is, if we think of how large a cast is implied by the opening scenes (both of those conditions stemming from a conviction that the manuscript was written for the real business of the theatre), we come upon Strange's men in the early 1590s as the company that probably originated it. They were an extraordinarily large company headed by at least one actor capable of an extraordinarily large role. On theatrical characteristics alone, they seem to be the company for which the original *More* was written – and if this hypothesis allows the evidence of handwriting and authorship to fit into place, so much the better.

THE REVISED PLAY: DATE AND COMPANY

The second stage of composition, consisting of the later revisions, was primarily carried out by Hands C and B, with a nice patch of writing from Hand E and perhaps another (see note 5) from Hand A. Many purposes are likely to lie behind the work of these writers. A necessary narrative link is provided by Hands B and C in what is known as Addition v. The characterization of More grows a little deeper with Addition III, by Hand C. A neat piece of dramaturgy combines the Faulkner and Erasmus episodes, originally held separate, in Addition IV, by Hand C. The staging of the play is sharpened by Additions IV and VI.[14] These other motives do not contradict or exclude what I take to be the primary motive that can be detected in all of the Additions except for Hand D's part of Addition II: the motive of easing the casting demands of an unusually large play.

The elimination of the three apprentices and Sir John Munday, together with the addition of a role for the Clown, has the effect of reducing the opening 500-line section to nineteen speaking roles. This is still a large play, but the casting can be managed by a normally constituted Elizabethan company. The revised text permits a test that is impossible for the original version with its lacunae: we can determine the minimum number of actors that would be required to play the speaking roles if all reasonable opportunities for doubling were taken. It is in charting the possible casting, incidentally, that one learns to respect the value of Hand E's additional patch of dialogue just before an influx of new characters, or the opportunity of doubling two important roles (Faulkner and Shrewsbury) which suddenly appears with the Erasmus and Faulkner episodes. It will be understood that this 'minimum cast' study is only a hypothesis. We have no evidence that a company actually seized all of the doubling possibilities in staging *More*. The minimum cast is not a statement of fact but an index of possibilities. It specifies the economical limit of casting – a limit towards which the business of professionals would aim without necessarily attaining it.

I have shifted the detailed casting list to an appendix in order to keep the narrative clear. All of the speaking roles in the revised *More* can be played by thirteen men and five boys, with the briefest costume change covered by over twenty lines of dialogue and most changes covered by upward of 100 lines. Most mute parts could also be covered by this group, although the insurrection scenes would require supernumeraries. There is no reason why a company of twenty cannot perform the entire revised play. This is not a small company by Elizabethan standards, but neither is it an outstandingly large one. In other words, the revisers were removing one of the original play's leading characteristics. Padded here and rewritten there, the new version takes on the shape of normal casting and makes our search for its theatrical provenance more difficult.

We are not entirely in the dark, however. The role of the title-character, exceptionally long in the original, does not seem to have been shortened at all in the revision. Addition III even provides a new soliloquy for More. We cannot compare the old and the new roles exactly (the lacunae in the original make this impossible), but it is clear that both versions run to over 800 lines and belong to the exceptional range in the plays of the period.

If the revised play was still intended as a star vehicle, we also know that a speciality role was being added for a comic actor and that both Hand B and Hand C designated this actor in speech prefixes as the 'Clown'. (Along with his obvious role in the revisions of the insurrection scenes, where the Clown is added as Betts's brother, note the prefixes for the Clown in Addition VI, l. 61 and l. 66, where Hand B must have had this comic actor in mind for the 'Vice' of the play-within-the-play).

Clown scenes, of course, are nothing new in Elizabethan drama. The generic designation is used by various writers throughout the period. I sometimes think that Heywood would not have written plays if he could not have written Clown scenes, and Heywood is usually taken as Hand B. We do know one further characteristic of the Clown in *More*, however, and that is his penchant for doing comic improvisations. One of the insurrection scenes in Addition II ends with the direction, probably by Hand C, 'MANETT CLOWNE', and although Greg thought this a mistake (Malone Society Reprint, p. 71) its purpose is clear to frequenters of vaudeville and burlesque houses. The Clown stays on after the others leave and improvises his gags. (This is in effect another Addition, which has always been overlooked because it lacked a text.)

In searching for the company responsible for the revised *More*, then, we are looking for an actor capable of exceptionally long roles, a comic known for the extemporaneous turn, and a group consistent with the hypothetical minimum cast of thirteen men and five boys for the speaking roles. If we find such a company, and it is consistent with our evidence about handwriting and authorship, we will not be disappointed.

When the Admiral's men moved to their new playhouse, the Fortune, in 1600, they were rejoined by their former leader, Edward Alleyn, one of the very few Elizabethan actors known to have played roles of over 800 lines, and the actor for whom, according to our earlier argument, the part of More was originally written. At that time, John Singer was the company's well-known comic actor, and in the plot of *Tamar Cam*, which dates from the Admiral's men in about 1602, his fictional name of Assinico alternates with the designation 'Clown'. I think it is significant that the very phrase that distinguishes the Clown in the revised *More*, 'Manett Clowne', appears at the end of a scene in the plot of *Tamar Cam*. I believe these are the only two occasions of this phrase in Elizabethan texts, and I see no reason to doubt that in both cases they refer to an improvised scene by a comic actor who can be trusted to do such things well.

That is not to say that the Clown's role in the revised *More* was written for John Singer. The evidence does not allow such trim conclusions. We know that the Admiral's men did designate comic roles for a 'Clown', that they did on occasion have their Clown do a 'voluntary' (the Elizabethan word for improvisation – Henslowe once paid Singer five pounds for his 'vallentarey'), and that one of their backstage documents uses the same phrase *More* uses as a signal, if my interpretation is correct, for such a comic turn. In other words, we know of a company that had both a leading actor capable of playing an extraordinarily long role and a capability in clownish improvisation that resulted in the phrase 'Manett Clowne, in one of their texts: that company, which may not be the only company to combine those traits, but is the only one we know of, is the Admiral's men in the years just after 1600.

What else do we know of the Admiral's men during these years?[15] Three of their most active writers, usually working in collaborative ventures and sometimes revising old plays, were Anthony Munday, Henry Chettle, and Thomas Dekker, who have been identified as three of the Hands in the *More* manuscript (S, A, and E). Thomas Heywood, thought to be Hand B of the manuscript, had been an actor and writer with the Admiral's men in 1598–1600, had then become associated with Worcester's men after the turn of the century, but had returned to do some collaborative writing for the Admiral's shortly before Henslowe's accounts came to an end in 1603 (he wrote *The London Florentine* with Chettle for the Admiral's in December 1602–January 1603). Of the six playhouse Hands discernible in the manuscript, then, four are known to have been associated with the Admiral's men after 1600. A fifth, the playhouse scribe known as Hand C, can fairly be added to the list if one follows Chambers's dating of another piece of C's writing for the Admiral's men, the plot of *Fortune's Tennis*, in 1602.[16] The only writer who cannot be connected to the Admiral's men after 1600 is Hand D.

Do we have any reason to suppose that the later Admiral's men would have attempted to refurbish an old play – and perhaps a play once denied by the censor – on the life of Sir Thomas More? As it happens, shortly after 1600 the Admiral's men performed a series of revivals from a decade before. When Alleyn returned to the company it was clearly in their interest to restore his great roles to the stage; and so revivals of *The Jew of Malta*, *The Spanish Tragedy*, *Doctor Faustus*, *Mahomet*, *The Blind Beggar of Alexandria*, *The Massacre at Paris*, *Tamar Cam*, *Friar Bacon* and *Longshanks* entered the repertory, all drawn from the earlier period of Alleyn's greatness. This in itself does not explain why a possibly unperformed play on More should have been taken up; but at the same time as revivals were forming the basic Admiral's repertory, the rather small number of new plays written for the company includes several on recent Tudor history, a subject generally avoided until the final years of Elizabeth's reign and the early years of James'. During 1601 Chettle and Munday participated in two plays concerning Cardinal Wolsey, and Samuel Rowley's long play on Henry VIII (*When You See Me You Know Me*) must have been written for the company shortly after Henslowe's records close in 1603–04.[17]

At a time when four or five of the writers of the *More* manuscript were preparing plays for the company, in other words, the Admiral's men were banking on revivals of old plays written for Alleyn and new plays on Tudor history. The evidence is taking shape; there is no reason to stop now. The text of *When You See Me* provides interesting comparisons with the revised *More*. Both plays divide their Tudor chronicle material into three sections, the first and third serving as an approach to Tudor state affairs and the middle taking the form of 'gests' (the King of *When You See Me* disguises himself, mingles with the rabble and intentionally lands in prison, in scenes no more beholding to fact than More's disguise prank with Erasmus and his impromptu acting in the play-within-the-play). The leading role in *When You See Me* runs to over 1,000 lines, which like More's constitutes about one third of the text and is a star vehicle. There is a major comic role for the Fool, Will Sommers. The possible doubling patterns of these two plays are remarkably similar. The revised *More* is by far the larger play in the first place, with nearly sixty speaking roles compared to forty in *When You See Me*, but the striking thing is that both plays reduce to about the same company structure if all doubling possibilities are taken into account: twelve adults and five boys in *When You See Me*, compared to thirteen adults and five boys in the revised *More* (see Appendix).

Other tests can be performed on the plays in order to compare their possible casting structures. From the welter of roles for adult actors in each play, the bit parts of under ten lines can be removed and the remaining 'distinct' roles for adults can be examined for doubling possibilities. *More* has twenty-seven distinct roles for adults; *When You See Me* has twenty-three. *More* calls eleven of these roles together in scene vi; *When You See Me* calls twelve together in the combination of exits and entrances at the juncture of scenes ix and x. The figures are again closely similar.

Can the eleven actors drawn together in scene vi of *More* double all twenty-seven distinct roles in the play? The answer is no: a twelfth actor would be required in scenes iii, v, and vi (the role of Cholmley requires the twelfth actor). These twelve actors could play all of the twenty-seven distinct roles for adults, in a pattern consistent with the doubling practices known from playhouse documents (three leading players would not have to double distinct roles at all, while the other nine would play two to four distinct roles each). In *When You See Me*, the twelve adult actors required for the largest scene can play all twenty-three distinct roles for adults, with six actors not doubling and the other six playing two to four roles. In other words, the hypothesis of maximum doubling for the distinct roles for adults (ten lines or more) produces exactly the same results for the two plays.

The other extant plays produced by the Admiral's men during 1600–05 for which reliable texts are extant are the two parts of *The Honest Whore*. The first part was published in 1604; the second not until 1630 (it is usually assumed to go back to the original production, but a note of caution should attend this text, which might reflect later revisions). Like most comedies, both plays are lighter in casting demands than the chronicle plays, and they do not have a single dominating role. They do reduce to approximately the same minimum cast as the larger plays, however, and perhaps the figures can best be seen in a table (detailed discussion in Appendix):

	Total speaking roles	Minimum cast	Adults	Boys
More	59	18	13	5
When You See	39	17	12	5
1 Honest Whore	31	15	11	4
2 Honest Whore	28	17–19	13	4–6

The chart shows that there is nothing improbable about the hypothesis that *More* was written for the company that played the other texts. It cannot be taken as positive evidence of that point until similar studies are performed on the texts of other repertory companies of the period. Not until then will we be able to evaluate the evidence for its positive results: if there are differences in the minimum casts of different companies, then positive discriminations can be made. For the moment, we may say that the reliable texts from the Admiral's men do reduce to approximately the same minimum cast as the revised *More*, keeping open the possibility that all four plays were written for the same company.

To summarize: in the Admiral's men of shortly after 1600, we find a star actor famous for his extensive lead roles, use of the word 'Clown' which accords exactly with the revisions to *More*, a minimum cast in the company's three reliable extant texts that agrees with the minimum cast of the revised *More* reliance on the revivals of older plays, a new interest in dramatizing the figures of Tudor history, a plot written by Hand C, busy writing from Munday, Chettle, Dekker, and Heywood, who were inclined to collaborate with one another and to revise plays for the company. In noticing that these fit exactly with the characteristics of the revised *More*, we are not proving anything; but I think we are building circumstantial evidence to a point that is rarely reached in matters of this sort.

The leading points of difficulty in this hypothesis require attention. Henslowe's *Diary*, which approaches completeness in naming the company's repertory until the death of Elizabeth, does not mention *Sir Thomas More*. Moreover, Thomas Goodale, named as an actor for one of the Additional passages, does not appear in the plots for the Admiral's men of 1601–2, and his absence from the plot of *Tamar Cam* is especially telling, for the production appears to have required the entire resources of the company. The first of these problems does not strike me as serious. If the *More* revision had been done after 1603, it would not have appeared in Henslowe's *Diary*; in this respect, too, it would resemble *When You See Me*.

Thomas Goodale presents more of a problem. He was with the earlier Strange's men and is named in Hand C's plot of 2 *Seven Deadly Sins*, but I do not believe that the appearance of his name in the *More* manuscript goes back to the original version; it seems clearly connected to Addition v, which Hands C and B combined to produce, according to my argument, during the later stage of revision. It is, of course, possible that Goodale joined the Admiral's men after 1603. We know nothing about him after 1599, so the possibilities are, at present, open. If he was with the Admiral's men after 1603, however, one could hope to find him on the extensive list of Prince Henry's men (successors to the Admiral's) in 1610, which appears to name more than the sharers; but he is not there. Perhaps he was dead by 1610, but such speculations seem to me no more satisfactory than resorting to the suspicions of fifty years ago that the marginal 'Goodal' was a forgery in the first place.[18] Dating the revision after 1603 for the Admiral's men does address the Goodale problem, but does not solve it.

On the other hand, one major problem does grow small on the assumption that the Admiral's men revived the play after Elizabeth's death. None of the writers of the manuscript shows signs of heeding the stern condition laid down by the Master of the Revels, Edmund Tilney: 'Leave out . . . the insurrection wholly'. On the older assumption that the revisions were performed soon after the original writing and in the face of recent censorship by Tilney, it cannot be understood why the writers were so nonchalant about their 'peril' (Tilney's word) as to leave the insurrection standing and even to touch it up. Greg declared such behaviour 'collective insanity' (Malone Society Reprint, p. xiv) and proceeded to argue that the revisions were written *before* the fist submission to Tilney, but his view has been properly challenged on grounds that Tilney had left no mark on any of the Additional pages. According to the present argument, however, Tilney's censorship of the original version, submitted to him by Strange's men in the early 1590s is far removed from the revision after 1603. Anti-alien disturbances, which seem the most plausible reason for Tilney's objections to the insurrection, were a major social problem in 1593, but not in the early years of James's reign.

More significantly, the Office of the Revels underwent some change of leadership in 1603. Early in the new reign, on 23 June 1603, Sir George Buc received a grant of the reversion of the Master's office to Tilney, and on the same day he was issued a new commission for the office, repeating the terms of the commission under which Tilney had operated since 1581, but replacing Tilney's name with Buc's. These documents cannot be taken to mean that Tilney was replaced by Buc in 1603. Tilney clearly continued to play some kind of supervisory role at the Revels office until 1610, and it appears likely that the authority of the Mastership was divided between him and Buc until then. Who was responsible for the licensing of plays after 1603 remains uncertain. Buc certainly licensed plays for the *press* after that became a function of the Revels Office in 1606, and there is evidence that he allowed *Juqurth, King of Numidia* for the stage in the early 1600s; but the exact division of authority between Buc and Tilney after 1603 remains uncertain. A change in the political climate occurred in 1603 in London – that much is certain; and it is also certain that a change in the Mastership of the Revels was in the offing at the same time, although the change may have been effected over a period of years.[19] A play that seemed dangerous a decade before may very well have seemed tame enough now, and it may be noted that an insurrection scene rather like *More*'s was incorporated in Chettle's *Hoffman*, written in 1602, apparently without fear of censorship.[20]

CONCLUSIONS

The evidence we have brought forward from the theatrical characteristics of *More* and other Elizabethan plays joins with long-established evidence of handwriting and authorship to produce the following outline of events in regard to *The Book of Sir Thomas More*.

The original play was written in the early 1590s for an uncommonly large acting company, Strange's men, and an uncommonly fine actor, Edward Alleyn. The writing was a collaborative effort, with the dramatists we now know as Hand S and Hand D sharing in the work. In at least one major scene, Hand D rewrote an episode first undertaken by Hand S. He wrote the revision on what are now called folios 8 and 9, joining up with Hand S's original version on what is now called folio 10. He may have written other passages as well, but if so, his contribution has been copied by Hand S.

Hand S, as is well known, was Anthony Munday. Hand D cannot be so readily identified. His one extant contribution suggests experience and skill at blank verse in a serious vein. We would look for him among the better known playwrights of the very early 1590s: Greene, perhaps, or Marlowe, Kyd, Peele, Shakespeare. Strange's men are thought to have performed at least one other play by each of these writers.

The original play was submitted to Tilney, who refused to license it for the stage unless major changes were made, especially the omission of the insurrection scenes. There is no evidence that these changes were made. The play was probably not performed by Strange's men.

A decade later, while the Admiral's men at the Fortune were reviving many of the plays that Alleyn had starred in during the 1590s (Alleyn having come out of retirement in 1600), and while they were also mining Tudor history for new plays, they took up the old play of *More*, had Hands B, C, E, and perhaps A patch together some revisions which would bring the piece down to proper casting scale from its luxurious original design, obtained licensing from the same authority who licensed such other plays on Tudor matters as their own *When You See Me* or (a few years earlier) the Chamberlain's men's play on *Thomas Lord Cromwell*, and mounted a production at the Fortune with Alleyn playing the title role.

The revision was carried out by Thomas Dekker (long recognized as Hand E), perhaps by Henry Chettle (long recognized as Hand A), perhaps by Thomas Heywood (the leading candidate for Hand B) and the playhouse scribe known to us as Hand C. Hand C had been with Strange's men at the time the original *More* was written and now (having travelled the same route as Alleyn, from Strange's to the

Admiral's) found himself rearranging this as well as other old plays for performance by Alleyn and his men. That Munday appears to have had no hand in revising his own play seems to me noticeable but not startling. Henslowe's writers were busy men who did not think of their plays as private property. That Hand D had no part in the revision can perhaps be explained by a glance at the candidates for his identity listed earlier: Greene, Marlowe, Peele, and Kyd were all dead; and Shakespeare, whose association with Alleyn ended with the formation of the Chamberlain's men in 1594, and who was now recognized as the leading playwright of the rival company, would simply have had no reason to be involved.

APPENDIX

Determining Minimum Casts

Only speaking roles have been considered, because the texts are indeterminate about mute parts for attendants and crowds. Elizabethan companies included supernumeraries for mute parts, of course, and these bit-players could have taken tiny speaking roles here and there. I have thought it best, however, to include all speaking roles without regard to the possibility that some of the smaller ones could have been played by walk-ons: the only exception is the role of 'Another' in *More*, scene ii, whose only line is 'And me'; this may be the tiniest speaking role in Elizabethan drama, and I have let it fall to the extras.

Roles normally played by boys have been distinguished from roles normally played by adults. Boys' speaking roles in *More*: Doll, Lady More, Mistress Roper, Other Daughter, Lady Vanity, Poor Woman. In *When You See Me*: Prince Edward, Young Dorset, Young Brown, Queen Katherine, Page, Countess, Lady Mary, 1 Lady, 2 Lady, Queen Jane. In *1 Honest Whore*: Mistress Fingerlock, Bellafront, 1 Prentice, 2 Prentice, Infelice, Viola. In *2 Honest Whore*: Bellafront, Infelice, Bride, 1 Prentice, Mistress Horseleach, Dorothea Target, Penelope Whore-hound, Catherina Bountinall.

Doubling possibilities are often defined by one's sense of the impossible. It is impossible for doubling to occur among characters who appear onstage together, and it is so improbable that an exiting character could be doubled with an immediately entering character that I have called this an impossibility too. Beyond that, given the evidence that costume changes were sometimes handled in the time covered by fewer than twenty-five lines of dialogue, with one example taking fewer than ten lines, anything is possible so long as the resulting doubling assignments do not outrun documentary evidence from the playhouses.[21] The actors sometimes played seven roles in one play, although the leading player did not usually double at all, and the boys did not double much. Below is a minimum casting pattern for each play, showing all speaking roles for the smallest number of actors who could play them according to these guidelines and indicating the briefest time for costume changes in each play.

Sir Thomas More

1. More
2. Shrewsbury. Faulkner
3. Surrey. Mess (vii). Porter (xv)
4. Lord Mayor. Horsekeeper (xv). Officer (xvii)
5. Lincoln. Roper
6. Lifter, Clown (iv, vi, vii). 1 Player (Vice). 1 Warder
7. DeBard. Suresby. Mess. (iii). Sgt. Downes. Officer (vii) Mess.-Sergeant (ix). Catesby
8. Betts. Erasmus. 2 Player. 2 Warder. Servant (xiii)
9. Caveler. Recorder. Mess. (v). Crofts. 3 Player. 3 Warder. *Gough

10. Williamson. Morris. Bishop. Gent. Porter. Servant (xvi). Hangman
11. Sherwin. 4 Player. Lt. of Tower
12. Palmer. 2 Officer (vii). *Randall. Brewer (xv). 2 Sheriff
13. Cholmley, Sheriff. Clerk. Butler (xv)
14. Doll. Lady Vanity
15. Lady More
16. Mayoress. Poor Woman
17. Mistress Roper
18. Other Daughter
*Briefest changes: 22 lines

When You See Me You Know Me

1. Henry VIII
2. Wolsey
3. Will Summers
4. Compton
5. Brandon
6. Seymour
7. Bonwit. Patch. Constable. Porter. Cranmer
8. DeMayo. 1 Watch. 1 Prisoner. Rookesby. Dr Tye. Emperor
9. Bonner. Prichall. 2 Prisoner
10. Dudley. Dormouse. *1 Servant
11. Grey. 2 Watch. *2 Servant
12. Gardner. Campeus. Black Will
13. Prince Edward
14. Queen Katherine. Countess of Salisbury
15. Young Dorset. 1 Page. 1 Lady
16. Young Browne. 2 Lady. Queen Jane Seymour
17. Lady Mary
*Briefest changes: 14 lines

1 Honest Whore

1. Hippolito
2. Matheo. Crambo
3. Candido. 3 Madman
4. Duke. Roger. Hippolito's servant
5. Castruccio. Fustigo
6. Sinezi. Dr Benedict
7. Pioratto. Porter
8. Fluello
9. 1 Servant. George. Sweeper. 2 Madman
10. 2 Servant. Poh. Doctor's man. Friar
11. Officer. 1 Madman
12. Bellafront
13. Infelice. 2 Prentice
14. Viola
15. 1 Prentice. Mistress Fingerlock.
No changes under 30 lines

2 Honest Whore

1. Hippolito
2. Orlando Friscoboldo
3. Candido
4. Matheo
5. Beraldo
6. Carolo
7. Fontinell. 1 Servant
8. Astolfo
9. Lodovico
10. Bryan. 1 Vintner. Master of Bridewell
11. Antonio Georgio. 1 Guest. Constable
12. Duke. 2 Vintner
13. 2 Servant. Bots
14. Bellafront
15. Infelice
16. Bride. Catherina Bountinall
17. 1 Prentice. Penelope Whorehound
18. Mistress Horseleech. Dorothea Target*

*Boys' roles could be reduced to four by doubling within the procession of prostitutes in v, iii, but this is an unlikely manoeuvre. The doubling of Mistress Horseleech and one of the prostitutes, shown above, would be avoided by a sixth boy.

No changes under 30 lines.

NOTES

1 *The Elizabethan Theatre and 'The Book of Sir Thomas More'* (Ithaca, N.Y.: Cornell University Press, 1987), chapters 1 and 2. The present article summarizes chapters 3, 4 and 7 of that book. © 1987, Cornell University, used by permission of the publisher, Cornell University Press. Aesthetic coherence is also discussed in Charles Forker and Joseph Candido, 'Wit, Wisdom, and Theatricality in *The Book of Sir Thomas More*', *Shakespeare Studies*, 13 (1980), 85–104.

2 '*The Book of Sir Thomas More* Re-Examined', *Studies in Philology*, 69 (1972), 168.

3 Or else where to begin. Since the first speech on the written side of fol. 9 carries the prefix 'all', D may have made a false start and then turned the page over.

4 I quote the modernization in *The Riverside Shakespeare*, ed. G. Blakemore Evans and others (Boston, 1974).

5 Hand A deserves further consideration. I continue to list him with the later revisers, because his revision (Addition 1) has the effect of removing from scene xiii one character who was present in the original, the secretary Gough. But other motives must lie behind A's extensive rewriting in this scene, and it may be that like Hand D's his work belonged to the original composition.

6 Melchiori, '*The Book of Sir Thomas More*: A chronology of Revision', *SQ*, 37 (1986), 291–308. For the Renaissance paper trade, see Dard Hunter *Papermaking: The History and Technology of an Ancient Craft*, 2nd ed. (New York, 1974), and Allan Stevenson, *Observations on Paper as Evidence* (Lawrence, 1961). G.R. Proudfoot kindly joined me in examining the watermarks of the Additional pages in the Manuscript Room of the British Library and verified my observation that the watermarks are different. This is apparently what Greg meant in *Dramatic Documents from the Elizabethan Playhouses* (Oxford, 1931), when he alluded to 'two distinct makes of paper' in the Additions (p. 244). Michael Hays appears to have seen the same thing when he mentioned 'some slight difference among these pot watermarks', in 'Watermarks in the Manuscript of *Sir Thomas More* and a Possible Collation', *SQ*, 26 (1975), 67. On questions of paper and watermarks, I have benefited from the advice of William Ingram.

7 Alfred Harbage and Samuel Schoenbaum, *Annals of English Drama, 975–1700*, rev. ed. (London, 1964). This is meant to be a gross factual test, without introducing hypotheses as to how doubling would be handled. I appreciate the help of David Thurn in this work. All speaking roles have been counted, no matter how small. Substantially different texts of the same play (*1 Contention of York and Lancaster* and *2 Henry VI*, for example) have been counted separately on grounds that each text probably represents a separate performed version. With manuscript 'plots' I have counted the characters named within the first 20% of the lines, omitting those attendant parts which are not singled out in any way. For example, in *2 Seven Deadly Sins*, I have omitted the attendants who enter with Ferrex and Porrex at l. 17, but have included the Warder who accompanies the Lieutenant of the Tower at l. 5 because he is singled out by function and was played by R. Pallant, who plays speaking roles elsewhere in this play, and I have included the single Servant at l. 11 because other characters enter 'to him' and apparently converse with him.

8 See my article 'The Queen's Men and the London Theatre of 1583', *The Elizabethan Theatre*, x, ed. C.E. McGee, (Pon-Credit, 1988).

9 For the date of the *Sins* plot, see my 'Plots of *The Dead Man's Fortune* and *2 Seven Deadly Sins*', *Studies in Bibliography*, 26 (1973), 235–244, which summarizes the arguments of Greg and Chambers on this point. Their attribution of this play to the Queen's men in 1585 is open to doubt, but this is not the place to debate the issue. For the constitution of the Chamberlain's men in 1594, see E.K. Chambers, *The Elizabethan Stage* (Oxford, 1923), II, 192ff.

10 See I.A. Shapiro, 'The Significance of a Date', *Shakespeare Survey*, 8 (1955), 100–105 and Pollard's introduction to *Shakespeare's Hand in the Book of Sir Thomas More*, ed. A.W. Pollard (Cambridge, 1923), p. 18.

11 Marvin Spevack, *A Complete and Systematic Concordance to the Works of William Shakespeare*, 9 vols. (Hildesheim, 1968–80); T.W. Baldwin, *On the Literary Genetics of Shakespeare's Plays, 1592–94* (Urbana, 1959).

12 *Timon of Athens*, not included on either list because it is not assigned to an acting company in the *Annals*, deserves special note as having a role of over 800 lines *and* having more than twenty speaking characters in the first 500 lines. *Timon* and *More* are the only (presumably) public-theatre plays, 1580–1610, which combine these characteristics.

13 More fully discussed in my 'Plots of *The Dead Man's Fortune* and *2 Seven Deadly Sins*'. The *Tamar Cam* plot also has many performers' names, but ten of these are restricted to the final procession (including 'the red-faced fellow') and probably came from the theatre staff.

14 Discussed in my *Elizabethan Theatre and 'The Book of Sir Thomas More'*, chapters 5 and 6.

15 Carol A. Chillington, 'Playwrights at Work: Henslowe's, not Shakespeare's Book of *Sir Thomas More*', *English Literary Renaissance*, 10 (1980), 439–79 gives a useful review of company practices before veering off to the question of authorship and finding Webster in Hand D. Gary Taylor's contribution to the present volume discusses the reasons for assigning a late date to *More*. We agree on most of the points, although not on the dating of Hand D's pages, which Taylor places at the same time as the other revisions.

16 *The Elizabethan Stage*, IV, 14. Greg, *Dramatic Documents*, p. 131 conjectures 1597–8, but his reasoning seems based on unproved suppositions about the meaning of 'Mr.' in the plots. Chambers has the stronger argument here.

17 Malone Society Reprint of *When You See Me* (Oxford, 1952), p. x.

18 See W.W. Greg, 'T. Goodal in *Sir Thomas More*'. *PMLA*, 46 (1931), 268–71.

19 Chambers, *Elizabethan Stage*, I, 99 thought that Buc became acting Master in 1603. That Tilney continued in office after 1603 is argued by Mark Eccles, 'Sir George Buc, Master of Revels', in *Thomas Lodge and other Elizabethans*, ed. C.J. Sisson (Cambridge, Mass., 1933), pp. 409–506, and W.R. Streitberger, 'On Edmond Tyllney's Biography', *Review of English Studies*, 29 (1978), 11–35. I agree with Gary Taylor's fuller discussion of this matter in his contribution to this volume.

20 I owe this point to Chillington, 'Playwrights at Work', pp. 476–7.

21 See the useful summary of evidence in Gary Taylor, 'Three Studies in the Text of *Henry V*', in Stanley Wells and Gary Taylor, *Modernizing Shakespeare's Spelling* (Oxford, 1979), pp. 72–84, along with David Bradley, *The Ignorant Elizabethan Author and Massinger's Believe as You List* (Sydney, Australia, 1977). The basic source for evidence about casting is David Bevington, *From Mankind to Marlowe* (Cambridge, Mass., 1962).

4

The Book of Sir Thomas More: dramatic unity

GIORGIO MELCHIORI

There seems to be little doubt that the original manuscript of *The Book of Sir Thomas More* was a fair copy and not foul papers.[1] The hand, it has been ascertained, is that of Anthony Munday, though he might not have been the sole author, but the transcriber of a text written in collaboration with others.[2] His crossing out, rewriting and expanding the very last speeches of the play – More's execution (fol. 22^r, 1954–86) – shows that he assumed the full rights of an author to improve on his own or anybody else's first draft and impose his ideological construction on the meaning of the play.[3] Munday's is undoubtedly the most important hand in the original text of *More*. Moreover, Meres's characterization of him as 'our best plotter' directs attention to the design of the play and its evolution from Munday's initial conception to its present form.

It looks to me as if the play as a whole had been plotted with a precise intention: that of showing the abuses perpetrated under cover of the absolute power of the king. The play opens with a graphic presentation of the overbearing behaviour of the strangers under the protection of local authorities towards the industrious London citizens, so that John Lincoln's reaction is fully justified:

It is hard when Englishmens pacience must be thus ietted on by straungers and they not dare to reuendge their owne wrongs.   (fol. 3^r, 24–5)

(It is significant that this speech was the first to be crossed out by Tilney before deciding that the whole scene must be left out 'att your own perrilles'). After this introduction the figure of More is built up as the very incarnation of the marriage of Wit and Wisdom,[4] just and humane, not a wily tribune of the plebs but 'the best freend that the poore ere had' (fol. 20^r, 1648). His integrity is never questioned, so that his death becomes the one inevitable and fully accepted solution of a case of divided allegiance: to moral (rather than religious) principles that were part of his very nature, and to an earthly sovereign whose orders he had sworn to follow unquestioningly. By never specifying the nature of the royal articles to which More refuses to subscribe, the author avoids raising the specific question of the conflict between the Roman and the English Church, replacing it with that of the freedom of the individual conscience from worldly authority; as More tells the Lieutenant of the Tower: 'I haue peace of conscience, though the world and I, | are at a little oddes' (fol. 20^v, 1741–2). Freedom of conscience was a question that interested the

Puritan and non-conformist London middle class even more than the Roman Catholic dissidents. This explains why the vindication of More, by then a martyr of the Catholic Church, was undertaken by Munday, a man who had fought with all means against that Church, to the point of becoming an informer against English Catholics in Rome and in London. His Puritan sympathies, inclining him increasingly to denounce the prevarications of Church and State against the rights of the individual, are apparent in his most successful plays, *The Downfall* and *The Death of Robert Earl of Huntingdon*.

Whatever his religious sympathies, Munday's decision to write or 'plot' a play on Sir Thomas More seems motivated not only by the growing popularity that the memory of the Lord Chancellor, friend to the poor, enjoyed among the people of London (in spite of Foxe's accusations in the *Book of Martyrs* and the slighting treatment of More in Hall's chronicles), but also by the impression Munday received during his stay in the English College in Rome from February to May 1579. It was on the first of May of that year, when Munday was most involved in the affairs of the Church of Rome, that the Papal constitution *Quoniam divinae bonitatis* proclaimed Thomas More and John Fisher, Bishop of Rochester martyrs of the Christian faith, and on this occasion the English College, directly concerned, commissioned from Pomarancio the fresco representing the martyrdom of Fisher, More and Margaret Pole. The fresco, most impressive in its theatricality, was destroyed at the beginning of the nineteenth century, but is reproduced in an engraving by G.B. de Cavalleriis included in *Ecclesiae Anglicanae Trophaea*, published in Rome in 1584. Obviously Munday would not mention the papal constitution or the frescoes in the college in his report on his stay there, *The Englishe Romaine Lyfe*, of 1582, since that pamphlet was meant to exonerate him from any suspicion of Catholic sympathies and to present his visit to Rome as the first step towards the new role he had assumed as informer against English Catholics at home and abroad.[5] It was in this role, as a close collaborator of Richard Topcliffe, 'the priest catcher', that Munday may have acquired further knowledge about More's life, not available in print but used in the later part of the play. In fact he seems to have known Nicholas Harpsfield's *Life of More*, written about 1557 (in Mary's reign), but published only in 1932 and considered now as the first formal biography in the English language, since it integrates in a scholarly way Roper's first hand biographical information, the testimony of More's own and Erasmus's writings and a number of other sources carefully sifted.[6] The most authoritative of the eight surviving copies of the manuscript, preserved in Emmanuel College, Cambridge, bears the inscription:

This booke was found by Rich: Topclyff in Mr Thomas Moare [Sir Thomas's grandson] studdye emongs other bookes at Greenstreet Mr Wayfarers house wher Mr Moare was apprehended the xiiijth April 1582.

Munday, at Topcliffe's direction, may well have scrutinized the manuscript for evidence against the English Catholics, and learnt many of the details he later included in *More*.[7]

I do not wish, in this paper, to deal exhaustively with the sources of the play; Vittorio Gabrieli has shown elsewhere that they are somewhat different from those pointed out by past scholars and that none of those used in the Original Text is later than 1588. Significantly there is no trace of a new recourse to the sources in any of the Additions: there are at most echoes from other plays, or topical references pointing to dates not later than 1593. But for the present what I want to underline is Munday's general choice of sources and his way of mixing and manipulating them. Looking for a biographical touch that would show More's popularity with the citizens of London (and with an eye for the current feelings and problems of the City in the 1590s) he hit on the marginal part More played in the pacification of the Ill May Day riots of 1517, and expanded it into a major role; he needed only to supplement the description of the riot and of its origins from an unimpeachable source, the Tudor historian Edward Hall, or rather Hall as reported in the 1586–7 edition of Holinshed's *Chronicles* with the substantial additions by Abraham Fleming, including a quotation from the solemn sermon delivered in October 1584 by Doctor Aylmer, Bishop of London, acknowledging that More was 'a man for his zeale to be honored' (p. 939). Commentators have been intrigued by finding that one episode of the play, that of More's confrontation with the long-haired ruffian Faulkner, is not part of More's biography but is an anecdote reported of More's arch-enemy Sir Thomas Cromwell, by no less authority than John Foxe in his *Book of Martyrs*.[8] I find this transposition typical of Munday's political strategy: having decided to make More the ideal statesman, witty and wise, above all factions, he turned to the pages of the most eminent protestant apologist in order to find examples of the same qualities in a statesman; Foxe's ideal statesman is of course Cromwell, whose outstanding qualities are 'flourishing authority, excelling wisdom, and fervent zeal'. The first two examples that Foxe provides of these virtues are, first, Cromwell's ability by his mere presence and the authority of his name to quench 'a certain notorious fray or riot, appointed to be fought by a company of ruffians in the street of London called Paternoster Row'; the second example is of Cromwell meeting a long-haired ruffian, whom he sends to prison, 'till at length this "intonsus Cato", being persuaded by his master to cut his hair . . . he was brought again to the Lord Cromwell, with his head polled according to the accustomed sort of his other fellows, and so was dismissed'. Foxe's comment on the latter episode is worth reporting:

If the same Lord Cromwell, who could not abide this servingman so disfigured in his care, were now in these days alive, with the same authority which then he had, and saw these new-fangled fashions of attire, used here amongst us both of men and women, I suppose verily, that neither these monstruous ruffs, nor these prodigious hose, and prodigal, or rather hyperbolical barbarous breeches . . . would have any place in England.

Foxe was writing in 1563, but the attacks against extravagant attire were as rife some thirty years later when, in 1592, a lawyer was imprisoned and struck off the roll because his apparel was unfit for the calling[9] and there raged a battle of pamphlets (as we can see from the *Stationers' Register* for the years 1590–3) on the

wearing of hair either too long or too short.[10] Munday, then, saw the topicality of
the two examples of the correct use of authority given by Foxe in connection with
Cromwell and fused them together, making of the long-haired ruffian (for whom
and for whose master he had to invent names) a participant and promoter of the
Paternoster Row fray.[11] His only miscalculation was the overly realistic presentation of yet another riot in the play.

All that has been said up to now points to Anthony Munday as something more
than a mere transcriber of a 'book' written in collaboration with a number of others,
although we cannot exclude that some playwright in the service of a company of
players may have contributed to develop part of the dialogue. The question now is:
what was Munday's purpose in writing out a fair copy of the book? What is
particularly striking is the exceptional consistency of the speech headings, for which
the same abbreviations are used throughout in the different scenes (except for a
couple of oversights) with a fine distinction between proper names (always in
Italian script) and titles or qualifications (e.g. *L.Maior*, *Ser.*) always in English script
like the rest of the text. This accuracy, together with the remarkable regularity of
the spelling and the already noted richness and precision of the stage directions,
goes well beyond the usual requirements of a prompt-book to be used in
performance. It seems rather to pursue a double aim: (1) to demonstrate the
theatrical functionality of the play; (2) to provide a readable text that could be
circulated not only among theatre people but also among men of letters who would
appreciate its topical implications.

As Peter Blayney demonstrated in his paper '*The Booke of Sir Thomas Moore* Re-
Examined'[12] – which is the most penetrating reconstruction so far of the manuscript
and of the revision process – the original in Munday's hand included, besides fols. 3^r
to 5^v, 10^r to 11^v, 14^r to 15^v and 17^r to 22^r in the present numbering, three more leaves
now lost, two of which (designated by Blayney as fols. W and X) between 5^v and 10^r,
and one (fol. Y) between 11^v and 14^r. Since Munday averaged 80 lines for each of his
pages, the 320 lines in folios W and X must have contained: (1) the continuation of
the now cancelled prentices' scene, with the wounding of the alderman Sir John
Munday (say, some 80 more lines); (2) a scene in the Guildhall equivalent to or
nearly identical with what is designated by Greg as scene va in Add. ii, Hand C
(now 55 lines, but probably more in the original); (3) the first part of scene vi,
presenting the May Day riot, the manhandling of the Sergeant-at-arms Downes and
the intervention of More (surely considerably more than the present 148 lines in
Hand D).[13] Fol. Y (160 lines) certainly contained the conclusion of the scene viiia
between More and Erasmus with the practical joke performed on the latter and the
protestations of friendship between the two (as rewritten as Add. iv this part of
scene viii is some 60 lines long); and, as a separate scene, the Paternoster Row fray –
presented directly on the stage – and arrest of the ruffian Faulkner (scene viiib for
Greg); it is impossible to evaluate the extension of this first part of viiib: if less than
80 lines, there would have been room – as Blayney privately suggests – for a brief
linking scene between viiia and viiib showing Erasmus's leave taking from More as

well as, in my opinion, More and Surrey being summoned to an urgent meeting with other 'Lords' (it is on his way there that More intervenes in the trouble in Paternoster Row, and the sudden summons may have suggested to Hand B the idea of Add. VI, when More is called from the entertainment he is offering the Lord Mayor to a hurried meeting of the Privy Council).

The question of how closely scene va copied in hand C (Add. II, 66–120) reproduces a missing scene in Munday's original cannot easily be settled. The scene itself sends out contradictory signals. The fact that it is modelled to a large extent on a scene devised by Munday is supported by: (1) the appearance at the beginning of '*Sr Iohn Munday Hurt*', which links up with the preceding prentices' scene (while the incident should have disappeared in the revision); (2) the way, typical of Munday, in which Holinshed's chronicle is used, reporting the different incidents of May Day in the order in which they are recorded there. After relating the assault on the alderman Sir John Munday and his flight from the enraged prentices, Holinshed goes on: 'Then more people arose out of euerie quarter . . . & brake vp the counters, tooke out the prisoners that the maior had thither committed for hurting the strangers, and came to Newgate, and tooke out Studleie and Petit committed thither for that cause'. The following paragraphs of the historian are devoted to the meeting at St Martin's gate of the crowd with 'sir' Thomas More's party (note 'S' in the opening stage direction of the scene) and the attack on Downes (the subject of scene vi), the assault on the strangers' houses, fortunately empty (described in scene iv), and the quelling of the rebellion. The narrative goes on: 'About fiue of the clocke the earles of Shrewesburie and Surrie, Thomas Dokereie lord of saint Iohns, George Neuill lord of Aburgauennie, and others, which had heard of this riot, came to London with such strength as they could make vpon that sudden'. Compare with this the speeches of More (II, 76–82), of the Messenger (II, 87–90) and of Shrewsbury (II, 96–101). It is just the way in which Munday would have arranged the information drawn from Holinshed. But against this there are the alterations introduced in the report, which contrast with the sympathy the author had shown for the oppressed citizens in the previous scenes: the prisoners released are not, as in Holinshed, the citizens guilty only of 'hurting the strangers', but common criminals, including 'fellons and notorious murderers', while the insolent strangers have become 'the amazed Lombards'. Throughout the original (and the rest of the additions) the word '*Lombard*' had been used only once in scene i (l. 41), while the foreigners had been called 'strangers' (ten times in scene i, once in scene iii, three times in scene iv, twice in scene vii, four times in Add. II in hand B and seven times in hand D), 'aliens' (twice in scenes i and iii, once in scenes iv, vii and in Add. II in hand B), 'French' (twice in scene iii, once in scene vii and three times in Add. II in hand B), 'Dutch' (in scene vii and Add. II in hand B), 'Fleming' (twice in Add. II in hand B); there is also the pointed reference to 'ffraunc or flanders' in Add. II in hand D, l. 250. None of these words appears in the re-written scene va, while '*Lombards*' figures in it twice (II, 82 and 104). This sudden reversal of sympathies, and the substitution of 'Lombards' for 'strangers' or 'aliens' suggests that this scene is an adaptation of one originally written by Munday with deliberate alterations and possibly cuts in order to transfer the blame for the rebellion from the unbearable insolence of the foreigners to the ignorance and irresponsibility of the populace. A further detail should be taken into account: upon his entrance at II, 95 Shrewsbury (closely echoing the already quoted passage in Holinshed) announces that 'his ma^{tie} receaving notice.|of this most dangerous Insurection|hath sent my lord of Surry and my self | Sr Thomas palmer and o^r followers | to add vnto o^r forces [emended by all eds. to 'yor]o^r best meanes | for pacifying of this mutinie'; there is no mention of Sir Roger Cholmley (too important to be considered just as a 'follower'), though he had appeared with Palmer and the rest in scene iii and is present in Munday's surviving part of scene vi (his exit is indicated at 493); besides, Cholmley is given no speech in va – he might as well not be there. It should be noticed that in the entrance direction at l. 95 Hand C had put a full stop after the words '*Enter Shrowsberie Surrie Palmer*', and the name '*Cholmley*' is added after it. It looks as if Cholmley had not been meant to take part in this scene as originally written by Munday or in its adaptation, and his name was an addition by the book-keeper C who, going over the reassembled text of the play, noticed his presence with Palmer in scenes iii and vi; but Munday had good reasons to leave him out of this particular scene: Holinshed, immediately before the already quoted passage on the arrival of Shrewsbury, Surrey and others, reads: 'The lieutenant of the Tower sir Roger Cholmeleie (no great freend to the citie) in a frantike furie, during the time of this vprore, shot off certeine peeces of ordinance against the citie. And though they did no great harme; yet he wan much euill will for his hastie dooing, bicause men thought he did it of malice, rather than of anie discretion'. It is significant that in the later scenes of the play (scenes xiv, xvi and xvii) Munday deliberately refrains from identifying the Lieutenant of the Tower sympathetic with More's plight with Cholmley, and does not mention his name.

It is now time to ask why and how a manuscript originally submitted to a company of players in such good order was subjected to so many mutilations, corrections and additions. One thing is clear to me: all this tampering with the text has in no way diminished the solidity of its dramatic structure, but on the whole it has actually enhanced it. In his acute analysis of the revisions, Blayney attributed them to censorial interference, and postulated two separate interventions of the Master of the Revels Edmund Tilney, each of them followed by a separate set of revisions and additions. What I am going to question is essentially the assumption that when the book was rejected a second time by Tilney, as Blayney puts it, 'with surprising optimism, the revisers seem to have considered it worth attempting to salvage the play' and wrote or added to other scenes in order to compensate for the elimination of scene i, required by Tilney.[14] On the other hand, in view of the fact that there are no marks in Tilney's hand in the Additions, G. Harold Metz has recently maintained that Tilney saw and commented on the play only once, when Munday's original manuscript was submitted to him,[15] and revisions and additions were made on the copy he had returned; this credits the revisers with an even greater dose of 'surprising optimism' than that attributed to them by Blayney. Metz's contention, though, that the revisions are improvements of the text based on strictly theatrical considerations is well worth entertaining. Which theatre or cinema producer nowadays, receiving from professional authors the perfectly polished and finished script of a play or a film would dream of staging or shooting it exactly as it stands? He would be sure to go to work on it with the director, and have it thoroughly overhauled by his own experts so as to adapt it to the circumstances of that particular production. This aspect of stage production has not basically changed since Elizabethan times. Once *More* was accepted for production by a company of players (presumably the Strange's men, or a combination of Strange's and Admiral's) the process of adaptation would start. I shall try to outline what I consider to be the different stages through which the 'book' passed before the players abandoned it following Tilney's injunction or for whatever other reason.[16]

Stage I

The company, having received the copy from Munday, sets about transforming it into a proper 'prompt-book',[17] something for practical use on the stage. In order to achieve this, they find that it needs altering in several places for two reasons. The first is merely of a theatrical nature: the play is a sequence of separate scenes that need linking together, there are abrupt transitions, loose ends and no decent part for the company's clown. The second reason has to do with the necessity of getting the book passed by the Master of the Revels for public performance: there are too many episodes of violence against the authorities in the play. The players may have sought in advance the advice of the Revels Office on the subject, or decided independently to exercise a form of self-censorship that was and is still far from uncommon among experienced show-business people. The revision has therefore a double aim, and the two can be easily combined.

The passages that might meet difficulties with the censor are not hard to identify: the prentices cudgelling Sir John Munday; the attack on the Sergeant-at-arms Downes; the street fight between the followers of two bishops (Munday had pointedly decided to transform the 'company of ruffians' mentioned by Foxe into the men of my lords of Winchester and Ely); allusions that might have sounded critical of royal behaviour (especially in scene xiii, 19^r, 1491ff.). They decide therefore; (1) to abolish altogether the prentices' scene; (2) to introduce some clowning that would both amuse the audience and discredit the seriousness of the rebellion; this could be combined with another requirement: (3) to develop the role of the Clown and the comic scenes in general; (4) there should be no show of physical violence to Downes, and More's intervention must contain a point by point rejection of the threats to the 'strangers' (large numbers of foreigners, many of them escaping from religious persecution on the continent, exercised their trades in London and were regarded with hostility by the local artisans – this is relevant, as we shall see, to the dating of the play); (5) as for the Paternoster Row fray, a way should be found to reduce it to a mere amusing anecdote showing More's sense of justice; and in the process care should be taken to join together more effectively the central scenes of the play, when More is at the height of his career; (6) to replace More's speech in scene xiii containing allusions to the behaviour of princes.

Stage II

Some actors or more or less experienced playwrights are allotted the task of basic revision. 'Hand A' (now definitely identified with Henry Chettle) is put in charge of seeing to point (6). Point (4) is entrusted to somebody considered able to deal with a scene of popular rebellion without incurring the censor's displeasure – since Shakespeare had done exactly that in the case of the Jack Cade rebellion in *2 Henry VI*, this is a possible reason for identifying 'Hand D' with Shakespeare. 'Hand B' has the more general task of creating the part for the professional clown of the company, as well as of providing comedy whenever the opportunity offers throughout the play (see points (2) and (3)). As for point (5), there is no immediate evidence as to whom it was entrusted in the first instance.

Stage III

The way in which A set about his task, as evidenced by Add. 1, has been admirably shown by Blayney in his essay of 1972. As for D, the case is different: he seems to have read the original scene rather hastily, with no reference to the sources used by Munday, but keeping in mind the main objective of his revisions; he therefore reduced the attack on Downes to indignant noises against an unnamed Sergeant-at-arms and incorporated into More's speech a thoroughly argued rebuttal of the threats to foreigners circulated in London in the spring of 1593, and in particular of the seditious rhyme posted on the wall of the Dutch Churchyard on May 5th, beginning: 'You, strangers, that inhabit in this land, |Note this same writing, do it understand, |Conceive it well, for safeguard of your lives, |Your goods, your children, and your dearest wives';[18] a threat that was taken so seriously by the Privy Council as to cause the arrest of a number of suspects, among whom was the playwright Thomas Kyd. (A further consequence was the interrogation and indirectly the death of Christopher Marlowe.) Finally D decided to follow exactly the same tactics used by the author of the Cade scenes in *2 Henry VI*: to present all the rebels, and especially their leaders, as clownish figures – from the indignant, dignified and purposeful character presented by Munday in the rest of the play, including the scene of his execution, John Lincoln is turned into an exact copy of the malicious and foolish Jack Cade, to the point of appropriating Cade's followers' characteristic use of *argo* for *ergo* in their preposterous pseudo-syllogisms; D in his addition ignores the characterization undertaken by Munday of the other rebels: he remembers the names of Doll, Betts and Sherwin, while ignoring Williamson (Doll's husband) and prefixing several speeches with the heading 'other', leaving to somebody else the task of identifying the speaker; besides he is unaware of the introduction into the play of a professional Clown identified with Ralph Betts.

The Clown is actually the invention of B, taking advantage of the fact that Hall and Holinshed mentioned the 'bretheren Bettses' among the participants in the riots, while Munday had written speeches for only one of these two characters.[19] B is so pleased with his invention that in scene iv he introduces so many new speeches for this character that they couldn't be fitted into the margin of Munday's manuscript, so he crossed out the whole scene on fol. 5^v and transcribed it on a new sheet (7^r), with the Clown's additions that lengthen it by one third. In scenes vi and vii the additional speeches of the clown can be fitted into the margins of the original fols. 10^r, 10^v and 11^r. Having created the part for a new professional actor, B decides to exploit his capacities in other roles, and, realising that after the cuts in other scenes, the play would be shortened, he invents a *coda* to scene ix, in which the players of the Interlude (among whom the one impersonating the Vice was traditionally a Clown) are cheated by a servant of More and receive redress from his master; this is Add. vi in hand B which contains many corrections and rewritings, but is presentable enough to be inserted as fol. 16 in the manuscript. This addition fulfils also a remarkable structural dramatic function. In the original the audience was left at the end of scene ix with the promise that the performance of the interlude would be resumed after the banquet (1140–4), but they got instead a brusque and unprepared transition to the Privy Council meeting. The addition makes it clear instead: first that the interlude is not going to be resumed and the actors are paid for the work already done, and secondly that More has been summoned 'In haist to cownsell' (Add. vi, 36); of course, this cannot be the same meeting of the Privy Council that we are going to watch in a moment, but the very mention of the Council makes plausible in our minds the change of location from More's house to the Council chamber. It is interesting to notice that in the first draft of the addition preserved on the same page of the manuscript (Add. iv, 21–3) there was no mention of the Council.

There are cases though in which the new contributions to the text are too confused to be inserted directly into the 'book'. It is at this point that a professional scribe is called in: C had already been working for the theatre; he had been responsible for transcribing the 'plot' of Tarlton's *The Seven Deadly Sins* for a revival in the very early 1590s by a company that included several members of the Strange's men; he also wrote the titles in gothic lettering on the vellum wrappers of both *Sir Thomas More* and Munday's *John a Kent and John a Cumber*, the latter datable round the year 1590 (both wrappers are from the same piece of vellum, proving that the binding was done at the same time); and in the case of *John a Kent* he acted as book-keeper, since it appears that the additional stage directions in that 'book' are in his hand; finally he was to write the 'plot' of *Fortune's Tennis* for the Admiral's men. Greg concludes that 'he was some one closely connected with the playhouse, possibly in the capacity of book-keeper', and that he 'acted as editor to the team of revisers' of *More*.[20] Actually he seems to have had in this case the task of what is called in modern cinema parlance 'continuity man' (more commonly 'girl') – the person in charge of seeing that there are no flagrant inconsistencies in costume, surroundings and so forth in consecutive scenes shot on different days and frequently in the wrong order.

The main job of C was that of copying out a long new scene (viii), the result of the fusion of the scene with Erasmus and of that with the long-haired ruffian. It is precisely because C transcribed it, that we have no way of guessing who had the idea of getting round the problems of eliminating the unseemly Paternoster Row fight by transferring the meeting of More with the ruffian Faulkner from the London streets to More's study: Faulkner is taken to him by the Sheriff and sent to Newgate, and after a certain time-lag turns up again duly shorn of his hair, and is pardoned; in the original Munday version the time-lag between the two appearances of Faulkner was filled with the arrangements made by More, the Lord Mayor, Surrey and Shrewsbury to re-establish public order; this was impracticable in the new setting, so the reviser has Faulkner's first entrance taking place while More is still arranging for the practical joke to be played on Erasmus, and the time gap between Faulkner's exit and his second entrance is filled by the performance of the joke and by the friendly exchanges between More and Erasmus. The reviser, then, leaves the text of the Erasmus scene practically untouched, except for breaking it into two unequal parts, transposing and inserting odd lines (e.g., at the arrival of Morris, when a new line addressed to him (Add. iv, 177) intrudes in a regular sequence of rhymed couplets spoken by More to Erasmus). The double interview with the ruffian instead is completely rewritten and – it must be acknowledged – vastly improved in respect of Munday's original version (most of which has remained, albeit cancelled, on fol. 14^r). Faulkner, from a semi-articulate moron who ends up with a verse speech of abject recognition of his folly, is transformed into a brilliant manipulator of verbal wit, pretentious and resentful – a fully rounded character.

C transcribes the dovetailed scenes on new sheets of paper, filling three sides (fols. 12^r and 12^v, 13^r) and the top part of another (some thirty lines on fol. 13^v) and adds the *exit*. It is at this point that Hand E (which most palaeographers are inclined to recognize as that of Thomas Dekker) suddenly emerges: it seems a pity to waste half a new page – E crosses out the exit and extends the final dialogue between Faulkner and his master Morris for thirty more lines, producing a little masterpiece of comic repartee, with the addition to Faulkner's part of a pathetical angry note and a subtle final allusion to beheading that fits perfectly not only with the mood of this scene but with the total meaning of the play. E had certainly read over the rest of the scene before making his addition – three words added to a speech in l. 193 (another improvement) are in his hand – but these last thirty lines are so much in keeping with the rest that it must be asked whether he was responsible for the whole new treatment of the Faulkner episode, in a style so different not only from that of the original, but also from that of all other revisers, including the 'comedy expert' B.[21]

Two puzzles remain in connection with the replacement of the Erasmus and

Faulkner scenes. One is the note in the left margin at the beginning of the original version of the Erasmus scene on fol. 11^v; '*this must be newe written*'; being in Italian script, it is difficult to determine the hand, certainly not Tilney's: Greg inclines for B, while Blayney inclines for A. It is no doubt a suggestion by a reviser, but it implies that whoever wrote it was leaving to somebody else the task of 'new writing' the scene; it may refer more specifically to the opening stage direction and the first 23 lines of the scene, the dialogue between More and his man Randall, supposing that the person in charge of rearranging the two scenes had not cared in the first draft of what is known as Add. iv to tackle this particular passage, since it was going to be at all events substantially preserved as the opening gambit to the new version. The reviser took the hint and also rewrote those lines, partly recasting Randall's speeches in order to reduce them from three to two, and modifying More's words about Erasmus's arrival so that the new scene could take place in the morning instead of at night as in the original. The new time-table allows for Faulkner to be brought in in the daytime and for Erasmus to take his leave also during the day, so that the evening is left free for More's entertainment to the Mayor of London, giving an impression of continuity to the scenic action.[22]

Also the second puzzle is a marginal note in Italian script, the words '*et tu Erasmus an Diabolus*' in the right margin not of the original but of the rewritten scene (Add. IV, 150–1), and in this case there is no reason to believe that the hand is other than that of C, who had copied the rest of the addition. The only reasonable explanation is that C was unthinkingly transcribing a note made by somebody (perhaps the same person who had written the instruction at the beginning of the Erasmus scene in the original) reading over the rough copy of the redrafted scene. Recalling the current anecdote about the first meeting of Erasmus and More (when still unknown to each other, after an argument at the Lord Mayor's table, Erasmus said 'Aut tu es Morus aut nullus', to which More replied 'Aut tu es Erasmus, aut diabolus'),[23] this unknown reader was suggesting a much more radical recasting of the scene: to replace the weak joke at the expense of Erasmus devised by the original author of the play with a more creditable anecdote. The suggestion was obviously not accepted.

Stage IV

The next stage in the process of revision is a demonstration of the care the revisers took to preserve and possibly improve the structural consistency, the dramatic effectiveness and the inner balance of the play. The experienced theatre scribe C was put in charge of seeing to the assembling the book with the new additions, providing the technical indications, such as essential stage directions, missing speech headings, etcetera. He was probably aided by at least one of the revisers who was reading over carefully the available material.

The revision of the first part of the play was no plain sailing for C. I shall summarize here some of the conclusions reached in a recent paper of mine based on a new recension of the Harleian manuscript (see note 21). It is most likely that D thought that the Guildhall scene (va) had been suppressed for good and all, so he conceived his contribution to the play as a continuation of scene iv, taking place in St Martin's, as it was before the introduction of the Clown. C in turn was handed the two leaves in hand D and, separately, fol. 7 on the recto of which B had transcribed scene iv with the clown's additions (7^v was as yet blank). The book-keeper went over B's work, providing the entrance stage-direction at the appropriate place and correcting a couple of speech headings (fol. 7^r, l. 41 and possibly 51) which B, with his habit of adding the prefixes only after writing all the speeches (see the cancelled draft of ll. 21–34 of Add. vi), had got wrong; then, moving on to fol. 8^r in hand D and noticing the clownish character of several of the speeches assigned to the anonymous 'other', he made sure that the new character should remain on stage and, while changing some of D's speech headings from 'other' to 'clown', he added at the end of the scene in hand B of fol. 7^r the words 'Manett Clowne'.[24] A change of mind intervened at this point: the revisers decided that the Guildhall scene was indispensable and, salvaging the discarded original version, introduced in it a number of changes and handed it to the book-keeper. C transcribed the revised text on the blank verso of fol. 7, but inadvertently included also the entrance direction for Sir John Munday and the first eight lines of the original version of the scene which, after the deletion of the prentices' scene, had no place in the play. The incongruity was noticed later and the eight lines marked for omission.[25] C forgot to cross out the now inappropriate 'Manett Clowne' on fol. 7^r, but was careful to add at the bottom of 7^v the entrance stage direction for the next scene (vi in hand D). I must refer once again to my study of 'Hand D in *Sir Thomas More*' for the numerous misunderstandings of D's text by C in the course of his revision. C managed to join fairly neatly the addition in hand D with the surviving part of scene vi in Munday's hand by simply crossing out the first three lines of fol. 10^r; but he did not notice that D had not recorded the entrance of More or, for that matter, of Palmer and Cholmley, who figured as present on the stage in this part of the scene. Instead he is careful, when Munday had recorded entrances inconspicuously in the right margin, to give them prominence either by enclosing them in a frame (*cf.* 523: Ent *Shrew.*) or by repeating them in the left margin (553: Enter Crofts).[26]

Add. iv, the new scene substituting two scenes in the original and acquiring the status of centre-piece of the play, was approached in a different spirit. The main preoccupation of the revisers was to secure effective links with what went before and after, so as to maintain the dramatic flux. The general structure to be underlined was extremely simple, but most effective: (1) More's rapid ascent to the highest position in the State, from London sheriff (scene ii) to knight and Privy Councillor (scene vi), to Lord Chancellor of England (announced at the end of scene vii); (2) the presentation of his state of extreme splendour (the meeting with Erasmus in viii and the entertainment to the Lord Mayor in scene ix); (3) his decline and fall, through his refusal to sign the royal articles (scene x), his retirement (scene xi), arrest (scene xiii), imprisonment (scenes xiv–xv) and execution. The link between phases 2 and 3 (splendour and beginning of decline) had been happily provided by

B's Add. VI at the close of scene IX, the cheating of the players and More's intervention on his way to the Privy Council, where he has been suddenly and ominously summoned: his brief passage prepares for what is to come. What matters now is to secure as smooth a transition from phase 1 to phase 2 – that is to say, from his elevation to the Chancellorship to his meeting with Erasmus – and to join together more firmly the two scenes presenting More at the height of his career, so that they would form a single block, the top of the dramatic parabola (the already noted change of 'timetable' for Erasmus's visit was going some way in that direction).

In the first case, the readiest means of effecting the link, since the appointment as Chancellor had been announced to the people of London (and to the audience) by Surrey in a scene where More himself does not appear, was to show his personal reaction to his new dignity in a monologue. This was duly provided, but there is no means of telling by whom, though there is a growing tendency to accept the suggestion based on stylistic analogies that the author was once again Shakespeare. I hesitate to credit it, finding unconvincing the parallel of the first line with one in *Othello*, in so much as, while More maintains that human nature depends exclusively on heaven's will, Iago's ''Tis in ourselves that we are thus or thus' (*Oth*, I.iii.317) implies exactly the contrary.[27] Besides, while this monologue is precisely suited to the dramatic context, serving perfectly the function I have tried to outline, the famous three pages in Hand D are the worst fitting in the total revision of the play, especially because of the grave inconsistencies in the characterization of Lincoln and the 'rebels'. The problem of authorship can never be solved in as much as, whoever wrote the monologue, C transcribed it on a half sheet of paper which he duly pasted on the lower part of the cancelled fol. 11ᵛ, with the laconic stage direction *Enter moore* – but he forgot to cross out More's name in the entrance direction at the top of the additional fol. 12ʳ which he had transcribed before.

Another monologue, in which More announces the departure of Erasmus and the visit of the Lord Mayor, was considered the best way of linking the two central scenes. Also this was transcribed by C on another half sheet of paper and pasted on the lower portion of the next cancelled sheet, fol. 14ʳ, with a half line at the end which picked up More's first line at the beginning of scene IX in the original, addressed to the servants, so as to show that the monologue should continue directly with his instructions for the entertainment of the Lord Mayor. What is really remarkable is that a close examination of the manuscript has satisfied me that the two monologues have been transcribed by C side by side on the two halves of a single upended leaf, and then separated and pasted on fols. 11ᵛ and 14ʳ respectively. I have set out the evidence in the already mentioned recent paper, and at present I wish only to underline the implication that the two monologues must have been written practically simultaneously by different authors at a fairly late stage of the revision. If Shakespeare is responsible for the first, and he is the author as well of the earliest of the additions (that in hand D), then all the revisions of the book must have been effected within a very narrow period.

At all events, even after the introduction of the second monologue, the transition from scene viii to ix seemed still too abrupt. B decided to introduce before it the announcement to More of the Mayor's visit. He drafted five lines for the purpose, jotting them down in a very rough state in the blank space left on the verso of the sheet containing his own addition to the players' scene (Add. VI, fol. 16^v), a sheet not yet inserted in its proper place in the manuscript. C, who had already stuck More's monologue on fol. 14^r, transcribed these lines, preceded by the direction 'Enter A Messenger to moore', up the left margin of the composite page, partly on page 14^r itself, partly at the side of the pasted-on addition; for clarity, also the beginning of the new More monologue is repeated at the end of the Messenger's words ('Moore why this is cheerfull &c.'), while at the beginning there is a mark (a cross enclosed in a circle) that sends us back to the same mark placed at the end of the Faulkner scene in the previous page. The overabundance of references and cross-references at this point is due to the fact that at first C himself had misunderstood the correct placing of the messenger's speech, and had thought that this announcement should be made to More at the moment of his exit in the previous scene; consequently he had added at that point (Add. IV, fol. 13^v, 203–4) the note in the left margin 'Enter a messenger |heere.', which he crossed out when he realized his mistake.

But the most extraordinary feature of this new functional insertion is represented by the words 'Mess T Goodal' added in front of the Messenger's entrance direction. After some misgivings Greg has positively identified the writer as the scribe C. The note can have only one meaning: the players were so sure that, with the modifications they had made, the play would pass the censor, that they had already proceeded to cast the different roles. Adding at the last moment the new, albeit minimal, part for a Messenger, they took care to indicate which of the actors, among those who already doubled other minor roles in the rest of the play, should take it. Note that in most cases the names of actors that creep into stage directions of plays are those of practically unknown players taking very small roles (see for instance 'Curtis' at first as messenger and then as an attendant, and 'T. Tucke:' as another attendant, in The Two Noble Kinsmen, IV.ii.70.1 and V.iii.0.1). All that we know of Thomas Goodale is that in 1581 he was a member of Lord Berkeley's men, imprisoned after a fray with the men of the Inns of Court, while in the very early 1590s he took several minor roles in the revival of Tarlton's The Seven Deadly Sins, presumably acted by Lord Strange's men; but Goodale was no longer with the Strange's men when they were reorganized into the Chamberlain's men in 1594. Neither was he among the Admiral's men or in any of the other companies acting after that date, though his profession is still given as 'player' in parish registers for the years 1594–5 and 1599.[28] If we take into account that the 'plot' of the second part of The Seven Deadly Sins, in which the names of Goodal and several other actors of the Strange's men appear, is written in the same hand C that transcribed several of the additions of More, it is not unreasonable to surmise that the latter play was meant to be performed by at least some of the same actors at a time not far removed from the revival of Tarlton's earlier morality.

We can now run through the rest of the play noticing in passing the other adjustments made by C or another reviser to render the book presentable in its final shape. Line 996 on fol. 15ʳ (scene ix) was crossed out because found supererogatory. On fol. 17ʳ of the original C crosses out the '*exeunt*' at the end of scene ix and adds in the left margin a mark and the note '*Enter To the player with a reward*', to indicate that the addition in hand B to this scene should be inserted at this point. In fact at the top of the addition itself (fol. 16ʳ) C repeats the mark and adds the stage direction '*Enter A Servingman*'; looking down the page he also notices that B had not bothered to mark the entrance of More, and so he introduces the appropriate stage direction, though omitting to regularize the very casual speech headings provided by B; he also forgets to introduce the new *exeunt* and to cross out the first draft of the messenger's speech for an earlier scene written by B on fol. 16ᵛ. From this point of the manuscript on, Hand C disappears. There is no telling whether Munday himself or somebody else decided that a second closing rhymed couplet to a speech of More in scene xiii (1457–8) was excessive, and also the crossing out of l. 1571 seems to be more than anything a matter of taste. It is more surprising that there are no specific marks indicating that the addition provided by hand A on a separate sheet (now 6ʳ) should replace the long speech of More (1471–516) in the same scene, which is not properly crossed out but merely marked for omission. This lack of precise instructions like those provided by C on other occasions, may account for the misplacing of A's addition in the manuscript as we have it now; Blayney, though, supplies good evidence that at some stage also this addition was in its proper place, but probably as a loose leaf.[29] Was it submitted to Tilney not as a definite substitution but merely as a possible alternative?

Stage V

The play is now complete, ready for rehearsal, even to the point of already having the parts assigned to the actors; Tilney receives the book for approval – not yet a prompt copy, but in such a state that it can be easily turned into one. But on the very first page he is struck by the talk of Englishmen having to revenge the wrongs received from 'strangers'. He crosses out at first some speeches by Lincoln, Doll and George Betts (fol. 3ʳ, 24–5 and 28–31) which are far too strongly worded, and too likely to raise sympathy for the May Day rebels. As he goes on he decides that the whole scene is seditious, but perhaps he does not write immediately his injunction. The second scene in itself is inoffensive: the two passages in More's speech (163–4) and in Lifter's (198–201) marked for omission probably reflect a decision by the author himself or the reviser for merely aesthetic reasons. But in scene iii, the recognition of the rightful indignation of the Londoners by a nobleman like Surrey (fol. 5ʳ, 372–8) is a dangerous matter, and must be omitted, and so are the words of Cholmley complaining that the king is misinformed (379–85) and the description of the threatening attitude of the crowd (388–93); Shrewsbury's remarks at the beginning of the scene instead (316–23) were thought at first to need only some toning down – Tilney had written '*Mend Yis*' in the margin

– but in view of what follows he marks that speech too with a cross. Tilney also requires the substitution in the same scene (fol. 5ʳ) of 'Lombard' for 'straunger' (364) and 'ffrencheman' (368), as well as of the noncommittal 'ma*n*' for 'Englishe' (352); by now he must have added his imperative note on the first page.

There are no objections to the substituted scenes iv, va and vi, since they now represent the folly of the rebels; but the speech of the Sheriff on 'these troublous times' in scene vii (fol. 10ᵛ, 583–96) is alarming, and perhaps it was again Tilney who crossed out Surrey's words later in the same scene (fol. 11ᵛ, 726–30) on 'awefull iustice' – but the passage is in itself weak and supererogatory, and the author or the revisers may have decided that it was better left out. Tilney's two other interventions in the remaining part of the play are highly indicative: they affect the ideological core of the play. The author(s) had been very careful not to specify the nature of the articles that More refused to sign – and I have already discussed the implications of this apparent vagueness (p. 77). But also Tilney realised that if on the one hand this caution prevented the play from becoming an apology for the Roman Church, on the other it made it politically much more dangerous in as much as it questioned the arbitrary use of power by the sovereign against personal conscience. This is why in scene x Tilney demanded that the passage where Palmer impeaches Rochester of 'capitall contempt', confines More to his house, and obtains a too ready submission from Surrey and Shrewsbury (fol. 17ᵛ, 1247–75), should be 'all altered'. Finally, in scene xi, Tilney, knowing his Latin, firmly crosses out the quotation from Seneca (fol. 18ᵛ, 1373) implying that the signing of the royal articles in order to save one's life was a 'foul medicine'; it is the most open condemnation of the prince's behaviour, though only educated members of the audience could realise this.

Tilney's imperative requests on the one hand, by abolishing the first scene, utterly destroyed the structural balance of the play, which the different additions and substitutions had been at pains not only to preserve but to improve; on the other they affected and practically nullified the deeper meaning of the play. Under such conditions, it is hardly possible that the author–revisers set to work again in order to comply with Tilney's injunction: it would have meant contradicting the very principles on and for which the play had been written, both on the formal and on the ideological level.

It is on the first of these two levels that I wish to insist now, considering the text in what I would call its definitive form – as it was submitted to Tilney, with the omissions decided upon by the revisers and the additions in their proper places. The modernized text provided by Harold Jenkins in 1953[30] is sufficient to show how well the play is constructed in its double movement – rise and fall – with only four characters present in both halves (More, Surrey, Shrewsbury and the Lord Mayor) while all the rest change:[31] the people of London dominate the first half, More's family the second. It is better though to see it developing through three phases or movements, as I have hinted before: the first – the rise – is logically the longest, the second – the achievement – the shortest, and the third – the fall – midway between the other two (about 39, 26 and 35 percent of the total length respectively). The most brilliant idea of the author was that of placing, as the culmination of the central part, the play within the play – theatre reflecting itself as in a mirror, so that the dramatic fiction becomes the emblem of truth; and the choice of the Interlude performed, its very title – *The Marriage of Wit and Wisdom* – as has been recently noticed, is in itself extremely meaningful.[32] There seems to be no doubt that Munday took the idea from Harpsfield's manuscript biography of More (we saw before how he may have come across it), where he speaks of young Thomas More's education:

[He], among many other tokens of his quicke and pregnant witt, being very yonge, would yet notwithstanding vpon the soden stepp in among the Christmas players, and forthwith, without any other forethinking or premeditation, playe a part with them himselfe, so fitly, so plausibly and pleasantly, that the Auditours tooke muche admiration, and more comfort and pleasure thereof then of all the players besydes; and especially the Cardinall, vpon whose table he wayted.[33]

The repeated mention in the scene of 'My Lord Cardinalls players' (908, 950, 994) is conclusive evidence of the source.

Munday, besides, had devised a subtle play of correspondences between the first and the last sequences, the most obvious of which is the conclusion of each with an execution followed by Surrey's words of forgiveness and compassion. The parallel between the figures of Lincoln, who in his noble final speeches acquires a truly heroic stature, and of More, is established in this way, and the fate of the London commoner and rebel becomes a prefiguration of that of the Lord Chancellor.

We have already seen how the rewriting and additions to the central section of the play (scenes viii and ix, Act iii for Jenkins) had improved it by conferring upon it a unity and continuity of action which was lacking in the original presentation of three separate spurious anecdotes. The first and last sections of the play are organized differently: the continuity of action is already there in the original, though each section is clearly divided into two parts. Taking the last section first, since it did not undergo any changes: scenes x to xiii (Act iv for Jenkins) move from the public to the private, from power in the Privy Council to retirement in the house at Chelsea, portending a decline without disgrace; scenes xiv to xvii (Act v) mark the consummation of the tragedy, described in actual theatrical terms (from 'a state pleader' to 'a stage player'), so that the centrality of the play-acting scene is vindicated, and they all take place under the incumbent shadow of the Tower, except for the indirect report of the trial which, by another magnificent dramatic intuition, is entrusted to the humblest characters in the play, More's servants.

The first and longest section of the play shows an even more marked division into two parts. Scenes i to iii (Act i) are the perfect protasis: each of them introduces a different group of characters, representing one of the 'estates' – though the Judiciary replaces the Clergy; to comply with Tilney's request to abolish the first scene would have rendered nonsensical the very careful social and political 'setting' of the whole play (the deliberate exclusion of the clergy is tantamount to taking a definite political stand).[34] Scenes iv to vii (Act ii) cover the events of the Ill May

Day, and the unity and continuity of action is obvious; but they are also the most tormented part of the play. The suppression of the prentices' scene, originally between iv and v, is a very definite improvement, not because it exorcises the threats of censorship but because it avoids the introduction of yet another set of characters with no part in the later scenes: its presence would have reduced the sequence to a series of isolated episodes, more or less faithfully derived from the official sources (Holinshed in particular), paralysing the inventiveness shown for instance in the Justice Suresby scene in the previous section, which was derived from a spurious anecdote inspired in turn by a passage in More's *The Four Last Things*. As it now stands, the City of London is the protagonist of the sequence, with the perfect characterization of the citizens as individuals, prepared by the first scene of the play. From this point of view, though, there is a weak link in the chain. The weak link (in contrast with the skilful addition of the Clown's part by Hand B in the rest of the crowd scenes, that enriches the original little gallery of characters) is the first part of scene vi, the three pages containing 147 lines in hand D, substituting the original version now irretrievably lost except for three lines;[35] it is surprising that those three surviving lines – the end of a speech – are in prose, and I wonder if that speech, offering the royal pardon, was intended (as is generally assumed) as More's; could not it be from a minor royal emissary, such as Downes, so as not to involve More in a definite promise of mercy which was only partly fulfilled?

The weakness of the addition in Hand D does not consist in its poor literary quality or in its interrupting the flow of the action; on the contrary, taken by itself it handles beautifully the rhetoric of persuasion and it is a masterly treatment of a crowd scene. The trouble with it is that it does not *belong* to the context created by the original author: this is a completely different crowd from that which had appeared in scenes i and iv or were to appear again – as people facing the gallows with dignity and even humour – in scene vii. The rioters presented by Hand D could be easily fitted into the crowd scenes of *2 Henry VI*, or even *Julius Caesar* or *Coriolanus*, but are at the opposite pole (as I have already had occasion to remark) from those so acutely and sensitively individualised by the original author of the 'book' in the other scenes.[36] As early as 1911 Greg, after recognising the 'undoubted literary merit of D's additions', perceptively added: 'it seems to me an eminently reasonable view that would assign this passage to the writer who, as I believe, foisted certain of the Jack Cade scenes into the second part of *Henry VI*.'[37] This contradiction has caused untold damage, rendering practically impossible a correct evaluation of the qualities of the play. From the time Simpson suggested that the additions in Hands D and C might be Shakespeare's, and an authority like Sir Edward Maunde Thompson in 1916 maintained that Hand D was Shakespeare, the critics' attention – and praise – concentrated on those three pages, and the rest of the play was at best disregarded, but more frequently considered badly structured and written, *because it did not fit in with the Shakespearian fragment*. In other words, they took the paradoxical view that the whole should suit the part, against all rules of common sense and practice.

94

The addition in hand D was written by an admirable craftsman who knew how to present a riot and its quelling, and could manipulate the technique of persuasion through verbal felicity and inventiveness as hardly anybody else could; but in applying his art to this special occasion he took very little notice of the context he was contributing to, to the point of not troubling to check the names and the individual roles of the characters taking part in the scene; he was informed only of the situation, and applied to it his own conceptions without realising that they were in contrast with the surviving parts of the script he had to add to. This, I think, renders utterly incredible, even apart from my doubts as to the reliability of stylometric tests, Tom Merriam's contention, conveniently summarised by Merriam himself with the words: 'The original of *More*, written in the hand of Anthony Munday, was copied from an original by Shakespeare. Of the additions, those in Hands C & D were also by Shakespeare. Of the total, it appeared that 90 percent of the play was Shakespeare's'.[38] It would be very extraordinary that, having witten the whole of the original text, Shakespeare should forget all about it when redrafting one scene.[39]

From what I have said up to now it must have appeared that I favour a comparatively early date – not later than 1594 – not only for the writing of Munday's original, but also of the additions.[40] There is no widespread agreement about the writing of the additions, for which a number of different positions can be listed. My own conclusions – based on a new recension of the manuscript, on re-examination of the political background for the composition and censoring of the play, and on reconsideration of topical allusions in the additions – require more space to set out than can be provided here.[41] This is the more regrettable since they by no means coincide with the dating of the Additions elaborately argued in some of the other papers in the present volume. The extent of the disagreement will appear from the following brief summary of my view of the development of the play.

Anthony Munday plotted the play, wrote it perhaps with the help of some other dramatist (Chettle? Dekker?)[42], and produced a fair copy of the original in late 1592 and/or early 1593, partly stimulated by the re-emergence of xenophobic feelings among Londoners. When he submitted it to a company of players – most likely some sort of amalgamation of Admiral's and Strange's Men – they asked Chettle, Dekker, possibly Heywood (if hand B is his)[43] and probably Shakespeare and others to make a number of alterations in order to improve the dramatic structure of the play, eliminating at the same time things in it that might have proved offensive. The scribe/book-keeper (Hand C) was put in charge of reassembling the text both for submission to the Master of the Revels and for use as a prompt-book. This process of revision must have coincided more or less with the second half of 1593. When the re-shaped play was submitted to Tilney in late 1593 or early 1594 the 'troublous times' were still too close to allow for a stage presentation – and justification – of anti-alien feelings (in 1594 Sir Thomas Mildmay moved to keep a register of all the strangers coming into the realm) or of the imprisonment and execution of a saintly Roman Catholic (Robert Southwell had been arrested by Topcliffe in June 1592 and, like More, in the prison where he remained till his execution in 1595 he wrote some of his most moving works).[44] Tilney's veto (for his note on the first page of the book amounts to that) induced the actors to set aside for the time being the idea of performing the play, and the radical re-organisation of theatre companies in 1594–5 made them practically forget about it.

NOTES

1 Line references to the Original Text do not reproduce the asterisk and the obelus used by Greg to designate the lines after the first and the second gap in the manuscript respectively. Greg's scene division has instead been adopted. Valuable new readings and suggestions have been privately communicated by Peter Blayney, full use of which will be made in the new modern spelling reconstruction of the 'final' text to be edited by Vittorio Gabrieli and myself for the Revels Plays (Manchester University Press). The present paper draws extensively on the material collected for our edition and on the conclusions reached in our work on the text.

2 MacD.P. Jackson ('Anthony Mundy and *Sir Thomas More*', *NQ*, 208 (1963), 96) argued that his misunderstanding 'fashis' for 'fashion' on fol. 216 (1847) could be an ordinary authorial 'penslip', and Richard Beebe (' "Fashis" in *The Booke of Sir Thomas Moore*', *NQ*, 216 (1971) 452–3) marshalled new evidence in favour of this view. John Jowett in this volume makes a good case for Henry Chettle as Munday's collaborator, but Munday was indisputably the senior partner.

3 In his contribution to the present volume, Harold Metz reports that the survival of the two endings of the play has been taken as evidence of 'a scribal transmission of original work not his [Munday's] own'. I find this unacceptable: it would imply that Munday was such a merely mechanical transcriber as to become aware of the duplication only after completing the copy.

4 See the title of the Interlude chosen for performance in scene ix, and the perceptive remarks about it by C.R. Forker and J. Candido, 'Wit, Wisdom and Theatricality in *The Booke of Sir Thomas More*', *SStud*, 13 (1980), 85–104.

5 See Anthony Munday, *The English Roman Life*, ed. by Philip J. Ayres, (Oxford, 1980); reminiscences of the Roman days may have crept into the play: a Doctor Morris was the master of the English College of which Munday was for a time a member, while the leader of the English students protesting against Doctor Morris's rule was Ralph Sherwin, who two years later was captured in England, tried and executed upon evidence provided by Munday himself.

6 *The life and death of Sr Thomas Moore, knight, sometymes Lord high Chancellor of England, written in the tyme of Queene Marie by Nicholas Harpsfield, L.D.*, ed. by Elsie Vaughan Hitchcock, (EETS, O.S. 186, 1932). The edition is based on the Emmanuel College copy which bears the inscription reported below.

7 As Vittorio Gabrieli and I demonstrate in our forthcoming Revels edition of *More*, there is ample evidence that the author of the play knew also those parts of Harpsfield's biography which are not derived from Roper's earlier *Life of More*, while in no case passages from Roper not included in Harpsfield are made use of. This renders supererogatory the case put forward by Michael A. Anderegg ('*The Book of Sir Thomas More* and its Sources', *Moreana*, XIV, 53 (1977), 57–62) according to which Roper's manuscript must have fallen into Munday's hands under circumstances similar to those in which Harpsfield's was found.

8 J. Foxe, *The Ecclesiasticall Historie, conteining the Acts and Monuments of Martyrs . . . Newly recognised and enlarged by the Authour* (London, 1583), II, 1188. My quotations are from the edition by J. Pratt (London, 1874), V. 395–6. In his contribution to the present volume Harold Metz suggests that the anecdote might originally have referred to More rather than Cromwell, and Foxe, learning it through oral tradition, 'adapted it to his purposes in his eulogistic presentation of Thomas Cromwell' (p. 32). The suggestion is attractive, but does not account for the fact that – as I illustrate here – Munday actually fuses together not one but *two* anecdotes related by Foxe of Cromwell, attributing them to More. In the context of the debate about the length of hair rife in the

years 1591-3, he may have been struck by the sentence which, in the 1586-7 edition of Holinshed, precedes by only a few lines the accounts of the executions of Fisher and More: 'On the eight of Maie [1535], the king commanded that all belonging to the court should poll their heads, & to giue example, caused his owne head to be polled . . . which fashion the courtiers imbraced, and would (no doubt) haue put in practise though they had not beene therevnto bound by precept: for the people imitate the prince' (III, p. 938). This might have put the author of *More* in mind of the anecdote reported by Foxe about Cromwell, and, looking it up in the *Book of Martyrs*, he used in the play, transferring it to More, also the anecdote about the Paternoster Row fray immediately preceding it.

9 G.B. Harrison, *An Elizabethan Journal, 1591-1594*, (London, 1928), p. 98.

10 See for instance the entry for 3 February 1593, to John Wolfe: 'Entred for his Copie vnder the handes of the Bisshop of London and master Stirrop warden. *A defense of shorte haire* &c.'. This seems to be part of the dispute about the Brownists that raged between 1590 and 1593. The last echo of it can be found in Shakespeare's *Twelfth Night* III.ii.31-3; Sir Andrew Aguecheek, so proud of his long hair, declares that he would be prepared under certain circumstances to sacrifice it: 'I had as liefe be a Brownist, as a Politician'.

11 The choice of Morris as the name in the play of the Bishop of Winchester's secretary, master of the long-haired ruffian, was surely conditioned by the fact that the 1583 edition of the *Book of Martyrs* relates at some length, only a couple of pages before the Paternoster Row episode (1185-6), the story of another bishop's (or rather archbishop's) secretary: 'How the Lord Cromwell helped Cranmers Secretary' – and a prominent marginal note (not in the 1563 edition) informs: 'The name of this Secretary was M. Rafe Morice, being yet aliue.' Besides the name was familiar to Munday since his Roman days, when the Welshman Doctor Morris was '*Custos* of the Hospitall or Colledge' where the writer lived (A. Munday, *The Englishe Romaine Lyfe* (London, 1582), pp. 55-66); see note 5 above.

12 *SP*, LXIX (1972), 167-91.

13 The addition in Hand D offers several elements for a conjectural reconstruction of the original version of the scene – a version that D had surely seen – while C, who revised D's pages, hadn't. For a detailed study of this problem see G. Melchiori, 'Hand D in *Sir Thomas More*: An Essay in Misinterpretation', *ShS*, 38 (1985), 101-14.

14 In his original paper Blayney suggested, noticing that the Addition in Hand D seems to begin *in medias res* with no entrance direction, that Shakespeare had written two more pages (fol. Z, between 90 and 100 lines) which preceded the present addition, and they were scrapped after Tilney's second intervention. He now tells me privately that he no longer holds this opinion and is rather inclined to think that only one sheet of the original is missing between fols. 5ᵛand 10ʳ.

15 G.H. Metz, 'The Master of the Revels and *The Booke of Sir Thomas Moore*', *SQ*, 33 (1982), 493-5.

16 W.B. Long in this volume stresses that Tilney's comments in the manuscript are suggestions for revision rather than a prohibition. Nevertheless, the manuscript does not bear Tilney's licence for performance. Long further suggests that the prohibition of playing on account of the plague prevented the play from reaching the stage.

17 In the Introduction to his edition of Anthony Munday's *John a Kent and John a Cumber* (New York, 1980; 13-18), Arthur E. Pennell argues that 'the term "book" was the name the Elizabethans gave to playhouse copies prepared for production', in other words, what are now designated as 'prompt-books', and that, at least in the case of *John a Kent*, Munday's original manuscript was meant from the beginning to be used as a prompt-book. It should be noticed, though, that also in *John a Kent* some playhouse directions (albeit very few and mainly repetitive) had been added in the left margins in hands different from Munday's, and that the words '*The Booke of*' are written on the vellum covers both of *John a Kent* and of *More* by a professional book-keeper (Hand C). It is reasonable to think that the binding took place when he thought the two plays were ready for production and therefore, in the specific case of *More*, after the inclusion of all the additions and revisions to the text originally witten by Munday as a fair copy.

18 See John Strype, *Annals of the Reformation* (London, 1725–31), IV.168.

19 Munday uses the surname Betts only in the text of speeches – for instance, l. 63: 'as these two bretheren heere (*Betses* by name) can witnesse' – and in some stage directions, while the only speech heading he uses for one of the two brothers is 'George' (*Geo.*), a first name of his own devising; as a speech heading 'Betts' is used in the additions by Hand D and occasionally C, while B (and in most cases C) sticks to 'George'. The speech heading for the other Betts brother in all the parts added by B and C is constantly 'Clown'; his first name is learnt from a speech of Doll Williamson in scene vii, ll. 682–3: 'now cheerely Lads, George Bets, a hand with thee, ⏐and thine too Rafe'.

20 W.W. Greg, *Dramatic Documents from the Elizabethan Playhouses*, (Oxford, 1931), 224–5.

21 As Harold Metz remarks in his contribution to the present volume, 'most scholars now accept Dekker as the author of all 242 lines of Addition IV'; while agreeing with them, I no longer believe that Dekker added the thirty odd lines in his own hand at this comparatively early stage in the revision of the 'book'. As a result of a first-hand re-examination of the Harley MS., I incline to think that Dekker's remarkable extension and improvement of the scene, which he himself had contributed to re-cast, was in the nature of a last minute after-thought, when all the rest of the additions and revisions of the book were already complete. See G. Melchiori, '*The Book of Sir Thomas More*: A Chronology of Revision', *SQ*, 37 (1986), 291–308.

22 The Original Text reads (743–48):

> The learned Clarke *Erasmus* is arriu'de
> within our Englishe Courte, this day I heare,
> he feasteth with an Englishe honourd Poett
> the Earle of Surrey, and I knowe this night
> the famous Clarke of *Roterdame* will visite
> Sir Thomas Moore,

The revisers substituted it with (Add. IV, 8–13):

> the Learned Clarke Erasmus is arived
> wthin or english court. Last night I heere
> he feasted wth or honord English poet
> the Earle of Surrey. and I learnd to day
> the famous clarke of Rotherdam will visett
> Sr Thomas moore,

23 Strangely enough, the anecdote is first recorded by More's great-grandson Cresacre in his biography published in Paris in 1630; see *The Life and Death of Sir Thomas More . . . written by M.T.M.* (Menston, 1971), 109–10; but the story must have been current before and I believe it originated in another anecdote on More's meeting at table an unnamed foreign visitor, related by Harpsfield (139: 1–14). The playwright may have heard such a garbled version of it that he retained only the fact that at their first meeting More and Erasmus hadn't recognized each other, so he invented another story in line with his conception of More's fondness of merry jests.

24 In trying to account for this Greg notes that 'the most likely explanation . . . seems to be that C intended to continue with a revision of scene v [the suppressed prentices' scene] and to carry the Clown over from the one to the other'. This in fact is very *un*likely. A more plausible though rather over-elaborate explanation is offered by Blayney: at an intermediate stage of the revision one of the collaborators had written a brief scene for the Clown to be placed between iv and va, but it was found expendable and eliminated.

25 It is difficult to decide whether C himself or another reviser is responsible for marking for omission two couplets in a speech by More (Add. II, 113–16) which had been rendered incomprehensible by the faulty punctuation in C's transcription.

26 The book-keeper Hand C had followed exactly the same practice – repeating entrance directions in the left margin – when preparing Munday's manuscript *John a Kent and John a Cumber* for use as a

prompt book; see the edition of the latter play by Arthur E. Pennell, especially Introduction, pp. 13–18.

27 It is curious that G. Blakemore Evans, who, in *The Riverside Shakespeare* (Boston, 1974), 1694–7, supports the attribution with a series of parallels from other Shakespearian plays, should forget to mention, for 'bottom' in the last line of the Addition (found in that acceptation only in *Shrew*, IV.iii.137), the significance of Bottom the weaver in the *Dream*.

28 See Greg, *Dramatic Documents*, p. 45. The hand is identified as C's by Greg in 'T. Goodal in *Sir Thomas More*', *PMLA*, 46 (1931), 268–71.

29 Blayney, 180–1. Blayney has also identified B as responsible for the one intrusion by a different hand in Addition I: B mis-corrects a passage that A marked for omission and substituted (private communication, 1983). On the basis of this identification which I checked on the ms, I advance in the paper mentioned in note 21 above the tentative suggestion that A submitted the draft of his Addition to B, altered it again when it was returned to him, but the book-keeper C did not consider the replacement of Munday's original with A's laborious re-elaboration any real improvement.

30 *The Complete Works of Shakespeare*, ed. C. J. Sisson, (London, 1953). Among modern editors of *More* attempting to apply to it the canonical five-act division, Jenkins is the only one that correctly identifies the proper distribution of the scenes, evidencing the consistency of the structure of the play. The best study of the structure of the play is Scott McMillin, '*The Book of Sir Thomas More*, A Theatrical View', *MP*, LXVIII (1970–1), 10–24; see also J. Doolin Spikes, '*The Book of Sir Thomas More*: Structure and Meaning', *Moreana*, XLIII (1974), 25–39; and Alistair Fox, 'The Paradoxical Design of the *Book of Sir Thomas More*', *Renaissance and Reformation*, n.s. V (1981), 162–73.

31 Also Sir Thomas Palmer puts in a brief appearance in scene x, as little more than a messenger, and surely, the identification of the summoner in charge of arresting More in scene xiii with Downes was meant to establish a relation with scene vi, where – in the part of the Original now suppressed – he appeared as the Sergeant-at-arms rescued by More from the fury of the crowd.

32 It is very interesting that, though the dramatist chose the title of an actually existing Interlude, the text performed is put together from two other Interludes, *Lusty Juventus* and *The Disobedient Child*; obviously the author was more interested in the emblematic meaning of the title than in the play itself; *cf.* the paper by Forker and Candido mentioned in note 4 above, and see G. Melchiori, 'The Contextualization of Source Material: The Play within the Play in "Sir Thomas More"', in *Le Forme del Teatro*, III, ed. G. Melchiori (Roma, 1984), pp. 59–94.

33 Harpsfield, 10:28–11:9.

34 It is significant that Cardinal Wolsey, the predecessor of More as Lord Chancellor, who played a decisive role in the repression of the Ill May Day troubles and in obtaining the pardon for the prisoners, should never be mentioned in the play, in spite of the fact that he is a dominating figure in all the sources used by the dramatist, not only the chronicles by Hall and Holinshed, but also Harpsfield's biography of More.

35 The lines in question are 473–5, marked for omission; what may be inferred from them, at all events, is that the previous parts of this scene must have been mostly in prose, and this implies that, as in scenes i and va, the speeches of the 'low' characters largely outnumbered those of the authorities.

36 For a discussion of the ideological unfitness of the Shakespearian addition see G. Melchiori, 'The Corridors of History: Shakespeare the Re-Maker', *Proceedings of the British Academy*, vol. 72 (London, 1986), pp. 167–85.

37 See Greg, p. xiii; his diffidence about the authorship of the Jack Cade scenes in *2 Henry VI* was largely overcome in later years, making it possible to identify Shakespeare's contribution to both plays.

38 I am quoting from Merriam's contribution to the programme of *The Booke of Sir Thomas Moore* presented by The Poor Players in Bristol, April 1981; it is the substance of his theses, amply publicized elsewhere and most recently in Thomas Merriam, 'The Authorship of *Sir Thomas More*', *ALLC Bulletin*, 10 (1982), 1–7.

39 I am inclined to the view that those 147 lines are by Shakespeare by the presence in them of at least three forms or expressions which seem characteristic of him: *argo* (fol. 8a, 127), *vppon thipp* (140), and the spelling *scilens* (173); as well as the extraordinary parallelism in tone and style with the Jack Cade scenes, the affinities in imagery and in what R.W. Chambers has described as 'the expression of ideas – particulaly political ideas' (in *Shakespeare's Hand*, pp. 142–87). But the most impressive case for Shakespearian authorship is that made by Charles Forker in the paper contributed to the present volume. The arguments of Carol Chillington, 'Playwrights at Work: Henslowe's, not Shakespeare's *Book of Sir Thomas More*', *ELR* 10 (1980), 439–79 for identifying hand D as John Webster's rather than Shakespeare's are conclusively confuted from different standpoints by Charles Forker and Gary Taylor in their papers here so I need not go into the subject.

40 Summing up in 1961 fifty years of research into the problems of the *Book*, Harold Jenkins in his 'Supplement to the Introduction' to Greg's edition (*Collections* VI, 189) concludes: 'All things considered, the dates which best fit the evidence seem to be *c*. 1590–3 for the original composition and *c*. 1594–5 for the revision'. As for the availability at an early date of the revisors, my findings largely coincide with those by Karl P. Wentersdorff, 'The Date of the Additions in the *Booke of Sir Thomas Moore*', *SJW*, (1965), especially his section on theatrical history, 314–25.

41 These points are treated more fully in my paper 'The Master of the Revels and the Date of the Additions to *The Book of Sir Thomas More*', in *Shakespeare: Text, Language, Criticism. Essays in Honour of Marvin Spevack*, ed. B. Fabian and K. Tetzeli v. Rosador (Hildesheim, 1987), pp. 164–79.

42 For Chettle see John Jowett's paper in the present volume. On the other hand the surviving fragment of the suppressed prentices' scene is the closest anticipation in Elizabethan drama of Dekker's treatment of City Comedy. Only in *The Shoemakers' Holiday* (1599) as strong a sense of locale is created through the mention of London place names. In the other scenes of the Original only place names found in the sources (Holinshed, Foxe) are mentioned. This inclines me to think that Dekker contributed the prentices' scene to the original play.

43 A very strong case for identifying hand B as Heywood's was put forward by S.A. Tannenbaum in '*The Book of Sir Thomas Moore*: a Bibliotic Study' (New York, 1927) and *Shakespeare and 'Sir Thomas More*' (New York, 1929), but it was somewhat weakened by his attempt to credit at the same time the identification of hand C with Thomas Kyd's, so that Greg expressed his scepticism (*Dramatic Documents*, 244): 'B in some ways resembles Thomas Heywood's, but cannot be identified as his', and further objections were raised by J.M. Nosworthy in 'Hand B in *Sir Thomas More*', *The Library*, 5th series, II (1956), 47–50. But the late Peter Croft supported on palaeographical grounds the identification of Heywood with hand B, and I find striking affinities between the Clown's part in *More* and Heywood's *The Four Prentices of London* – notably the Clowns in both plays echo the ballad 'Mary Ambree' circulated shortly after 1584. If the most recent editor of *Four Prentices*, M.A. Weber Gaisor (New York: Garland, 1980), is right in dating it 1593–4, the case for Heywood as B is much strengthened, and so is that for 1593 as the latest possible date for the Addition.

44 For Mildmay's request (which resulted in the taking of yet another census of the strangers in London) see Strype, *Annals*, IV, Item CXLVIII, 212–15; for Southwell see *Annals*, IV, Item LXXXIX, 132–3, a letter of Richard Topcliffe to the Queen, dated 22 June 1592, concerning the 'taking and keeping' of this 'dangerous Conspirator'.

5

The date and auspices of the additions to *Sir Thomas More*

GARY TAYLOR

Heresies sometimes become orthodoxies; orthodoxies tend to fall asleep, and occasionally need to be awakened by the pinprick of a new heresy. For the first half of the twentieth century, the attribution to Shakespeare of three pages in *The Booke of Sir Thomas Moore* was a heresy in the process of becoming an orthodoxy. Three decades later that orthodoxy had settled comfortably down into the torpor of a received idea: Hand D was ripe for shaking. Carol Chillington's provocative re-examination of the problems had the immediate and substantial merit of dividing the scholarly consensus.[1] Most scholars who had done any specialist work on *More* were at the best sceptical, at the worst blisteringly rude, about the details of Chillington's argument, and tended to dismiss the whole because of the manifest deficiency of some of its parts. But there was a very different reaction from scholars who had, as it were, no vested interest in the play. Such readers were much more receptive to the clean 'common sense' of Chillington's central contentions. For Chillington did more than snipe at some of the evidence for Shakespeare's authorship of the three pages: she offered an apparently plausible alternative account of the date and history of the manuscript, which claimed to resolve several of the enigmas which had bewildered previous investigators. Chillington was, I believe, wrong on both counts; but she was at least originally and provocatively wrong.

Chillington's alternative hypothesis rests upon a series of negatives. First, and most important, her attribution of Hand D to Webster is based upon the fact that no certain example of Webster's handwriting is known to survive. As W.W. Greg said, if Hand D is not Shakespeare, then neither is he any playwright whose signature or handwriting is extant.[2] Since Webster is the only plausible candidate in this unfortunate situation, in order to reject Shakespeare Chillington must champion Webster. The discovery of a single Webster fragment could confirm – or demolish – her hypothesis in a twinkling.[3] In the absence of such a manuscript, there is no clear palaeographical evidence which would rule out Webster. His candidacy must therefore be seriously entertained. However, this purely negative plausibility should not obscure, or be allowed to outweigh, the positive plausibility of the palaeographical evidence for identifying Hand D with Shakespeare. E. Maunde Thompson, W.W. Greg, C.J. Sisson, Harold Jenkins, Peter W.M. Blayney, G.B. Evans, P.J. Croft, and R.E. Alton – who between them represent a tremendous storehouse of palaeographical expertise – have all examined the manuscript itself (rather than facsimiles or photographs), and all agree on D's similarity to Shakespeare's hand, both as it survives in manuscript and as it may be inferred from the evidence of his printed works. No palaeographer of similar eminence and experience has upheld the contrary view. The fact that, even so, this palaeographical evidence would not be considered strong enough to convict someone of murder does not render it valueless; we are necessarily dealing, in all such investigations, with probability rather than certainty. Moreover, if the ascription to Shakespeare would not stand up in court, the ascription to Webster would probably not even get a hearing, because the 'evidence' for it is entirely circumstantial.

Not only is there no surviving specimen of Webster's handwriting; there is no evidence (1) that Thomas Dekker or Thomas Heywood had begun writing plays before 1596, (2) that Munday, Chettle, or Heywood had any association with the Chamberlain's men, or (3) that Shakespeare had any association with Henslowe, after 1594.[4] These are facts of some interest and importance, but they do not – despite Dr Chillington – constitute 'external evidence' against the identification of Hand D as Shakespeare.

Chillington's argument is in two stages. First, the play belonged, from first to last, to Henslowe's company; secondly, at the time when it was written Shakespeare could have had no association with that company. Neither of these contentions is justified by the evidence. What this collection of negatives instead demonstrates is that we know little about the repertoire of Shakespeare's company, and a lot about the repertoire of Henslowe's.

Ignoring for a moment the plays of Jonson and Shakespeare, the known repertoire of the Chamberlain's/King's men from 1594 to 1604 consists of: *Alarum for London* (1598–1600), *A Warning for Fair Women* (1598–9?), *Thomas Lord Cromwell* (1599–1602), *Satiromastix* (1601), *The Merry Devil of Edmonton* (1599–1604), and *The Malcontent* (1603–5).[5] All but two of these plays are anonymous – as would be most of Henslowe's surviving repertoire, if we did not have recourse to his diary. The two exceptions are by Dekker (whom Chillington regards as a Henslowe hack) and Marston (who wrote almost exclusively for the children's companies – and in 1599 for Henslowe). Marston's play had, admittedly, been 'stolen', and supplied with new material for the King's men by John Webster – another 'Henslowe hack' who, to our knowledge, did not write for the King's men again for a decade.[6] Besides Shakespeare, then, the only dramatists we can identify with the Chamberlain's/King's men from 1594 to 1604 are Jonson, Dekker, and Webster – all of whom figure in Henslowe's diary, on collaborative projects, for the same period. The fact that Dekker, Heywood, Chettle, and Munday (Hands E, B, A, and S) all had associations with Henslowe therefore proves nothing; we might realize that they all had associations with the Chamberlain's men, too, if we knew more about that company's repertoire. Dekker clearly did; Chettle's agreement, on 25 March 1602, to write regularly for the Admiral's men thereafter has usually been understood to imply that he had been freelancing before that date; his complete absence from

Henslowe's diary from 19 June 1600 to 31 March 1601 encourages the same assumption.[7] Heywood was probably writing for other companies by 1599, and is not thereafter certainly identified with Henslowe at all until December 1602.[8] The other three dramatists who can be identified writing the additions to the manuscript therefore hardly constitute 'external evidence' that rules out an association with any company but Henslowe's.

In fact, only one piece of evidence apparently links the manuscript with Henslowe: Hand C. Though she pays it surprisingly little attention, Hand C is the true linchpin of Chillington's case, for it is now usually identified as the hand of Henslowe's scribe. Naturally, this anonymous workaday hand has received less intense palaeographical scrutiny than the more glamorous literary hands of A, B, D, E, and S; Chillington's argument has now made it all-important. Would the identification of Hand C with Henslowe's scribe stand up in a court of law? If not, the 'external evidence' that *More* belonged to Henslowe is no more secure – indeed, much less secure – than the 'internal evidence' that Hand D looks like Shakespeare. In particular, Hand C's link with Henslowe's later operations is based upon a single fragmentary plot in the British Library (MS. Addit. 10449, fol. 4), conjecturally identified by Greg as *2 Fortune's Tennis*. Greg conjecturally assigns this plot to the Admiral's men in the winter of 1597–8.[9] If Greg's identification of the hand, or of the company, or of the date, were incorrect, we should have no particular reason for assigning the *More* manuscript to Henslowe. I am personally inclined to accept Greg's arguments on all three issues, but Chillington is hardly in a position to do so. After all, those who reject Greg's palaeographical judgement about Hand D – a judgement supported by many other experts – can hardly accept as gospel Greg's judgement about Hand C. All of Chillington's alleged 'external evidence' is in fact 'internal evidence', because it depends upon the identification of certain hands with certain persons. Moreover, even if Greg is right about Hand C and *2 Fortune's Tennis*, such evidence only establishes that in 1597–8 the scribe was working for Henslowe; at some other time he may have been working for the King's men. Actors and playwrights, about whom we have more information, certainly did switch companies from time to time, and our complete ignorance of the day-to-day operations of the King's men makes it impossible to pass judgement on such possibilities. Our only knowledge of anyone who served as a prompter for Shakespeare's company before 1611 is an anecdote about 'Thomas Vincent', described by John Taylor in 1638 as 'a Book-keeper or prompter at the Globe playhouse' (*Taylors Feast*, sig. E4^v); this anecdote associates Vincent with the actor John Singer, who was the principal Clown for the rival company. Whether or not Hand C was Thomas Vincent, he was certainly not the scribe who prepared for Henslowe the plots of *Frederick and Basilea* (1597), *Troilus and Cressida* (1599), and *The Battle of Alcazar* (1598–9?); nor, as far as we can tell, does he appear to have been responsible for *1 Tamar Cam* (1602). Greg, who identified Hand C in *2 Fortune's Tennis*, believed that these last three Admiral's men's plots were all prepared by the same scribe. Unless we conjecture that Henslowe deigned to keep two scribes employed full-time, then it would appear that Hand C was definitely *not* working full-time for Henslowe from 1598 to 1602.

But even if Hand C was Henslowe's scribe and remained Henslowe's scribe all his life, those facts would only establish that the manuscript passed through Henslowe's company at some point in its history. By no stretch of the imagination does it follow that the play can have had no associations with any other company, at any other point in its history. We have already seen two plays transferred from other companies to the Chamberlain's/King's repertoire; in 1613, Robert Daborne (another 'Henslowe hack') wrote to Henslowe threatening to take his new play to the King's men if he could get a better deal from them.[10] In 1611 Dekker's *If This Be Not A Good Play, The Devil Is In It* was performed at the Red Bull after being turned down by Henslowe's company at the Fortune.[11] In July 1602 Henslowe made two payments for Dekker's *Medicine for a Curst Wife* (apparently for the Admiral's men), but by August or September it had been transferred to Worcester's men.[12] Then as now, plays intended for – or specifically commissioned by – one theatre sometimes wound up being produced at another. This is, of course, especially likely to happen when the playwright(s) involved have professional relationships with more than one company – as some of the *More* playwrights clearly did. Nor is it difficult to understand, in this instance, why one company might have decided to abandon the play, either before or after the censor saw it.

Hand C annotates or transcribes some of the additions (including, of course, Hand D's); Hand C must have possessed the manuscript after these additions were written. Therefore, if C is Henslowe's scribe, and D is Shakespeare, and Shakespeare never wrote for Henslowe, then at some unknown point in time the play apparently passed from Shakespeare's company to Henslowe's. Certainly, Hand D shows no signs of having returned to the manuscript after Hand C went to work on it. But Hand C himself provides us with a further piece of evidence about the company for whom he was preparing the play: he wrote the marginal instruction 'Mess T Goodal' opposite the entrance direction for a messenger at the beginning of Add. v. Thomas Goodale was an actor. The date of his death is unknown, but he was alive until at least November 1599, when one of his children was buried.[13] Goodale is named in the plot of *2 Seven Deadly Sins*, which Greg believed was performed between September 1588 and spring 1591, probably by Strange's men, and certainly by a company which included Richard Burbage, Thomas Pope, John Holland, and John Sinclo, all actors with strong associations with Shakespeare. Otherwise Goodale's theatrical affiliations are completely unknown, except for this marginal mention among the additions to *More*. If the additions were written early in the 1590s, then Goodale's name is of little significance in identifying the play's auspices – although it makes a connection with Shakespeare entirely reasonable. But if the additions date from the period favoured by Chillington – after 1600 – then Goodale's name is crucial. For although we do not know exactly who Goodale *did* work for in this later period, we know that he did *not* work for one man in particular: Henslowe. The complete absence of

Goodale's name from Henslowe's voluminous records constitutes in itself sufficient proof that Goodale 'the player' worked for someone else in the late 1590s and up to at least the end of 1602. Since he was no longer a boy, he must have acted for one of the other adult companies in London, and given his known connection with Burbage *et al.*, it would be simplest to suppose that he was a hired man regularly employed by the Chamberlain's men. The connection with Shakespeare's company must remain speculative; what can be ruled out is any connection with Henslowe's operations *c.* 1597–1602. In this the evidence of Goodale's name potently reinforces the evidence of C's presence: neither of these men can be connected with Henslowe in the period 1597–1602.

In order to prove that the manuscript was at some point in the possession of Shakespeare's company, we would have to identify one of the hands in the manuscript with a figure who can *only* have worked for the Chamberlain's men at the period in question. Only two such figures exist: the Chamberlain's men's theatrical scribe at that time, or their attached dramatist (Shakespeare). Nothing in the hand of the first of these figures is known to survive; since some annotations in the manuscript cannot be confidently identified, this otherwise unknown hand might or might not be present in *More*. Indeed, after 1597 Hand C might himself have been the company's regular scribe, but in the absence of corroborative evidence we cannot assume so. Consequently, *only* the presence of Shakespeare's hand in the manuscript could prove that it had some association with the Chamberlain's men, and the presence of Shakespeare's hand would be *sufficient* to establish a connection with that company – if we accept that an attached dramatist never wrote anything for a rival company. Chillington therefore cannot claim that the absence of other links with the Chamberlain's men rules out the attribution to Shakespeare, because the whole question of the play's relationship to the Chamberlain's men itself turns on the identification of Hand D.

However, even those who accept that Heywood, Dekker, and Chettle could all have had connections with the Chamberlain's men might still doubt whether the Chamberlain's men regularly relied on the system of play-botching and hack-work, often collaborative, so evident in Henslowe's operations. Here, again, however (as G.E. Bentley has observed) the absence of any parallel for Henslowe's diary distorts our picture of theatrical conditions elsewhere.[14] Of the twenty-four plays surviving in whole or part which Harbage and Schoenbaum assign to the Admiral's men from 1594 to 1603, all but five would be anonymous, or misattributed, or assignable only on the basis of internal evidence, if the diary did not exist. This includes all five plays which we know to be collaborative; another six, which to this day remain anonymous, might also be collaborative. In short, without Henslowe's diary we would know nothing about the way Henslowe commissioned and procured plays; since we lack such a document for the Chamberlain's men, we are hardly justified in assuming that their methods radically differed. Once again, our view of the company has been distorted by the predominance of Shakespeare himself, who as a sharer and 'attached playwright' clearly represents a special case. But Shakespeare alone could hardly have kept the company solvent, in a theatrical system based on short runs and (therefore) a constant supply of new plays. The number of anonymous plays in the Chamberlain's men's early repertoire certainly suggests an operation similar to Henslowe's (always excepting the fact that Henslowe did not have a sharer-dramatist like Shakespeare). Moreover, of the non-Shakespeare plays whose authorship we do know something about, one (*Satiromastix*) may have been initiated or planned by Marston before being wholly taken over by Dekker;[15] another (*Malcontent*) was adapted by the 'hack' Webster; a third (*Sejanus*) was originally written as a collaboration between Jonson and an unknown second playwright.[16] Thus, of the five non-Shakespearian Chamberlain's men plays from this period which can be attributed, two certainly (and a third possibly) were collaborative. The later history of the company tells the same story: witness the notorious authorship problems in the Beaumont and Fletcher canon, and Shakespeare's own possible-to-certain collaborations in *Timon of Athens, Macbeth, Pericles, All is True, Cardenio,* and *The Two Noble Kinsmen*.

There is, then, nothing anomalous in suggesting that the kind of collaborative hack-work evident in *More* could have taken place under the auspices of the Chamberlain's men; nor anything extraordinary in suggesting that Dekker, Chettle, and Heywood might have done work for Shakespeare's company. In Dekker's case, in fact, this is certain; for Chettle and Heywood, there is more evidence that they were working for someone else in 1600–1 than there is evidence that they were working for Henslowe. Nor is there anything anomalous about the Chamberlain's men taking an interest in this sort of subject matter: *Thomas Lord Cromwell*, after all, dates from 1599–1602. Nor is it difficult to explain Shakespeare's late involvement in the manuscript: an 'attached dramatist' might be expected to do just this sort of thing, where necessary, for plays produced by his company. All of the evidence so far considered would allow us to assume that the play was adapted for the Chamberlain's men.

The fluidity of relationships between playwrights and companies – and the essential similarity of the operations of the Admiral's and the Chamberlain's men – must be taken into account by anyone surveying possible explanations for the manuscript as it stands. This principle applies to the original play, as well as the additions. Anthony Munday wrote the fair copy of the original text; this in turn implies that, at the very least, Munday had a hand in the original composition. There is no evidence that Munday wrote plays for the Chamberlain's men. This absence of evidence may be misleading, but Munday nevertheless must be distinguished from Dekker, Chettle, and Heywood, who clearly did work for other companies. If we assume, on this basis, that the presence of Munday is *prima facie* evidence of a connection with Henslowe, then we must conclude that the original play was intended for Henslowe's theatre. But even this conclusion – which does not seem to me warranted by the meagre facts at our disposal – would still permit the hypothesis that the play was eventually adapted by another company, namely Shakespeare's.

In fact, Munday's link with Henslowe is less secure than might be supposed. Like so much else, it depends entirely upon the evidence of Henslowe's diary. None of the printed texts of the plays in which we know, through Henslowe, that Munday had a hand – *The Downfall of Robert Earl of Huntingdon, The Death of Robert Earl of Huntingdon, 1 Sir John Oldcastle* – names Munday as author. Munday disappears from the diary altogether between August 1598 and October 1599, and his appearances generally are far less frequent than those of Chettle, Dekker and others. Munday might easily, even during this period, have been writing for other companies. But even if we assume Munday's fidelity to Henslowe during these years, that tells us nothing about Munday's theatrical connections before 1598 or after 1602. At the beginning of his career Munday was apparently associated with the Earl of Oxford's men. This company performed at Court several times in the early 1580s, but after 1583 can only be traced in provincial records, and it seems likely that Munday confined his literary favours to Oxford's men after 1585. For Munday's theatrical connections in the years between *c.* 1585 and December 1597, we are entirely dependent upon the evidence of two autograph manuscripts: *More* and *John a Kent*. Scott McMillin elsehwere in this volume offers what seems to me a compelling argument that *More* was originally witten for Strange's men. If so, then Munday's presence in the manuscript tells us nothing about the theatrical provenance of the additions. Strange's men, after a brief existence, split up and reorganized into two companies: the Admiral's men (associated with Henslowe) and the Chamberlain's men (associated with Shakespeare, Burbage, etc.). An unperformed script written for Strange's men might have become the property of either company, depending upon the exact division of spoils. Even if Munday wrote exclusively for Henslowe *after* 1594, that fact would have no relevance to the latter disposition of a play written for Strange's men *before* 1594. Since the entire issue of provenance resolves around whether Shakespeare's company or Henslowe's owned the play, attribution of the original to Strange's men effectively deprives Munday's presence of any conceivable significance in determining the provenance of the additions. In fact, if Munday after 1594 wrote only for Henslowe, then one could even take his absence from the additions as indirect evidence that his original script went to the other company.

The provenance of *John a Kent* is just as conjectural as the provenance of *More*. It has sometimes been said that *John a Kent and John a Cumber* is an alternative title for a play which Henslowe variously describes as *The Wise Man of West Chester, Wise Man, Wise Man of Chester*, and *Westchester*, performed numerous times between 3 December 1594 and 18 July 1597. On the first of these occasions the play is annotated as 'ne', which means either that it was literally new or had been adapted. Munday's play can hardly have been brand-new in December 1594; Shapiro has shown that it almost certainly dates from 1589.[17] Given the obvious disparity in titles and dates, the conjectural identification of Munday's play with Henslowe's rests upon the flimsiest of foundations. A 1598 inventory for the Admiral's men – who performed *The Wise Man of West Chester* – includes 'Kentes woden leage'.[18] No such property is required by Munday's text, but E.K. Chambers explains this lacuna by saying that 'two or three leaves of the MS. appear to be missing'.[19] In her later Malone Society edition of the manuscript, M. St. C. Byrne demonstrated that Chambers's supposition was false, and that almost nothing of the text has been lost. As she concluded, 'there is no secure basis for speculation' about the relationship of Munday's play and Henslowe's.[20] Hence, 'there is no secure basis' for connecting Munday with Henslowe before 1598.

Our uncertainty about the provenance of Munday's other transcript has considerable bearing on our conclusion about the provenance of *More*. At some stage in their history the two manuscripts were bound together, and provided with titles by a single hand. That hand is 'perhaps . . . Hand C' who transcribes and annotates the additions to *More*; 'it is possible' that Hand C also added a handfull of stage directions to *John a Kent*; William Long believes that C was also responsible for the date written at the end of *John a Kent*.[21] If all of these equations are correct, then the company which at some unknown date adapted *More* also apparently owned at that time *John a Kent*, and may even have been considering a revival of it. However, since we do not know who owned *John a Kent*, the conjectural identification of Hand C in that manuscript tells us nothing about the date or provenance of *More*. No-one knows what the date 'Decembris 1590' means, at the end of *John a Kent*; the two Munday manuscripts were clearly written on different paper at different times.[22] No-one supposes that *More* dates from 1589 or 1590. Unfortunately, the physical connection between the two manuscripts fails to illuminate the date or provenance of either the original composition or the adaptation of *More*.

What may be more important than the undeniable connection between *More* and *John a Kent* is the apparent absence of any connection between them and the extant Henslowe manuscripts. Henslowe's diaries and papers passed into Edward Alleyn's collection, and thence to the library of the College of God's Gift at Dulwich; Alleyn's part for *Orlando Furioso* and the plot of *2 Seven Deadly Sins* also wound up at Dulwich; the other five extant plots, all dating from Henslowe's later operations, are all bound together in British Library Add. MS. 10449, and probably also at one time belonged to the Dulwich collection. None of this material was known or referred to before 1780.[23] By contrast, *More* can be traced back to October 1727, when it was in the possession of John Murray, from whom it apparently passed to the Earl of Oxford, and from there to the Harleian collection which reached the British Museum in 1753 (Jenkins, in Greg, p. xxxiii). Compared to the undisputed Henslowe and Admiral's men papers, *More* not only sufaces much earlier, but from a different direction.

By contrast with the Henslowe and Alleyn papers, the few theatrical documents which we can associate with the King's men tend to be mentioned early, and to come from a number of different directions. *Believe as you list* (British Library, MS Egerton 2828) is mentioned in the Stationers' Register on 9 September 1653 and again on 29 June 1660; it was again mentioned, in 1750, by W.R. Chetwood, prompter at Drury Lane from 1722 to 1741. *The Soddered Citizen* is mentioned in the Stationers' Register on the same two dates as *Believe as you list*. *Sir John van Olden Barnavelt* (British Library MS Add. 18653) already belonged to the Earl of Denbigh in 1697. *The Second Maiden's Tragedy* (British Library, MS Lansdowne 807) was mentioned in the Stationers' Register on 9 September 1653, and in the eighteenth century owned by Warburton. *Cardenio* was also included in the list of 9 September 1653, and allegedly owned in 1727 by Lewis Theobald; in 1770 we are told that the manuscript was kept in the 'Museum of Covent Garden Playhouse'. A manuscript of *Macbeth* must have been available in the 1660s to Sir William D'Avenant, who clearly drew on some theatrical document (now lost) in preparing his adaptation. *The Little French Lawyer* was printed in the 1647 Beaumont and Fletcher Folio, apparently from a promptbook. I have deliberately excluded from this list private transcripts, which were prepared for the libraries of particular readers; of the texts mentioned here, all but *Cardenio* – whose status is uncertain – are, or seem very probably to have been, annotated theatrical manuscripts, like *More* itself. The cohesion of the King's men broke down at some unspecified point in the 1640s, after the closure of the theatres; at that time their manuscripts were probably dispersed, and if we have any knowledge of those manuscripts at all it tends to surface before 1750, and to come from many different directions, reflecting the dispersal of the company's assets. By contrast, the Henslowe and Alleyn papers were not dispersed, and do not resurface until 1780. We do not possess a single significant theatrical document clearly traceable to Alleyn and Henslowe which is not also clearly traceable to Alleyn's bequest to Dulwich. If we judge *More* strictly from the point of view of the provenance of the manuscript, we have no reason to locate the provenance of the additions with Henslowe, and considerable reason to doubt any such connection.

Neither the known history of the manuscript, nor the known history of Anthony Munday, gives us any right or reason to assume that the play ever belonged to Henslowe. The specification of Goodale and the presence of Hand C also argue against attribution to Henslowe, if the additions date from 1598–1602. The presence of Chettle, Dekker and Heywood is compatible with production by companies other than Henslowe's; the methods of collaboration and adaptation evident in the manuscript must have been as frequent outside Henslowe's circle as within it. The almost universal assumption that the play belonged to Henslowe, a belief Chillington triumphantly seizes upon as the immoveable 'external evidence' upon which the identification of Hand D with Shakespeare must come to grief, has no basis either in fact or in reasonable inference.

Let us nevertheless, for the sake of argument, for safety's sake, assume, despite all the evidence to the contrary, that Chillington is right in attributing the play to Henslowe. Even if that unlikely assumption should prove correct, the play's alleged connection with Henslowe is incompatible with Shakespeare's authorship of one or more of the additions only if (1) the additions were written *c*. 1600–3, and (2) Shakespeare, as an 'attached dramatist', could not and would not have written for anyone else. Only the combination of both these propositions would veto a Shakespearian contribution to *More*.

Shakespeare clearly wrote all of his own extant plays, from 1594 onwards, for the

Chamberlain's/King's men; just as obviously, after Shakespeare's death several other dramatists (Fletcher, Massinger, Shirley, Brome) seem to have had similar arrangements, probably contractual. Interestingly, for three of these four dramatists we know of one certain exception – involving a full-length play – to the rule of exclusivity.[24] Moreover, all the available evidence suggests that Shakespeare was the first dramatist to have such a sustained special relationship with an acting company; for that very reason, the relationship may never have been contractualized. The earliest documentary evidence of a contract binding playwrights to write exclusively for one party comes – unsurprisingly – from Henslowe's diary; even so, the three examples (in 1598, 1599 and 1602) are all, in different ways, ambiguous.[25] In the circumstances, we can hardly claim that the Chamberlain's men had a contractual monopoly on Shakespeare's labours, and then use the existence of that alleged monopoly as 'external evidence' against the identification of Hand D as Shakespeare; again, our conclusions about Shakespeare's participation in *More* must determine our view about his precise relationship with his company, not vice versa.

Even if the authorship of an entire play were in question, the single anomalies in the record for Shirley, Massinger, and Brome would forbid us from denying Shakespeare's claim to authorship of an Admiral's men play. When only part of a single scene is at stake, the force of an alleged contractual obligation becomes even more difficult to assess, and even less reliable as 'external' evidence for authorship. Certainly, we have no evidence that Shakespeare ever elsewhere wrote brief passages in a play for another company; but in the nature of the case, such evidence could only derive from an autograph manuscript, and autograph manuscripts of Shakespeare are not overly abundant.

The conclusion that Shakespeare *would* not, in any circumstances, have written such an addition for another company's play rests upon psychological, rather than legal, premises (or 'external evidence'): 'Since Shakespeare was a sharer in the Chamberlain's men, he would have had a strong personal interest in the financial well-being of that company; since the Admiral's men were a rival company, he would have had no particular interest in the success of plays written for them'. These premises are simple and attractive, but they may also be simplistic and misleading. Most investigators have assumed that Hand D (whoever he was) did not contribute to the original version of the play.[26] If this assumption is correct, then the author in question was approached either because he was particularly good at this sort of scene, or because he was on hand, or both. After *Contention* or after *Julius Caesar*, Shakespeare's qualifications for the proposed scene would have been obvious. Whether he would have been 'on hand', in any personal or professional sense, depends in large part on our view of the operations of the Chamberlain's men. Certainly, the fluidity of professional relationships between most playwrights and most companies in this period gives us no right to rule out the sort of personal and professional link which could have led one of the *More* collaborators to approach Shakespeare. I cannot prove that such relationships did exist; but nor can Chillington prove (or presume) that they did not.

Even if he had no interest in adding to the estate of Philip Henslowe, Shakespeare might have been willing enough to do a favour (paid or unpaid) for one or more fellow playwrights with whom he had, on occasion, professional contacts for the Chamberlain's men. Certainly, if he did write half a scene for *More*, it would be hard to contend that by doing so he was seriously damaging the interests of his own company. Robert Armin was certainly a sharer in Shakespeare's company by 1603, and probably earlier. But in 1609 he published *The History of the Two Maids of More-Clacke*, which both the title-page and Armin's own preface tell us was '*acted by the boys of the Revels*'. These performances must date from 1607–8, when Armin's relationship with the King's men cannot be doubted.[27] If a whole play by a sharer in the King's men could come to be performed by a rival company, then we have no confident grounds for denying that three pages written by a sharer in the King's men might come to be performed by a rival company. And after all, human beings have from time to time been known to betray the corporate interest for reasons of personal gain, financial or otherwise. The conviction that Shakespeare could not have written 147 lines for Henslowe in 1600–3 rests upon assumptions about his contractual status (about which we know nothing) and his character (about which we know nothing).

In short, nothing in the external record would rule out the identification of Hand D as Shakespeare, *even if* the additions were written for Henslowe in the early seventeenth century. We must therefore compare the internal evidence for Webster with that for Shakespeare, and consider each on its intrinsic merits.

Chilington's attribution to Webster itself depends on certain 'external' assumptions. In order to make that attribution plausible (and not subject to the same objections she had herself levelled against a 1592–5 date for the play), she must postpone the play's composition until the first record of Webster's association with Henslowe, in 1602. Since the diary is relatively complete for 1599–1602, Henslowe's failure to mention *More* effectively rules out composition or production during those years, if the play indeed belonged to Henslowe: it must be earlier or later, and Chillington plumps for later. But this dating, even if correct, need not invalidate the attribution of D's addition to Shakespeare. Shakespeare's participation might be particularly easy to explain in spring 1603: the Queen was dead, the theatres were closed by plague, the political and theatrical future was uncertain. We simply do not know enough about Shakespeare's career or his character to rule such possibilities peremptorily out of court.

Chillington's conjectural 1603 date makes Webster possible (though it does not rule out Shakespeare); but the internal evidence for Webster is not very convincing. The amateurishness of Chillington's discussion of authorship – not only in respect to Hand D, but more generally in her elaborate reconstruction of the alleged shares of the five dramatists in the original play – must forcefully strike anyone who has examined either the cumulative stylistic evidence for attributing Hand D to Shakespeare, or any reputable modern scholarship on the attribution of anonymous or collaborative Jacobethan plays. Webster's claims are evaluated at length by Charles Forker elsewhere in this volume, and I will therefore confine myself to the palaeographical evidence. I have found not a single example of 'a' misread as 'or' or 'oi' or 'li' in any of Webster's known or suspected works, whether of single or collaborative authorship.[28] The particular form of 'open spurred a' which encourages such misreadings is, of course, one of the strongest palaeographical links between the Shakespeare signatures, the Shakespeare quartos, and Hand D; the complete absence of such misreadings in Webster's known work in itself virtually vetoes his candidacy for the authorship of the addition.

The immediate appeal of Chillington's rejection of Shakespeare's claim rested heavily on her provision of an apparently plausible alternative; if that alternative proves illusory, then we are forced back to the conclusion R.C. Bald enunciated: *et tu Shakespeare an diabolus* (*ShS* 2, p. 60). Certainly, the internal evidence for Shakespeare is much better than the evidence for Webster. Chillington echoes Schücking in complaining that D's portion contains a number of words and expressions not found elsewhere in Shakespeare's work;[29] but this in fact reinforces Shakespeare's claim, since all of Shakespeare's recognized works contain an unusually high proportion of new and/or unique vocabulary.[30] She makes much of recent doubts about the strength of the palaeographical argument; but, although it is true that the palaeographical argument cannot, in the nature of the evidence, be by itself conclusive, it is at least extremely suggestive of Shakespearian authorship. As to the links in metrical practices, thought and imagery, Chillington objects that such parallels link Hand D's additions more strongly to the early seventeenth century, than to the early 1590s; yet she herself has argued, on quite other evidence, that the play must date from that later period. The metre and style and imagery, in short, suggest that whoever wrote D's portion was thinking and writing in much the way Shakespeare himself was thinking and writing at the time when, according to Chillington's own argument, the additions were written.

But is Chillington right about the date? She may be; certainly, the evidence for dating the play needs to be re-examined dispassionately. The starting point for any such enquiry must be the recognition that the additions are later than the remainder of the play. I accept the arguments of other contributors to this collection that the original play dates from *c.* 1592–5. We do not know when the additions were written, but they may be considerably later. The evidence of watermarks makes it objectively verifiable that the additions were written on different paper.[31] Munday the author-scribe and Tilney the censor, who between them copied and responded to the main text, make no appearance in the pages of the additions; as R.C. Bald pointed out (pp. 50–1), the use of 'Lombards' twice in the additions (11b, 82, 104), in place of the consistent identification of the aliens as French or Dutch in the main text, certainly suggests that at least some of the additions were written after Tilney made at least some of his comments, insofar as Tilney had insisted on exactly this substitution in scene iii (ll. 364, 368), for fairly obvious political reasons. Such evidence makes it impossible to assume or assert that the play and the additions to it date from the same moment in time. Consequently, evidence for the date of the original play tells us nothing about the date of the additions, and vice versa. This principle is as simple as it is self-evident.

As Jenkins says, 'the problem of the date is twofold. Failure to appreciate this has sometimes confused the meagre and uncertain clues'.[32] Chillington fell into this trap by assuming that a late date for the additions implied a late date for the original; others have committed the reverse error. G.B. Evans, for instance, concludes that 'two things make a later dating difficult'. First, 'Munday's hand (Hand S) in the *More* manuscript is considered by handwriting experts to show a much closer relationship with his hand as it appears in the holograph manuscript of *John a Kent* (about 1590) than with his hand in another holograph manuscript (*The Heaven of the Mind*) which he wrote in 1602'. This is of course an argument only relevant to the date of original composition. Evans commits Chillington's error in reverse. Secondly, 'By 1597 [Hand C] was certainly associated with the Admiral's Men alone', and hence if we accept the identification of D with Shakespeare then 'the association of D . . . with C' argues against a letter dating.[33] Evans here commits the same error as Chillington, postulating that a conclusion about theatrical provenance justifies and indeed requires a conclusion about authorship. Chillington accepts the conclusion about provenance, but rejects that about authorship; Evans accepts the conclusion about authorship, but not that about provenance; both assume a direct relationship between the two. But as I have tried to show in this essay, unless we succumb to complete circularity of reasoning, the presence of Shakespeare's hand in a play manuscript of 1600–3 need not be incompatible with a Henslowe connection. We must therefore attempt to judge the evidence for the date of the additions without being influenced by unwarranted assumptions about Shakespeare's professional conduct.

We may begin with the evidence of datable allusions in the text of the additions. The additions contain twenty-seven profanities of a kind forbidden by the *Acte to Restraine Abuses of Players* (*3 Jac. I*, c. 21): each addition sports one or more of these profanities, and we can therefore be confident that the additions were written before May 1606. The only acknowledged verbal evidence which may link the additions to a datable event outside the theatre occurs in one of Faulkner's speeches, written by Hand E (Dekker): 'Moore had bin better a Scowrd More ditch, than a notcht mee thus' (Add. IV, 215–16). Percy Simpson drew attention to the scouring of Moreditch in 1595, and Bald noted that it was scoured again in 1603.[34] Jenkins simply notes that this reference 'would have particular applicability in 1595', thus ignoring the 1603 parallel, and then minimizes the significance of the allusion by claiming that 'the condition of the ditch was notorious' (Greg, p. xlii). But Stow only records three efforts to clean the ditch in his lifetime: in 1549, 1569, and 1596. To these we may add the cleansing authorized on 15 February 1602/3 (too late to be mentioned in Stow's 1603 edition).[35] Of these four occasions, the first two can obviously be discounted, leaving only 1595 and 1603 as dates when the allusion would be 'particularly applicable'. Unfortunately, we do not know the time of year of the 1595 scouring; since Stow treats the year as beginning on 21 March, if the allusion was intended and if the additions date from 1595 then they must have been written between late March and June (when further riots and executions made it impossible for anyone to imagine that the play could be salvaged). But Stow also records that the 1595 effort was an almost total and immediate failure, which is why the job had to be undertaken again so soon after, in 1603. In terms of the severe haircut apparently inflicted on Faulkner, the scouring of 1603 is at least as appropriate as that of 1595, if not more so. And one of these two dates seems likelier than any other.

The Moreditch allusion has been noticed before – though not, I think, properly appreciated; but another group of possible allusions has to my knowledge not been noticed, and I therefore offer it with some diffidence. Chettle's addition replaces part of More's conversation with his wife, in scene xiii. In the original More says almost nothing about the King, and literally nothing about the court. Chettle's emphasis is very different:

> the Court like heauen
> examines not the anger of the [king;] Prince
> and being more fraile composde of guilded earth
> shines vpon them on whom the [Prince] king doth shine
> smiles if he smile, declines if he decline   (Add. 1, 12–16)

These lines are marked for omission; others, however, remain:

> as commonly disgraes of great men
> are the forewarnings of a hastie death . . .
> . . . Perchance the king
> seeing the Court is full of vanitie   (1, 23–4, 26–7)

Such complaints about the court become commonplace soon after the accession of James I. In December 1603 Sir Walter Raleigh was convicted of treason, although he was not in fact executed until fifteen years later; ten other 'conspirators', however, were executed that month. Essex was executed in February 1601. All of this may be coincidence, of course. So may an apparent pun in another passage – one, like the first, marked for omission:

> Great lords haue onely name; but in the[ir] fall
> [the] Lord Spend-alls Stuart's master gathers all
> But I suspect not thee admit thou hast
> Its good the seruants saue when Masters wast.   (I, 58–61)

Chettle would undoubtedly claim that the spelling 'Stuart' stands for the word we would spell 'steward'; but someone nevertheless decided that the passage should be omitted.[36] It seems to me that the writing of these passages, and the deletion of some of them, make more sense after than before the execution of Essex and the accession of James Stuart.

Only one study of the stylistic evidence of the additions has suggested that any of them is of an early date. The second half of Peter Blayney's 'The Booke of Sir Thomas Moore Re-examined' is concerned with parallels between the text of and additions to More and the works of Chettle; he notes for instance that Kind-Heart's Dream, entered in the Stationers' Register on 8 December 1592, was 'found to contain more echoes of the main text of Moore than the other three works put together,' and that the pattern of links 'points to *Moore*'s being the source rather than the recipient' (p. 182). In the absence of a published list of such resemblances we can hardly accept such evidence as conclusive proof that the main text dates from before 8 December 1592, but it does lend support to a date already attractive on other grounds. But Blayney's evidence for dating the additions is less persuasive. As Richard Proudfoot concluded, in reviewing the article, 'Blayney is least convincing on the subject of the likely chronology of the revisions, where he attaches undue weight to the existence of certain verbal similarities between parts of the play, including Hand D's addition, and Chettle's *Kind Heart's Dream*'.[37] However, because Blayney's work has never been extensively examined in print, and has had some influence, it merits more attention than Proudfoot – in a survey of the year's work in textual studies – could have been expected to give it.

Since Chettle may himself have collaborated on the main text of *More*, a compilation of parallels between his other work and the main text is of obvious potential value, in terms both of authorship and influence. But in trying to date the additions Blayney is only concerned with links between Chettle's published work and a passage he clearly did *not* write (Hand D's addition). Identity of authorship can therefore be ruled out, and only the possibility of influence investigated. Blayney's case for dating the addition is, essentially, a variety of source study: he proposes that Hand D's brief addition is an important source for *Kind-Heart's Dream*. Naturally, since one of the elements in this equation is of uncertain date, the credibility of this proposition depends upon establishing not only that there are numerous and unusual links between the two texts, but particularly that those links can only be explained by influence in one direction rather than the other. In fact, in this case we must also consider a third possibility: that the author of *Kind-Heart's Dream* influenced the author of D's addition. Chettle may well have collaborated on the main text, and if so it is always possible that he wrote the original scene which Hand D was asked to replace. Since that original is now lost, we have no way of knowing what it contained, and whether Hand D was influenced by any of its verbal details. If – as Blayney's own evidence encourages us to believe – Chettle contributed to the main text not long before he wrote *Kind-Heart's Dream*, then we might expect a certain number of verbal correspondences between the pamphlet and a lost scene written by Chettle, and some of those verbal correspondences may in turn have influenced Hand D's revision of the scene. Consequently, in the absence of proof that Chettle did *not* collaborate on the main text, Blayney's entire reconstruction is built upon a profoundly uncertain foundation.

To the orthodox accumulation of parallel passages Blayney appends a more unusual form of evidence; the identification of certain 'key words' in D's addition, which recur in significant 'clusters' in *Kind-Heart's Dream*. Blayney believes that D's addition is so much better than the rest of the play, and the other additions, that anyone involved in the collaboration must have been deeply impressed by it, and that certain conjunctions of key words would have exercised an unconscious influence upon his next piece of writing. This seems to me a somewhat implausible postulate. Modern scholars know Hand D's addition far better than they know the rest of the play; modern scholars take it for granted that even in 1592 Shakespeare was a unique genius, whereas Munday *et al.* were common drudges; modern scholars are much concerned with the critical concept of 'key words'; but Henry Chettle was not a modern scholar, and for all we know he might not even have read Hand D's addition. If Blayney's method were empirically valid, it should work in cases where direct influence has already been reliably established by other means; moreover, it should *not* work in cases where influence can be reliably ruled out by other means. Blayney supplies no such controls for his experiment, and without such controls we should not place much confidence in his results. To me, it does not seem very surprising that words like 'authority' and 'order' occur in proximity to one another ('Cluster E'); or that 'authority', 'innovation', 'sin', 'hurly burly', 'rout', 'barbarous', and 'magistrate' all occur in one passage, describing riots at a theatre ('Cluster C').

We are on safer, more familiar ground – ground easier to evaluate – in Blayney's list of significant parallels between D's addition and Chettle's pamphlet. Of the two parallels to which he gives most weight, one is:

> in ruff of yor opynions clothd (II, 202)
> in the ruffe of ribaudrie (*KHD*, 02)

Despite the surface similarity, the two phrases have completely different meanings. Hand D figuratively describes an abstract attribute in terms of clothing imagery, the *ruff* being a 'circular outstanding frill on the sleeve of a garment; a ruffle' (*OED. sb.*² 1) or 'An article of neck-wear, usually consisting of starched linen or muslin arranged in horizontal flutings and standing out all around the neck, worn especially in the reigns of Elizabeth and James I' (*sb.*²2). Indeed, Hand D may have deliberately chosen *ruff* because the finery of the clothing contrasts with the usual wear of More's onstage audience: their opinions are as inappropriate to their station as ruffs would be.[38] Chettle, by contrast, is using a common idiom of an entirely different meaning; in *Kind-Heart's Dream* a *ruff* is 'the highest pitch or fullest degree of some exalted or excited condition. Usu. *in the ruff of*' (*sb.*⁶ 1). *OED* cites, among other examples, Gabriel Harvey's *Four Letters* (1592): 'in the ruffe of his freshest iollity'. Chettle is in fact describing two ballad-singers, who 'carowse out' lewd ballads. Clearly, these two 'parallel' passages have little in common.

Two other parallels depend upon single words: *hurly* (II, 236) and *innovation* (II, 216). Hand D's use of *hurly* by itself is indeed unusual, but *Kind-Heart's Dream* contains only the commonplace doublet, *hurley burley* (E4). Blayney notes that, if D's addition was written before 1596, it is 'among the first known occurrences with the specific sense of "insurrection" (*OED sb.* 1b, first example *1 Henry IV*, v.i.78, 'hurly burly Innovation'). But although the word clearly has this meaning in *More*, in *Kind-Heart's Dream* it refers to a fracas in a theatre (E4). Again, the similarities between the passages hardly compel the hypothesis of direct influence.

A comparable dissimilarity of context affects another parallel:

> . . . they breed sore eyes and tis enough to infect the
> Cytty wt the palsey   (II, 132–3)

. . . They that intend to infect a riuer poison the fountaine, the Basiliske woundeth a man by the eie, whose light first failing the body of force descends to darknes.

These Basilisks, these bad minded monsters, brought forth like vipers by their mothers bane, with such lasciuious lewdnes have first infected London the eie of England, the head of other Cities,

(*KHD*, C1^v)

The *OED* gives other examples of *eye* used figuratively, 'Applied to a city, country, province, etc.' (*sb.*[1] 3e) and in *Pierce Pennyless* – entered in the Stationers' Register on 8 August 1592 – Nashe described London as 'the fountain whose riuers flow round about England' (D3^v).[39] Chettle had clearly read Nashe's pamphlet, for his own derives from it, and as both passages refer to 'ballad singers' (*KHD*, C1) and 'Ballat-makers' (*PP*, D3), it seems likely that Nashe's image lies behind Chettle's. As for the image of the basilisk, it is, of course, a literary commonplace, and although Shakespeare never speaks of its effect as venomous, others do: 'O, that it were the basseliskies fell eye, / To poyson thee' (Henry Porter, *Two Angry Women of Abingdon*, l. 121). The basilisk was, after all, a serpent. Moreover, as early as 1549 writers were figuratively comparing evil influences in the body politic to basilisks (*OED*, *sb.* 2). But Chettle, while drawing throughout this passage on a series of conventional images, seizes upon the basilisk here for a very particular and obvious reason: for the 'bad minded monsters' he is upbraiding are 'ballad singers', and more particularly the printers who print their lewd ballads. Readers thus take infection through the eye; London, moreover, is the 'eye' of England; these ballads therefore, by a natural progression, 'infect' the whole country. In its context, Chettle's image is self-explanatory, and no influence from *More* need be suspected. What is unusual about the passage in *More* is the conjunction of 'sore eyes' with 'palsey' (which recurs in *Troilus and Cressida*, v.i.19–20) and the unparalleled, apparently ludicrous claim that such diseases are caused by the parsnip.[40] Neither of these elements recurs in *Kind-Heart's Dream*.

Finally, Blayney draws attention to 'a very interesting group of parallels at the end of the cluster D [F1, l. 25-F1^v, l. 12], where sandwiched between a near-quotation of Lincoln's bill of wrongs (*Moore*, fol. 3b) and a clear echo from More's "Nature hath sundry mettalles" speech (fol. 19a), appears a "bestiary" commonplace which may well have been suggested by a combination of an Aesop allusion in the Council debate (fol. 17) and Shakespeare's "men lyke ravenous fishes" image (ll. 207–10)' (pp. 183–4).[41] Only one of these four alleged links with *More* occurs among the additions; consequently, only it is of value in dating Hand D's contribution. Blayney admits that Chettle's image is commonplace; the unusual element in *More* is Hand D's specification of 'ravenous fishes', an emphasis memorably exploited in Shakespeare's acknowledged work but not present in *Kind-Heart's Dream*. Consequently, the one link with Hand D seems to me unreliable evidence of D's influence on Chettle's pamphlet. Nor do the other cited 'parallels' convince me of any link between the play and the pamphlet.

Given Blayney's contention that D's 'ravenous fishes' influenced Chettle, it seems surprising that he does not mention Chettle's use of the identical phrase in *The Tragedy of Hoffman*:

> woold shark on you and men lyke ravenous fishes
> woold feed on on another   (II, 209–10)
>
>   I think these woods and waters are
> common wealthes . . .
> . . . there lives vpon the earth more beasts
> With wide devouring throates, then can bee found
> Of rauenous fishes in the Ocean:
> . . . the Whale has a wide mouth
> To swallow fleeting waters, and poor fish,
> But we have Epicures and Cormorants,
> Whom neyther sea, nor land can hardly serve   (*Hoffman*, 34–5, 41–3, 45–9)

This is, I believe, a closer parallel with D's addition than anything in *Kind-Heart's Dream*: within a brief passage the phrase 'ravenous fishes' is juxtaposed with comparisons of the sea to a commonwealth and of human with marine omnivores.

Striking as it is, this isolated parallel in *Hoffman* is less important than a clutch of resemblances between 3.1 of *Hoffman* and More's quelling of the riot. John Jowett, *Hoffman*'s most recent editor, notes that 'Like More, Hoffman interposes himself between ruler and rebels and prevents the retribution of authority in the latter by addressing them, persuading them to abandon their action. He uses part of More's argument: that if the rebels surrender they will benefit from the clemency of the prince (who is compared with God in *Sir Thomas More* as he is implicitly compared with Christ in *Hoffman*), but by failing to do so, the rebels will inevitably bring retribution upon themselves'.[42] Hoffman appeals to the Duke to pity

> Those silly people, that offend as babes,
> Not vnderstanding, how they doe offend
> And suffer me chiefe agent in this wrong,
> To plead their pardons with a peacefull tongue . . .   (1210–13)

He then turns to the rebels:

> O I beseech you save your lives and goods . . .
> This act of yours by gathering to a head,
> Is treason capitall, and without grace
> Your lives are forfeit to extreamest law . . .
>   cast your weapons downe,
> And arme your selves with mercy of your Prince
> Who like a gracious shepheard ready stands
> To take his lost sheepe home in gentle hands.   (1249, 1255–7, 1261–4)

Moreover, as in the scene in *More*, the cause of the riot is 'a stranger', 'an arrant Alien', 'a mere peregrination' (1218, 1239, 1240).[43] The crowd is also similarly characterized. The speakers make the grounds of the insurrection ludicrously comic; the text refers to their 'garlike-breath' (1191); when offered pardon they first refuse (1215–25); Hoffman asks 'but heare me' and the leaders of the crowd urge their followers to listen (1244–6); after his speech one responds 'Mas he saies true' (1258).

In combination the links between D's addition and Chettle's play seem too numerous and striking to arise from coincidence. Since *More* was never published, and *Hoffman* only published in 1631, normal literary influence cannot explain it, either.[44] Even if Chettle wrote the original scene that Hand D revised, it is difficult to believe that D's revision followed its original either in its portrayal of the crowd or in so many of its verbal details. Even if it did, why should Chettle echo so vividly a passage he had written a decade before? On 29 December 1602 Henslowe paid Chettle five shillings 'in parte of paymente' for *Hoffman*; since a completed play would have been worth £6, the payment of only $\frac{1}{24}$ of the full amount suggests that Chettle was probably not too far advanced on the play. Henslowe's records become increasingly scanty from this point, until they stop completely in March 1603, and the play is not again mentioned; but it seems fairly reasonable to suppose that it was completed in 1603 or early 1604. It therefore appears that at some time between December 1602 and spring 1604 Chettle was strongly influenced by one of the additions to *Sir Thomas More*, and since he contributed to those additions himself it would be most logical to suppose that the additions were written during this time. The evidence that Hand D influenced Chettle in 1603–4 seems, to me at least, better than the evidence that he did so in 1592.

The internal evidence of the additions themselves strongly suggests that they date from the early seventeenth century. D.J. Lake has shown, on the basis of stylistic evidence, that Dekker's contribution must date from 1600 or after.[45] Although Chettle's addition is metrically more regular than we might expect from *Hoffman*, 'the verse . . . shows a facility and control that do not suggest its author is at an experimental stage of his career. Moreover, [Chettle] is entrusted with the alteration of an important and by no means easy scene'.[46] This was the opinion of Harold Jenkins half a century ago, in the only book-length critical study devoted to Chettle, and Chettle's role in the alterations has since been dramatically increased by Blayney's suggestion that, on the basis of handwriting, Chettle was responsible for many of the cuts.[47] Although Chettle's addition remains more difficult than Dekker's to date, such considerations do reinforce the parallels in *Hoffman*, in suggesting that Chettle's engagement with the additions occurred in the period of his artistic maturity.

For two of the playwrights who helped to reshape *More*, Chettle and Dekker, independent internal evidence dates the additions after 1600. For Heywood no such internal evidence is available: Heywood's works have received relatively little scholarly scrutiny in this century, and we are as yet in no position to judge their dates of composition on the basis of internal evidence. But Heywood was probably born between 1573 and 1575, probably entered Pembroke College, Cambridge in 1591, and probably came to London only after the death of his father, in 1593.[48] Since plague closed the London theatres for all but a few weeks between June 1592 and

June 1594, this would hardly have been an opportune time to establish himself as a playwright. His earliest extant work, and his earliest connection with London, is probably *Oenone and Paris*, by 'T.H.', entered in the Stationers' Register on 17 May 1594, and described in its preface as 'the first fruits of my indeuours and the Maiden head of my pen'.[49] Not until 14 October 1596 is there any record of Heywood as a playwright.[50] We can thus hardly rule out, as Chillington peremptorily does, Heywood's authorship of B's additions in the first half of 1595. Any date earlier than June 1594 seems to me relatively unlikely; but this is admittedly a matter of judgement. Of extant plays unquestionably by Heywood, only *The Foure Prentises of London* (printed 1615) can be confidently dated in or before 1600.[51] Almost by definition, then, if B is indeed Heywood it will be difficult or impossible to date his contribution on internal evidence alone.

By contrast, the fourth hand, even more than Chettle's and Dekker's, can be confidently dated on the basis of internal evidence; indeed, for the fourth hand the internal evidence is various and overwhelming. MacD. P. Jackson has recently shown that, if Hand D is by Shakespeare, then the linguistic evidence points to it having been composed shortly after the turn of the century.[52] E.K. Chambers pointed out, decades ago, that the versification of D's portion suggests a late date, and Lake confirms this: feminine endings, run-on-lines, speeches concluding with a half-line, alexandrines, and unsplit lines with pauses all occur in frequencies associated with Shakespeare's early seventeenth-century plays.[53] MacD. P. Jackson also demonstrates that the distribution of pauses within verse lines clearly places Shakespeare's addition in the period from *Twelfth Night* (1601–2) to *Macbeth* (1606).[54] J.M. Nosworthy argued that the vocabulary points to the same period; Jackson has now put this vocabulary evidence on a more systematic and objective foundation, capable of mathematical evaluation, which demonstrates a statistically significant association with the group of plays from *As You Like It* (1599) to *Timon* (1604–5).[55] Hand D's addition has predictable links with crowd scenes throughout Shakespeare's career (*Contention, Julius Caesar, Coriolanus*). But if we ignore such parallels, which are dictated by subject matter, then R.W. Chambers's impressive analysis of sequences of thought and imagery in D's addition found the most impressive Shakespearian parallels in *Hamlet, Troilus and Cressida, Othello*, and *Lear*.[56] The two closest verbal parallels between the additions and Shakespeare link *More* with *Othello* (1603–4) and *Coriolanus* (1607–9).[57] More's argument with the crowd takes the rhetorical form of a special case of *comparatio* in which the hearer is placed in the position of the accused; the most emphatic and clearest examples of this argument in Shakespeare occur in *Measure for Measure* (1603–4), where both Isabella and Escalus direct it at Angelo.[58]

A more extensive stylistic test of my own points to the same conclusion. This 'colloquialism-in-verse' test, which I document and describe in greater detail elsewhere, depends upon Shakespeare's use of a whole series of contractions and colloquial or poetic forms, each of which individually shows a strong correlation with the basic outline of the known chronology, but which occur much more frequently either in the plays after 1600, or in those before 1600.[59] All the occurrences in the verse, within a play, of features which occur more often after 1600 (*th'*, *t'*, *'em*, *'ll*, *'rt*, *'re*, *'d*, *'ld*, *'lt*, *'st*, *'ve*, *I'm*, *'as*, *this'*, *'a'*, *ha'*, *o'*, *'s*, *has*, *does*) are added together; from this figure is subtracted the total number of occurrences in verse of features which occur most often before 1600 (third person singular verbs ending in -*eth*, syllabic *ed*, disyllabic -*ion* and other obsolescent syllabic licences in individual words). The resulting total is then divided by the number of words of verse in the play. This test gives all the plays written before 1600 (i.e. all those up to and including *Henry V*, *Julius Caesar*, and *As You Like It*) negative values; all those after 1599 have positive values. Here is the relevant section of the chart:

Henry V	−.23
Caesar	−.16
As You Like It	−.01
Hamlet	.52
Troilus	.18
Twelfth Night	.23
Hand D	.31
Measure	.52
All's Well	.81
Othello	.83
Timon (Shakespeare's portion)	.86
(Middleton's portion)	1.81
Lear (Q)	.85
Macbeth	1.01
Antony	1.06
Pericles	.51
Coriolanus	1.57

Once we have taken into account the well-established suspicions of collaboration in *Timon* and corruption in *Pericles* (suspicions which this test reinforces), the regularity of this pattern, and its general agreement with other evidence for the dating of individual plays, can hardly be ignored.

Our only certain evidence of the dating of most of the early plays is Francis Meres's 1598 list; no play named by Meres has, by this test, a value higher than −.06. Likewise, no play which can be or has been dated in or before 1595 has a value higher than −.06. This test not only clearly places Shakespeare's alleged additions after 1600, as do all the others; it also provides a specific point for the play's composition, in a continuum which agrees remarkably well with the accepted chronology of the canon. On this scale, Shakespeare's contribution to *More* was written after *Twelfth Night* and *Troilus* (1601–2) but before *Measure for Measure* (late 1603–4). This conclusion exactly corresponds with the entirely independent evidence that Chettle was influenced by the additions to *More* between December 1602 and spring 1604. By contrast, as with all the other independent internal evidence, this stylistic test makes it extremely improbable that Shakespeare could have written Hand D's addition at any time before 1595.

It must be emphasised that such internal evidence is our only basis for dating any of the additions. If only one such test were available, or if the tests conflicted with one another, it would be possible to dismiss them. But for all those authors where such internal evidence is available, that evidence points unequivocally to the first few years after 1600; the most precise indicators both point to 1603–4. The consistency of this evidence tends to weigh against Scott McMillin's suggestion, advanced elsewhere in this volume, that Hand D's addition might belong to the period of the play's original composition, and hence be unrelated to the other additions. Certainly D's addition does not fit easily with some of the others. On the other hand, neither does D's addition fit very well with the original play: it is in certain respects anomalous, however we construe it. Moreover, because the material which D's addition replaced is now lost, we cannot judge the relative casting requirements of the original and revised material: for all we know D, like the others, might have reduced the number of actors needed. Likewise, although the coincidence of watermarks between fols. 9 and 12 cannot prove composition at the same date, the coincidence does favour that supposition. On balance I do not see any reason to suppose that the additions date from two periods rather than one, although the possibility cannot be ruled out.

If Hand D is Shakespeare, then the independent evidence of six different metrical licences, of linguistic preferences, of vocabulary, of imagery, of exact verbal parallels, of rhetorical parallels, and of colloquialism in verse all point to the same period. Those who reject this evidence for the play's date must also reject the identification of Hand D with Shakespeare.

If a work is dated at a period when author X could not have written it, then either the date is wrong or the attribution is wrong. The internal evidence for dating the additions to *More* is entirely consistent. Those who date the additions earlier than this do so for one reason: as Jenkins says, summing up the orthodox view, 'if we accept the three pages as Shakespeare's, the conjunction of Hands D and C makes . . . a date after 1597 extremely difficult to credit'.[60] In other words, the attribution to Shakespeare is taken as a fact which must be accommodated in any conjecture about dating. But the attribution to Shakespeare is of course not a fact but a conjecture: it cannot be made the basis for rejecting all of the independent evidence which argues for a date after 1600. Indeed, the prime reason for accepting the identification of D with Shakespeare has been the variety and independence of the strands of evidence which support this identification. 'The real strength of the case for Shakespeare's authorship . . . rests, then, not on any single piece or kind of evidence but on the quite remarkable manner in which several independent lines of approach support and reinforce one another' (Evans, *Riverside Shakespeare*, p. 1684), so that 'the combination of resemblances outstrips any credible coincidence' (Jenkins, Greg, p. xxxviii). Exactly the same reasoning makes it impossible to ascribe to 'coincidence' the internal evidence for the date of the additions. Except for the palaeographical evidence – for which we have no basis for chronological judgements – all of the evidence which links the two passages to Shakespeare also puts them in the period 1600–5. If all of that evidence must be dismissed as misleading in respect to date, it can hardly be credited as reliable in respect to authorship. To reverse A.W. Pollard's dictum, 'If [the additions to] *More* can be proved [not] to be as late as 1599, I shall regard the date as an obstacle to Shakespeare's authorship so great as to be . . . fatal'.

The consistent internal evidence for a date of *c.* 1603 for the additions also resolves a fundamental problem in the history of the manuscript's development, a problem which Jenkins calls 'an enigma' and which Evans includes among those which are 'complex' and perhaps 'insoluble'. Tilney's comments on Munday's part of the manuscript would require the omission of something like a quarter of the play. But everyone agrees that 'the revisions do not meet his objections, and cannot have been designed to' (Jenkins, p. xxxix). Those scholars who would date the revisions before 1595 therefore face the considerable problem of explaining why the revisions do not meet Tilney's objections, and why anyone should have gone to the trouble of making minor dramatic improvements to a play which had been effectively disembowelled by the Master of Revels. This is the insoluble 'enigma', and various expedients have been offered, all involving some combination of naivete or disbelief or 'surprising optimism' on the part of the playwrights, or special relationships between the playwrights and the censor, or unusual undocumented implausible procedures.[61]

This entire problem disappears if the original play comes from 1592–5 and the revision from 1603–4.[62] As Pollard said,

after the Queen had wreaked this really savage revenge [in July 1595] . . . Henry VIII's clemency would inevitably be contrasted by the spectator with his daughter's cruelty, and the hope of mercy abundantly held out by More would inevitably be taken as implying that the same hope had been held out by the Lord Mayor (in 1595).[63]

But after March 1603 the Queen, with the Tudor line, was dead, and the executions in question were eight years old. It would have been perfectly reasonable to assume that the politically sensitive issue of anti-alien riots was no longer especially sensitive. It would also be reasonable to assume that Tilney might have forgotten about the original play, which he had read ten years before. In the interim he must have licensed hundreds of plays; if Henslowe's *Diary* is at all representative, Tilney might have seen at least a thousand plays between 1593 and 1602. In order to facilitate such oblivion it would be wise to prepare a new transcript of the play: it would be foolish to return the manuscript to him with his original comments still on it. It would thus be desirable, in any event, to prepare a new transcript. But it would also be desirable to alter the play. *Sir Thomas More* was, by now, probably ten years old, and Henslowe's play-factory regularly rehashed plays which were more recent than that. As others have recorded, the additions and alterations seem designed to make *More* a better play. But there might also be another, less honourable motive for revising the text: for if Tilney did vaguely remember having seen and rejected once a play about More, then the players could honestly claim that the play had been considerably revised. The original had been in Munday's hand; the new transcript, prepared for resubmission, would certainly not be, for Munday was not even one of the new collaborators. By such means the playwrights could discourage, as effectively as possible, any memory of the earlier play. Of course, the play is still basically the same, and Tilney *might* have remembered it; but even if he did, the grounds for objection in 1603–4 were no longer very pressing or serious. And if Tilney did not remember the earlier incident at all, so much the better.

Tilney may in fact never have seen the revised play at all, or the playwrights may have hoped that he would not. On 21 June 1603, Sir George Buc received the reversionary grant of the mastership of the revels. Exactly when Buc began to exercise any or all of the functions of the office we do not know, but he clearly assumed primary responsibility long before Tilney's death in 1610. He began to license plays, as Master, by 21 November 1606; his hand is present also in the anonymous manuscript play *Charlemagne*, which on the evidence of paper and topical allusions is usually dated in the first years of James I's reign. Even if Buc did not assume any of Tilney's functions until after 1603, the players and playwrights might have expected him to. They might also reasonably have anticipated a change in the Revels Office months before Buc's appointment was announced: so important a figure in the royal household might well be replaced by the new monarch. A new Master of the Revels would, of course, have no memory of the earlier submission of *More*. Consequently, even if the playwrights preferred not to risk resubmission to Tilney, in 1603 there must have seemed an excellent prospect that they would never have to.

The hypothesis that the revisions date from *c.* 1603 resolves all of the difficulties caused by the disregard of Tilney's objections. But it does not solve the problem of who revived the play. Scott McMillin, elsewhere in this volume, provides independent theatrical evidence that the additions date from 1603–4; he assumed that the Admiral's men were responsible, and he certainly demonstrates that they could have been. But an equally plausible case could be made for revival by the King's men. Burbage could have played the lead role as well as Alleyn; indeed, the lead role might originally have been written for Burbage rather than Alleyn. Both companies produced new plays on early Tudor themes early in the new century; Henslowe's companies appear to have presented more such plays, but that may simply be due to the fact that Henslowe's Diary supplies us with evidence of lost plays, whereas for the King's men we must depend solely upon the evidence of those texts which survived into print. Audiences at the Globe saw as many clowns as those at the Rose. Either company would have had an incentive for reducing the casting demands of the original play, and I doubt that the size of the two companies was very different. As happens in so many spheres of life, the two rivals tended to imitate one another. If one had a play about Sir John Oldcastle or Troilus and Cressida, the other soon acquired one. If one was successfully reviving plays from the previous decade, would the other ignore the commercial possibilities? When, after all, did Burbage stop (or start) playing Hieronimo? Given *More*'s probable origins with Strange's men, it could have descended to either Alleyn's company or Burbage's. Given the perhaps unresolvable dispute about the dating of the plot of *2 Fortune's Tennis*, Hand C could have belonged to Henslowe's operations only before 1597, or only after 1602. In either event, Hand C and Thomas Goodale conspicuously *cannot* be associated with Henslowe in the very years when Dekker, Chettle, and Heywood can (1597–1602). Even without the problems over the identity of Hand D, the evidence is inconsistent. Moreover, if McMillin and I are right in thinking that the revival belongs to 1603–4, then it dates from a period when Henslowe ceases to help us, when the documentary source dries up, and when consequently the detailed operations of both the Rose and the Globe are shrouded in equally impenetrable obscurity. In the current state of our ignorance I do not believe it is possible to arbitrate over which company revived the play. It seems best to assume nothing about theatrical provenance, and to let the internal evidence for Shakespeare's authorship of Hand D's addition stand or fall on its own merits.

This scenario is necessarily speculative and conjectural, but these limitations should not obscure the solidity of the foundations on which the scenario is built. The additions must be later than the rest of the play; all the internal evidence dates them after 1600; much of that evidence strongly suggests 1603–4; in 1603 there was a change of monarch and the prospect (or fact) of a change of censor. Moreover, these years saw a sudden boom in plays about the early Tudors. Shakespeare's company performed the anonymous *Thomas Lord Cromwell* between 1599 and 1602. In 1601 *Cardinal Wolsey* was such a success for Henslowe that a sequel was written later that year; the following autumn Henslowe had another Tudor success with *Lady Jane*, for which again there was a sequel. Chettle was deeply involved in all these Henslowe projects.[64] After his successes with Tudor chronicle plays in autumn 1601 and 1602, resurrecting *More* in 1603 makes excellent theatrical sense.

Finally, revision in 1603 helps explain Munday's complete absence from the revision – surely rather surprising, if he had just collaborated in writing the play. Henry Chettle's earliest appearances in Henslowe's *Diary* involved collaboration with Munday; in 1596 he wrote an epistle to Munday's translation of *Primaleon of Greece*, and in 1592 an epistle to Munday's translation of *Gerileon*, in which he refers to Munday as his 'good friend'. On the basis of twelve lines he added to the manuscript of *John of Bordeaux*, Chettle clearly began his playwriting career early in the 1590s, and had a particular fondness for chronicle plays;[65] there is, I think, nothing implausible in the suggestion that he had been a collaborator on the original play. Both Oliphant and Nosworthy concluded that Chettle had a hand in the original.[66] If he did, that would explain why the manuscript of an unperformed play remained in his possession, to be revamped by him (and others) perhaps as much as a decade later. After 1598, though Munday and Chettle continue to write for Henslowe, and to collaborate with other Henslowe dramatists, they only once again worked together (1601); moreover, in *England's Mourning Garment* (1603) Chettle calls on ten contemporary poets (including Shakespeare and Dekker), but does not even mention Munday. For whatever reasons, the erstwhile collaborators seem to have gone their separate ways. Hence, perhaps, Chettle's presence and Munday's absence from the additions.

Much about *The Booke of Sir Thomas Moore* remains a mystery. We cannot know the exact circumstances of the composition or production of either the original play or the additions to it. But so long as we acknowledge the limitations of our knowledge, they need not disturb us. What we do 'know', what at least we accept as hypotheses so probable that we may accord them the status of temporary facts, are: that Anthony Munday transcribed the original, and presumably wrote at least part of it; that Tilney objected to it; that Chettle, Dekker and two other playwrights wrote additions to it; that those two other playwrights seem most likely to have been Heywood and Shakespeare. Among these 'facts' I would include the conclusion that the additions were written after 1600, probably in 1603–4. These 'facts' might have a variety of causes, about which we can only speculate – but the need to speculate about the causes in no way diminishes the plausibility of the central propositions. In particular, speculations and deductions about the circumstances of the play's production cannot be made the criteria for dating the additions or identifying their authors. The place where does not predetermine the time when, or the man who.

NOTES

1 Carol Chillington, 'Playwrights at Work: Henslowe's, not Shakespeare's, *Book of Sir Thomas More*', *ELR*, 10 (1980), 439–79.
2 'Shakespeare's Hand Once More', *TLS*, (24 November and 1 December 1927), pp. 871, 908.
3 Since this essay was originally written Felix Pryor has claimed to discover just such a manuscript: see his *John Webster: The Duke of Florence* (auction catalogue: Bloomsbury Book Auctions, 20 June 1986) for a description, transcript, photographic reproduction, and discussion of the four pages of the Melbourne manuscript. Whatever its absolute merits, Pryor's case for Webster's authorship of the Melbourne manuscript is far stronger than Chillington's case for his authorship of Hand D's addition.
4 Chillington notes that Henslowe first mentions Chettle and Dekker in 1598–9 (p. 454). Dekker is first mentioned on 8 January 1598; but in Francis Meres's *Palladis Tamia* (entered in the Stationers' Register on 7 September, 1598) he is included among those 'best for Tragedie' – a reputation hardly likely to have been earned in a mere eight months. Chapman, also mentioned by Meres, had a phenomenal theatrical success as early as 12 February 1596 (*The Blind Beggar of Alexandria*); Jonson is first mentioned in July 1597. It would therefore be reasonable to assume that Dekker's career began no later than 1596–7. Whether it is reasonable to extend Dekker's career back to 1592, on the assumption that this popular and prolific writer left no traces of his presence for a full six years, seems to me rather more open to question.
5 Alfred Harbage, *Annals of English Drama, 975–1700*, rev. S. Schoenbaum (London, 1964). Dekker is also probably the author, in whole or part, of *The Merry Devil of Edmonton*: see the edition by W.W. Abrams (Durham, 1942), pp. 62–103.
6 For Webster's share in the additions, see G.K. Hunter's Revels edition (1975), pp. xlvi–liii, and D.J. Lake, 'Webster's Additions to *The Malcontent*: Linguistic Evidence', *NQ*, 226 (1981), 153–8.
7 *Henslowe's Diary*, ed. R.A. Foakes and R.T. Rickert (Cambridge: 1961), p. 199. For the interpretation of Chettle's agreement with Henslowe, see Harold Jenkins, *The Life and Work of Henry Chettle* (London, 1934), pp. 25–6.
8 Almost all scholars attribute to Heywood the anonymous *Edward IV*, entered in the Stationers'

Register on 28 August 1599 as 'lately acted by the right honorable the Erle of Derbye his seruantes'.

9 *Dramatic Documents from the Elizabethan Playhouse* (Oxford, 1931), *Commentary*, 130–7. (Statements about the other plots also derive from Greg; not everyone accepts Greg's conclusions.) Michael L. Hays, upon whose arguments Chillington draws extensively in challenging the palaeographical basis for Shakespeare's claim, has also urged that Hands C and D are only one hand, that of an unidentified playwright: see 'Watermarks in the Manuscript of *Sir Thomas More* and a Possible Collation', *SQ*, 26 (1973), 66–9.

10 *Henslowe Papers*, ed. Greg (Oxford, 1907), pp. 76, 84.

11 Cyrus Hoy, *Introductions, Notes, and Commentaries to texts in 'The Dramatic Works of Thomas Dekker'*, 4 vols. (Cambridge, 1980), III, 80–1.

12 *Henslowe's Diary*, pp. 204, 214–16.

13 See Emma M. Denkinger, 'Actors' Names in the Registers of St Bodolph Aldgate', *PMLA*, 41 (1926), pp. 100–1.

14 *The Profession of Dramatist in Shakespeare's Time, 1590–1642* (Princeton: 1971), p. 65.

15 Hoy, *Commentaries*, I, 191.

16 Ben Jonson, *Works*, ed. C.H. Herford, Percy and Evelyn Simpson, 11 vols. (Oxford, 1925–52), II, 3–5.

17 I.A. Shapiro, 'The Significance of a Date', *ShS*, 8 (1955), 100–5.

18 *Henslowe's Diary*, p. 320.

19 *The Elizabethan Stage*, 4 vols. (Oxford, 1923), III, 446.

20 *John a Kent and John a Cumber*, ed. Muriel St. Clare Byrne, Malone Society Reprint (1923), p. vi.

21 Harold Jenkins, 'Supplement to the Introduction', in Greg, p. xli; *John a Kent*, p. vii.

22 E.M. Thompson, 'The Autograph Manuscripts of Anthony Munday', *Transactions of the Bibliographical Society*, 14 (1915–17), 324–53.

23 Greg, *Dramatic Documents*, pp. 4–10; *Henslowe's Diary*, p. xi.

24 Bentley, *Profession of Dramatist*, pp. 114–17. Fletcher is the only dramatist of the four for whom there is no anomaly; but as Bentley says, in his case 'the evidence for date of production and original ownership is less complete than for Shirley or Brome' (p. 117) – or Massinger. Bentley is I think wrong in asserting that Fletcher's contractual relationship with the King's men began at the time of Shakespeare's retirement: see John Jowett and Gary Taylor, 'With New Additions: Theatrical Interpolation in *Measure for Measure*', forthcoming.

25 Bentley, *Profession of Dramatist*, pp. 118–20. Bentley acknowledges that only the third example looks at all like the contractual agreement Brome later signed; however, five months later Chettle was writing for Worcester's rather than the Admiral's men (Jenkins, *Chettle*, p. 26).

26 For an exception, see Thomas Merriam, 'The Authorship of *Sir Thomas More*', *ALLC Bulletin*, 10 (1982), 1–8. See also Scott McMillin's essay elsewhere in this collection.

27 Armin also says that the play '*perchaunce in part was sometime acted more naturally in the Citty, if not in the hole*' (the last word punning on 'whole' and the name of a debtors' prison). Even if this obscure passage does refer to earlier performances by some other company, the Chamberlain's/King's men acted not in 'the Citty' but the suburbs until they began using the Blackfriars late in 1609 or after. Nor does it seem likely that Armin himself had any connections with 'Citty' theatres prior to his association with the King's men. Armin's emphasis on the distinction between '*in part*' and '*in the [w]hole*' suggests that the latest performances were based upon a revised version of the play, a hypothesis independently supported by internal evidence. For the fullest discussion see *The History of the Two Maids of More-Clacke*, ed. Alexander S. Liddie (London, 1979), esp. 13–24.

28 In searching for such misreadings I have relied upon the collations of the Revels editions of *The White Devil* (rev. edn. London, 1966) and *The Duchess of Malfi* (London, 1964), both edited by J.R. Brown, on the Regents Renaissance Drama edition of *The Devil's Law-Case*, ed. Frances A. Shirley (Nebraska and London, 1971), and on *The Complete Works of John Webster*, ed. F.L. Lucas, 4 vols. (London, 1927).

29 'Shakespeare and *Sir Thomas More*', *RES*, 1 (1925), pp. 44–5.

30 See G. Sarrazin, 'Wortechos bei Shakespeare', *Shakespeare Jahrbuch*, 33 (1897), 121–65, and 34 (1898), 119–69; Alfred Hart, *Stolne and Surreptitious Copies: A Comparative Study of Shakespeare's Bad Quartos* (Melbourne, 1942), pp. 28–40, and 'Vocabularies of Shakespeare's Plays', *RES*, 19 (1943), 128–40; MacD. P. Jackson, *Studies in Attribution: Middleton and Shakespeare* (Salzburg, 1979), pp. 148–58.

31 Hays', 'Watermarks'. See Scott McMillin's essay, elsewhere in this collection.

32 Jenkins in Greg, p. xl.

33 *The Riverside Shakespeare* (Boston, 1974), p. 1684.

34 Simpson, '*The Play of Sir Thomas More* and Shakespeare's Hand in it', *The Library*, III, 8 (1916/17), 94–5; Bald, *ShS* 2, p. 52.

35 John Stow, *A Survey of London*, ed. C.L. Kingsford, 2 vols. (London, 1908), I, 20; G.B. Harrison, *An Elizabethan Journal, 1599–1603* (London, 1933), p. 317.

36 Before 'Lord' something at the beginning of the line has been crossed out, first by the scribe and again later in black ink.

37 *ShS*, 26 (1973), p. 183. Several years ago Blayney told me that he had come to share Proudfoot's reservations about the second half of the article.

38 See for instance *Rollo Duke of Normandy; or, The Bloody Brother* (By John Fletcher and others, *c.* 1617–19), 4.2.67: 'dip your wrist-bands,/(For ruffes you ha' none)'. Nashe speaks disparagingly of a newfangled 'Aldermans ruffe' (*The Unfortunate Traveller*, in *Works*, ed. R.B. McKerow, 5 vols. (Oxford, 1904–10; rev. edn. 1958), II, 300). Phillip Stubbes, after a scathing catalogue of varieties of elaborate ruff, concludes: 'Thus euery one pleaseth her self with her foolish deuices . . . euery one thinketh his own wayes best, though they leade to distruction of body and soule, which I wish them to take heed of'(*The Anatomy of Abuses*, ed. F.J. Furnivall, 2 vols. (London, 1877–82), I, 71).

39 *Works*, I, 193. On the same page Nashe includes 'merry sir *Thomas Moore*' among 'the chiefe pillers of our english speech' (I, 194).

40 Evans, *The Riverside Shakespeare*, p. 1687.

41 It may be simplest to quote in full the passage Blayney identifies as 'Cluster D':

> his monument, till Macke, Maw, Ruffe, Noddy and Trumpe, had beene no more vsde, than his charitie is felt. Pitie it is such Wolues are not shakte ot of sheeps cloathing. Elder times detested such extremitie: the Gospels liberty (howsoeuer some Libertines abuse it) giues no such license: by their auarice Religion is slandered, lewdnes is bolstered, the suburbs of the Citie are in many places no other but darke dennes for adulterers, theeues, murderers, and euery mischiefe worker: daily experience before the Magistrates confirmes this for truth. I would the hart of the Cittie were whole, for both within and without, extreame crueltie causeth much beggerie, Victa lacet Pietas, and with pietie pittie. Selfe loue hath exiled charitie: and as among beastes . . . (F1–F1ᵛ).

I am unable to pinpoint any parallel here with the 'Nature hath sundry mettalles' speech; from Lincoln's bill of wrongs the only relevant phrases are 'wherof proceedeth extreame pouertie to all the Kings subiects, that inhabite within this Cittie and subburbs of the same . . . crafts men be brought to beggerie' (ll. 81–2, 85). Chettle is complaining about landlords, not aliens.

42 '*The Tragedy of Hoffman*: An Edition' (unpublished Ph.D. thesis, University of Liverpool, 1983), p. 380. There are no known sources for Chettle's play, and while More's quelling of the mob is crucial to *More*, the insurrection in *Hoffman* is only loosely related to the plot.

43 Chettle puns on *arrant* in the senses 'notorious' and 'itinerant, nomadic' (*errant*).

44 On the traditional hypothesis, dating *More* before 1595, the play was never acted, which means that influence through performances or revivals would also be ruled out. But if the additions do date from *c.* 1603, then Chettle might have seen as well as read D's addition.

45 'The Date of the *Sir Thomas More* Additions by Dekker and Shakespeare', *NQ*, 222 (1977), 114–16. E.H.C. Oliphant, one of the first scholars to urge the identification of Hand E with Dekker, also

argued that 'The prose of E's addition is precisely that of part 2 of *The Honest Whore* 1604–5, and the characterization of Faulkner is distinctly reminiscent of that of Orlando Friscobaldo': 'Sir Thomas More', *JEGP*, 18 (1919), 229.

46 Jenkins, *Chettle*, p. 69.

47 Blayney, '*The Booke of Sir Thomas Moore* Re-Examined', *Studies in Philology*, 69 (1972), pp. 171–2, n. 8.

48 See Arthur M. Clark, *Thomas Heywood, Playwright and Miscellanist* (1931), pp. 1–7.

49 *Oenone and Paris By T.H.*, ed. Joseph Quincy Adams (Washington, 1943), pp. xxvi–xlv.

50 *Henslowe's Diary*, p. 50.

51 Chambers, *The Elizabethan Stage*, III, 341. Chambers's summary was written before the publication of G.E. Bentley's correction of Collier's documentary error in identifying Thomas Heywood 'a player' in Southwark records of 1590. (See *TLS*, 15 November 1928, p. 856.) Chambers therefore inclined to push the play, which Heywood says was written 'in my infancy of iudgement in this kind of poetry, and my first practice', to as early as 1592. The Epistle in which Heywood makes this statement cannot have been written earlier than 1610; if, as he says, he wrote the play 'some fifteene or sixteene yeares' before, the play can hardly be earlier than 1594–5 (and may date from 1599–1600). A date in the mid-1590s agrees perfectly with the evidence accumulated by Clark and Adams, dating the beginning of Heywood's London career *c.* 1594.

52 'Linguistic Evidence for the Date of Shakespeare's Additions to *Sir Thomas More*', *NQ*, 223 (1978), 155–6; 'Hand D of *Sir Thomas More*', *NQ*, 226 (1981), 146.

53 Chambers, *William Shakespeare: A Study of Facts and Problems* (Oxford, 1930), I, 509, n. 2. See also Lake, 'The Date'.

54 Jackson, 'Some Thoughts on the "Shakespearian" Additions to *Sir Thomas More*', forthcoming

55 Nosworthy, 'Shakespeare and *Sir Thomas More*', *RES*, 6 (1955), 12–25; Jackson, 'Some Thoughts'.

56 'Some Sequences of Thought in Shakespeare and in the 147 Lines of *Sir Thomas More*', *MLR*, 26 (1931), 251–80, and R.W. Chambers, *Man's Unconquerable Mind* (London, 1939), pp. 204–49. These expand upon his contribution to *Shakespeare's Hand*.

57 *Coriolanus*, 1.i.188, 'Would feede on one another' (II, 210, 'woold feed on on another'); *Othello* 1.iii.319–20, ''tis in our selues that we are thus and thus' (III, 1, 'It is in heaven that I am thus and thus').

58 I am grateful to John Velz for pointing out this parallel.

59 See my article on 'Canon and Chronology' in Stanley Wells, Gary Taylor, *et al.*, *William Shakespeare: A Textual Companion* (Oxford, 1987). Though published earlier, that article contains a revised version of the evidence presented here.

60 Greg, p. xlii.

61 For the latest example in a long line of such reconstructions, see G. Harold Metz, 'The Master of the Revels and *The Booke of Sir Thomas Moore*', *SQ*, 33 (1982), 493–5.

62 See Chambers's conjecture that '*Sir Thomas More* was laid aside when Tilney sent it back, and taken up later by new writers, with different literary notions from Munday's, in the hope that the political cloud had blown by and that Tilney might now be persuaded to allow the main original structure to stand' (*William Shakespeare*, I, 511–12). I suspect they hoped to deceive Tilney, not persuade him.

63 *Shakespeare's Hand*, pp. 24–5.

64 Jenkins, *Chettle*, pp. 236–7, 239–40, 241–4.

65 Jenkins, *Chettle*, pp. 248–9.

66 Oliphant, 'Sir Thomas More', pp. 226–35; Nosworthy, 'Shakespeare and *Sir Thomas More*', pp. 12–25. See John Jowett's thorough re-examination, elsewhere in this volume.

6

Henry Chettle and the original text of *Sir Thomas More*

JOHN JOWETT

When the handwriting of an addition to *Sir Thomas More* can be recognized as belonging to a particular dramatist, one may assume (unless the dramatist is reproducing lines from the original text) that he is the author of the passages concerned. Sometimes scribal features encourage such a belief: in particular, alterations which show the writer rethinking his material as he writes. The original text of *More* is another matter: its character is that of a fair copy, though it too was prepared by a dramatist, Anthony Munday. Munday was not, to our knowledge, involved in the extensive revision attributed to Chettle, Dekker, Heywood and Shakespeare, but his activity as scribe of the original text strongly suggests that he was involved in its composition. Elsewhere in this volume G. Harold Metz outlines the reasons why various scholars have suspected that Munday was not the sole author of the original text, and gives an account of the provisional authorship attribution first proposed by Oliphant and subsequently endorsed, with varying degrees of confidence and various modifications, by Jenkins, Bald, Partridge and Chillington (pp. 11–44). Oliphant identified three styles, one 'somewhat old-fashioned', the second 'much jerkier and less regular', and the third 'much finer and more impressive verse than either of the others'.[1] These three styles are said to belong to Munday, Heywood(?) and Chettle respectively. Oliphant divides the play as follows:

Scenes i–vii	:	Munday
Scene viii	:	Dekker or Munday
Scene ix	:	Heywood(?)
Scenes x–xiii	:	Chettle
Scenes xiv–xvii	:	Heywood(?)

He was disposed to include Dekker amongst the collaborators because he was also one of the revisers (though a similar deduction was not applied to Shakespeare). His criteria are obviously subjective and unverifiable. They are oriented towards verse, and have limited applicability to scenes mostly or entirely in prose. Furthermore, the most extensive prose passages are attributed to Munday, who is not thought to favour that medium in his dramatic work.[2]

Partridge appeared to present more concrete evidence for Munday and, more particularly, Chettle; he too was cautious about the case for Heywood.[3] His material is considered below in the context of the main body of the present work, an attempt to put the case for Chettle as part-author of the original text on a firmer footing. I am primarily concerned to distinguish between Chettle and the dramatist who has by far the best claim to be involved in writing the original text, Munday. A full investigation of the claims of Dekker, Heywood, and Shakespeare lies outside the scope of the present study. A positive claim can be made on Chettle's behalf without undertaking such an investigation, for some of the most telling evidence not only establishes material which is unlikely to have been written by Munday, but specifically points towards Chettle as its author. My approach to the authorship problem does not close the door on the other collaborators; it does, however, narrow its aperture.

It has been suggested that Henry Chettle's 'first scribbles' were published as early as 1579, two years after he was apprenticed as stationer. In that year the verse tract *The Lamentation of the Pope for the Death of Don John* was published, with the title-page attribution 'H.C.'. Celeste Turner Wright showed the significance of the fact that the work was licensed by the printer Charlewood, who also licensed an early work by Munday. Wright envisages the two young apprentice stationers turning to writing at an early age with the paternal help of Charlewood.[4]

From Henslowe's *Diary* we learn that Chettle collaborated with Munday on *The Death of Robert Earl of Huntington* (1598), *The Funeral of Richard Coeur de Lion* (with Drayton and Wilson, 1598); probably also on *Chance Medley* (1598), and *The Rising of Cardinal Wolsey* (1601). But in 1598 Francis Meres described Chettle as 'the best for Comedy amongst vs', which indicates that he must have been writing plays for some time before that date. In 1592 he supplied an epistle to the second part of Munday's translation *Gerileon*, addressing the author as his 'good Friend' (but falsely signing the epistle 'T.N.'). In the same year, in his pamphlet *Kind-Heart's Dream*, Chettle affectionately mocked Munday as 'Old Antony Now now', a singer of ballads. Both Chettle's literary activity (including the part he evidently played as revising editor or perhaps even author of *Greene's Groatsworth of Wit*), and his relationship with Munday demonstrably precede the Henslowe records.[5]

Munday was the senior partner in this relationship; he was also, on the (admittedly somewhat dubious) evidence of Francis Meres, 'our best plotter'. Professor Melchiori's essay in this volume shows how well-placed Munday would have been to secure access to the play's less readily-available source material, and how details in the play apparently recollect his time at the English College of Rome (p. 78). If *More* is collaborate in its original version, we may imagine Munday drawing together sources, plotting the play, and allocating work on it; after the text was assembled, he would scrutinize it with a view to consistency and coherence, then, perhaps still making minor alterations, transcribe the foul papers to create the extant text. In one instance we can see Munday making a fundamental revision which he added after transcribing his copy: the second version he supplied of the play's final lines. This revising activity, together with the initial fact of Munday's role as the scribe, the play's sources, the terms of Meres's praise, and perhaps too the seniority of Munday to any likely collaborator, indicate that Munday was in charge of the play, especially at the stages of its inception and its completion.

Authorship tests require control texts. There are two criteria for control texts for an attempt to distinguish Chettle's hand in the play from Munday's. The texts should be plays, and they should be generally accepted as of single authorship. Though both Chettle and Munday wrote prolifically, this leaves one extant text for each dramatist (I exclude Munday's *Downfall of Robert Earl of Huntingdon*, in which Chettle may have had a hand). Chettle's *Hoffman* was written in 1602–3, but survives only in the quarto of 1631: a badly-printed book evidently prepared from Chettle's foul papers (probably annotated in anticipation of preparing copy for a new promptbook some years after the original composition, or in the printing-house itself). The compositors were evidently inexperienced, but this has the advantage that they treated their copy with a naive conservatism. For example, it is unlikely that they seriously altered Chettle's forms of contractions. For Munday the control text is *John a Kent and John a Cumber*. Like the original text of *More*, *John a Kent* is extant in a manuscript in Munday's handwriting. The similarities between the two texts are therefore bound to be more striking than the differences, and other hands in *More* correspondingly more difficult to detect. Spellings may be valueless. It is an open question how far Munday sophisticated what he may have regarded as other accidentals of his copy, the very kinds of feature that Partridge studied – though it would be astonishing if Munday consistently altered them all. But these complications are inherent to *More*, not to *Kent*, which is an ideal control in that it introduces the minimum number of variables. One such variable is date – multiply so, in that the date of neither play is firmly fixed. The complications of dating *More* are discussed elsewhere in this book. At the end of *Kent* Munday signs his name; the date which follows his signature is probably 1590, but it has sometimes – probably wrongly – been thought to read 1596. When Partridge observes an increase in the use of *has* and in the variety of contractions between *Kent* and the scenes in *More* he assigns to Munday, he is able to refer 'to the fact that Munday's contribution to *Sir Thomas More* was probably written seven years later than his *John a Kent*'.[6] The interval may not have been one of seven years, but most recent investigators agree that there was a gap of several years, and that *More* is the later manuscript.

The following search for evidence of Chettle's part in *More* begins with a survey of potentially and actually valuable material readily available from the work of other scholars; after a note on transcription errors, my own authorship tests follow.[7]

There is one passage of the original text of *More* – to be more accurate, a succession of short passages – which forms a special case and is excluded from the analysis. W.W. Greg noted that the author(s) of *More* modelled the interlude *The Marriage of Wit and Wisdom*, which is performed as a 'play within the play' in scene ix, on passages from *Lusty Juventus*, adding a Prologue taken from *The Disobedient Child*.[8] Here at least Munday is not originating the text (though he did need to adapt his copy). The lines taken more or less directly from the older interludes are: 1029–36, 1042–53, 1056–8, 1062–3, 1065–7, 1072–8, 1085–9, 1093–1101 and 1104–8, a total of 534 lines. Their inclusion would go some way towards confusing the indications of the scene's authorship.

Partridge and Chillington

Had Partridge had access to a concordance he would have been less confident about following Oliphant in assigning scenes x–xiii to Chettle. This may readily be illustrated by considering material he put forward in support of Chettle's claim to these scenes.[9] Upon examination, his analysis of 'Chettle' forms proves all but valueless. The following table samples Partridge's forms accredited to Chettle in scenes x–xiii by taking the first entry under each of his grammatical classifications of forms. The first and second columns are from Partridge; the third provides comment on the limitations of each entry.

Articles: *The*	1542 th'other	Also: 416 th'enforced (scene iv), 563 th'appeaser (vi), 756 th'imperfect (viii), 834 th'offenders (viii) *Th'other* is itself found in *Kent* but not in *Hoffman*, though Chettle twice contracted *the* to *th'* in his play.
Prepositions: *To*	1247 t'appeare	Also 853 t'abuse (viii)
Adverbs	1224 oft	One other instance in scenes x–xiii; eight instances elsewhere
Auxiliary verb: *Will*	1264, etc. weele	Seven instances in scenes x–xiii; 16 instances elsewhere
Verb 'to be': *Is*	1611 ther's	The only instance in scenes x–xiii; 11 instances elsewhere

In other cases, such as the spelling *bin, yond* as opposed to *yon*, and *a one* as against *an one*, the 'Chettle' form is the only one found in the play. With the supposed preference for *whilste*, rather than *while*, there is actually an equal number of *while* and *whilste*, both in scenes x–xiii and in the play as a whole. *Wast* as 'third person singular' pronoun would be singular indeed; it is actually second person in the instance Partridge cites; the same form is also found at l. 458 (scene v). *Does*, rather than *doth*, promises to be distinctive, but is found twice in scenes x–xiii (ll. 1332 and 1434; scenes xi and xiii) and three times elsewhere (ll. 651, 1018 and 1122; scenes vii and ix (2)).

Either much of the evidence fails to discriminate, or Chettle's hand is more widely spread than Partridge supposed. However, the following are worth noting: (1) *Twixt* clusters in scene xiii (3 instances); the only other occurrence is in scene x. (2) *Nere* also clusters heavily in scene xiii, with eight out of twelve occurrences found here. Other scenes with this contraction are vi, vii, xi, and xiv (one each). (3) Three out of five instances of *yond* are in scenes x and xiii; the other two are in scenes vi and viii. (4) Of six occurrences of *for to*, three are in scene xiii;

other instances are in scenes vi, x and xi. Despite Partridge's somewhat random information, he established that some forms are concentrated particularly in scenes x and xiii. But Partridge's attribution of scenes x–xiii alone to Chettle is demonstrably insecure. Even the clustering features are found elsewhere, in particular in scene vi.

Nevertheless, Chillington assigns the same scenes as Partridge to Chettle (with the exception of the second half of scene xiii), using different criteria. She describes Chettle's addition to the play as characterized by its regularity, its light end-stopping, its tendency to avoid feminine endings, and its frequent use of an inverted first foot, features which give the passage a 'ceremonial' quality. Readers of *Hoffman* will recognize this quality, but will recognize it as only one of a range of stylistic effects: indeed some passages in that play would be better described as rugged.[10] As for the metrical features, neither the recurrence of inverted first feet nor feminine endings establishes a sufficiently strong pattern of contrast to be significant.[11]

Blayney's Parallels

In attempting to date *More*, Peter W.M. Blayney found a number of parallels between the Hand D addition and Chettle's only prose work, *Kind-Heart's Dream*.[12] Blayney drew attention also to a passage in *Kind-Heart's Dream*, towards the end of his 'Cluster D' which ends at sig. F4, which, he claims, is in succession reminiscent of Lincoln's bill of wrongs (scene i), *More*'s 'Nature hath many mettalles' speech (xiii), and the 'bestiary' imagery in scene x. Of these, the only convincing parallel is the 'bestiary' image:

> As in the morrall hunting twixt the Lyon,
> and other beastes force ioynd
> frighted the weaker sharers from their partes.   (*More* ll. 1197–9)

as among beastes the Lyon hunteth the Wolfe, the Wolfe deuoreth the Goate, and the Goate feedeth on mountaine hearbes: so among men, the great oppresse the meaner . . .   (*KHD* p. 46)

Austin's Chettle-favoured Words

In his study of the authorship of *Greene's Groatsworth of Wit*, Warren B. Austin records a considerable number of computer-assisted tests.[13] Most of these cannot be repeated on other texts without similar extensive use of computer facilities, including computer concordances of the works of the authors concerned. One test, however, may simply be applied to *More*. Austin establishes a list of words particularly frequent in Chettle as compared with Greene. None of these words necessarily distinguishes between Chettle and Munday, but it is possible that some do so. The words are: *admire, censure, beseech, however, hurt, immediate, preserve, remedy, reprove, rude*. These words occur more than twice in only one scene of *More*: scene i, which has three instances of *hurt* and two of *remedy*, giving a total of five occurrences. *Hurt* and *remedy* may therefore effectively discriminate between Chettle and Munday. *Hurt* also occurs once in scene ii. But Austin's list of Chettle-favoured words gives no more than a dubious indication of Chettle's possible authorship of scene i.

Errors of transcription

For the most part, those in *More* are common mistakes that can occur whether or not the scribe is as familiar with the text as its author would be. The most famous exception is *fashis* at l. 1847. Greg believed that this meaningless form was a representation of copy *fashiõ*, and so indicated that Munday did not understand his copy. MacD. P. Jackson pertinently objected that the required word could be inferred from the context, and that Munday is unlikely to have made a letter-for-letter transcription of what he believed he saw it if resulted in nonsense. He conjectured that Munday simply anticipated the initial letter of *sits* (though as this required an entirely different form of letter it is perhaps as likely that the end of the word was anticipated).[14] *Fashis* is not therefore good evidence for copy in another hand.

Scene viii presents a reading more likely to arise from misinterpretation of copy. At l. 757 the second syllable of *Lordship* is interlined. The original error *Lord* is best explained as an inadequate representation of a copy abbreviation 'L.' or 'Lo'.[15] Munday is likely to have known instantly what was signified if he originally wrote such an abbreviation. The interlineation indicates that Munday probably did not write this part of the text (though naturally it gives no indication of who actually did).

Asseverations, Contractions, and Other Discriminants

As there is low incidence of most individual forms, only those which occur in one control text but not the other are admitted as potential discriminants.[16]

Asseverations in *More* and *Hoffman* but not *Kent*

	More (scenes)
Bodie of me	ii
God (*with* morrowe, *etc.*)	xiii(2)
God saue	vii(4), viii
Oh God	i, vii, xi, xiii(4)
yfaith	i, ii(2), vii

Asseverations in *More* and *Kent* but not *Hoffman*

More (scenes)

bir Lady	i, ix
for Gods sake	i
God blesse	xi, xii, xv(2)
gramercies	ix, xiii
in faith	xi
on my faith	ii

These asseverations all provide potentially good evidence: they are resistant to changes in transcription, and the more apparently trivial ones are grouped in opposing pairs (*yfaith*/*in faith*; *God saue*/*God blesse*). Out of the nine scenes in which they occur, five have evidence pointing only one way, and another two show a strong preference. The evidence is particularly strong for Chettle in scenes vii and xiii, and reasonably strong for Munday in scene ix.

Other Discriminants in *More* and *Hoffman* but not *Kent*

More (scenes)

am/um ('em)	xiv
does	vii, viii, ix(2), xi, xii
hee's	iii, v, vii, viii(3), ix, x, xiv
I (ay)	i(2), ii(3), iv, v, viii, ix(2), xiii
Ide	ii, ix
on't	ii, v
th'art	ii
that's	ii(2), vii(2), viii, ix, xi(2)
theyle	ix
to't	ii
twas	ix, xi, xv
twill	v, viii, ix, xiii(2)
twould	vi
whilste	i, viii, x, xi, xiii, xvii
who's	x, xi
yes	viii(2)
you'r	ii

Other Discriminants in *More* and *Kent* but not *Hoffman*

More (scenes)

beside	ii
if't	ii
oft	ii, vii, viii(2), ix, x(2), xi, xiv, xvii
tane	xiv
th'other	xiii

137

Most of these items are practically valueless, as indicated by their complete failure to discriminate in any meaningful way. *Beside* is unopposed by any occurrences of *besides*; similarly – and puzzlingly, in view of Munday's preference for the form in *Kent – yea* is not found in *More*. It seems that *whilste* and *does* are scattered at random; in relation to each other they establish neither an opposition nor significant overlap. The remainder consists of common contracted forms which almost any writer of the period might introduce casually as required.[17]

Rhymed Words

Both Chettle and Munday are fond of rhymes. Their general prevalence in *Hoffman* and *Kent* makes the mere fact of rhyming couplets a useless indicator. But both dramatists repeat their more favoured rhymes, and although there is a certain amount of overlap between the rhymes used, the rhyming habits of the two dramatists are sufficiently distinct, and the samples involved sufficiently large, for the rhymes in *More* to be tested for links with each dramatist. The test has its limitations – most obviously it cannot be applied to prose scenes – but a remarkably consistent picture begins to emerge.

For the purposes of the test I compared pairs of rhymed words, not the rhyme elements themselves. Homophones counted as a single form. Plurals and the *-s* verbal inflexions were treated as the root form, but prefixes and suffixes were held to establish separate words. So *farewell* was not considered equivalent to *well* (though *well* was considered a separate element in *fare-ye-well*). The order of the rhymed words was regarded as irrelevant and no attention was paid to whether they fell in couplets or not. A positive link was recorded either when a rhyme in *More* occurred in one of the control plays but not the other, or when it was found in both plays but in one of them was counted over twice as often as in the other.

The test may itself be tested on Addition 1 to *More*, which is agreed to be in Chettle's hand. Of the rhymes in this passage the following occur in *Hoffman* and *Kent*:

Hoffman	*Kent*
death/breath (2)	
thee/mee (2)	thee/mee (1)
fall/all (4)	

A passage undisputedly written by Chettle has two rhymes found in *Hoffman* alone and one found more often in *Hoffman* than in *More*. By the criteria outlined above, the rhyme *thee/mee* would not be admitted as evidence of authorship, for the *Hoffman* count does not sufficiently exceed that for *Kent*. But by any criteria the test can be seen to work well, even for a passage of only 71 lines.

The Original Text's links with *Hoffman* and *Kent* are set out below. The count indicates the number of occurrences in the play under which the rhyme is listed, with the count from the other play (where there is one) added after a colon.

Scene	*Hoffman* links			*Kent* links		
	Line	Count	Rhyme	Line	Count	Rhyme
iii				355	1	alone/none
vi	492	2	breath/death			
	509	4	good/blood			
	529	1	kneele/steele			
	552	4	blood/good			
vii	679	3:1	hart/part			
				686	3:1	see/me
viii	764	3:1	parte/hart			
	772	2	grace/place			
				886	1	best/rest
ix				928	2	part/arte
	969	2	breath/death			
				998	3:1	prooue/loue
				1030	1	land/hand
				1070	2	walke/talke
	1119	2	hand/stand			
				1127	4	so/goe
x	1179	4	good/blood			
	1181	1	King/sing			
	1231	1	losse/crosse			
	1250	3:1	parte/hart			
				1280	2	too/doo
xi				1359	3	before/Moore
				1361	1	rest/best
	1374	4:1	all/fall			
xii	1386	3:1	hart/part			
	1409	1	you/adiewe			
xiii	1414	2	craues/graues			
	1423	3	rather/father			
	1485	3	earth/birthe			
	1515	1	well/hell			
xv	1721	4:1	fall/all			
xvi				1792	1	all/shall
xvii	1963	1	teare/feare			
				1974	3	more/before
	1981	1	teare/feare			

The first point to note is that, although *Kent* has over twice as many rhymes as *Hoffman*, *More*'s links are predominantly with Chettle's play. It does not automatically follow that Chettle wrote most of the play (the links can be broken down into six groups totalling less than 700 lines), but the inference that Chettle contributed to the play's verse is almost impossible to dismiss. Except for scene ii, the scenes not represented in this table are either short or are predominantly prose.

The linked rhymes fall in alternating clusters, and these clusters are clearly connected with the scene units. One scene gives ambiguous results (vii). In five scenes we have at least an indication of possible authorship (scenes iii, xi, xv, xvi, xvii), and in six scenes what appears to be a strong association between a scene and a dramatist: scenes vi (Chettle), viii (Chettle), ix (Munday), x (Chettle), xii (Chettle) and xiii (Chettle). The grouping in these scenes can scarcely be the product of coincidence. In five 'Chettle' scenes there are 38 links with *Hoffman* to five with *Kent*; two of these five would be explained if Munday contributed the last few lines of scene x (for example, the eight lines following the exeunt of Rochester and Palmer). Scene ix displays thirteen links with Munday to five with Chettle. But the author of scene ix may not be accountable for two of the five Chettle links: ll. 1119–20 may simply echo the rhyme at ll. 1066–7, which derives straight from *Lusty Juventus*.

'You' and 'Ye'

The forms used for the second person plural pronoun in the original text of *More* are of decided significance. The pronoun occurs regularly, and its forms fluctuate widely in their incidence from scene to scene. In *Kent* and *Hoffman*, Munday and Chettle establish contrasting preferences. Chettle uses *ye* just 24 times. In many scenes *ye* is absent, and in all scenes *you* outnumbers *ye* by well over three to one. *Ye* tends to concentrate in two consecutive scenes; elsewhere it is a relative rarity. Similarly, in Chettle's addition to *More* there are five instances of *you* to one of *ye*. Munday has a relative predilection for *ye*, using it 166 times in *Kent* as against 133 instances of *you*.

Such a predilection might naturally influence his transcription of material he did not originally write, so obscuring the usage of his copy.[18] In his transcript of *More* Munday writes 122 instances of *ye*: a high enough number to suggest Munday's hand, indeed a figure only surpassed in Lake's tables by *Kent* itself and Fletcher's plays. This total remains, in a text some 700 lines longer than *Kent*, markedly lower than the total for that play. On this evidence Munday's copy for *More* at least in part may have differed from his own practice, and in transcribing it he may have passed on some if not most of its forms. The inference is supported by Munday's practice in adapting his copy for *The Marriage of Wit and Wisdom*: the copy form is usually followed, but *ye* once becomes *you*, and *you* twice becomes *ye*.

The breakdown by scenes of occurrences of *you* and *ye* in *More* is as follows:

Scene	you	ye	you/(you+ye) as%
i	9	11	45
ii	25	27	48
iii	1	2	33
iv	1	4	20
v	4	3	57
vi	14	0	100

vii	11	2	85
viii	13	5	72
ix	24	30	44
x	8	0	100
xi	5	5	50
xii	3	4	43
xiii	23	2	92
xiv	5	1	83
xv	0	6	0
xvi	15	3	83
xvii	5	13	28

Scenes vi, vii, x, xiii, xiv, and xvi show an overwhelming preference for *you* which is most unlikely to originate with Munday. A more modest, but still strongly marked, preference for *you* is also found in scene viii. Scenes i, ii, v, ix, xi and xii are fairly evenly balanced. Surprisingly only scenes iv and xv markedly favour *ye*, though a preference is also expressed in scenes iii and xvii.[19]

Some of the fluctuation recorded here may arise from variation in practice according to the tone of a scene: one may suspect that *ye* was felt to be more informal, idiomatic or intimate. Certainly *ye* tends in *Hoffman* to be associated with either mad Lucibell or foolish Jerom and his companions, and there is considerable fluctuation from passage to passage in *Kent* itself. However, the discrepancy between *Kent* and the strongly-marked scenes in *More* is equally apparent if proportions of *ye* to *you* in *Kent* are divided into successive batches of (*ye*+*you*) totalling 30 in each batch; only one batch exceeds 54% *you* (the last 300 lines, which have 11 *ye* to 18 *you*, the latter therefore making 62% of the total). Despite Munday's transcription of *More* it has six scenes each with an incidence over 20% higher of *you* to (*you*+*ye*) than any batch of 30 (*you*+*ye*) in *Kent*; the average incidence of *you* in these scenes is 90% as compared with a peak of 62% in the anomalously high batch in *Kent*. Whereas the evenly balanced scenes may offer no indication of authorship, those where *you* strongly predominates are well outside the range expected of Munday, and are entirely consistent with Chettle's practices.

Parallels with 'Hoffman'

Individually some of the parallels offered below may have limited significance; cumulatively they provide a convincing indication of Chettle's authorship of several scenes, and more than a hint of his hand in some others. The parallels are of greatest value where they combine two or more factors such as vocabulary, image-patterns, and dramatic situation. One could scarcely gainsay that in writing the insurrection episode in *Hoffman*, Chettle was heavily influenced by the sequence of insurrection scenes in *More*. Some of the links might be explained as conscious or unconscious borrowings from another dramatist's work, but some of the detailed correspondences suggest the creative habits of an individual mind and therefore are not so easily dismissed. Moreover, the correspondences are by no means confined to the insurrection scenes in either play. Even taken in isolation, the parallels between *More* and *Hoffman* suggest that Chettle had a hand in the former play.

Scene i

Links of theme and vocabulary with the insurrection episode in *Hoffman* suggest that they share in their author. The rebels in both scenes revolt against *strangers*, and their *saucie presumption* (l. 33) in *More* compares with their *presumptuous hearts* (l. 1234) in *Hoffman*.[20] Interestingly, both scenes use a euphemistic sense of *tickle*: the bill against the strangers will *tickle* them (*More* l. 70), and Old Stilt praises himself as a *tickler* (*Hoffman* l. 1155). In both scenes there are references to eating bread: 'straungers eate the bread' (*More* l. 83), 'the bread of quiet eate' (*Hoffman* l. 1298). The cause of the insurrection is, in a sense, the same: in *More* the citizens rebel against the privilege of *Aliens* (ll. 83 and 90); in *Hoffman* Jerom, the legitimate but disinherited heir to the dukedom, leads '*a rabble of poore souldiers*' against Hoffman (disguised as Charles) who is thought to be 'an arrant arrant *Alien*' (l. 1239; my emphasis). When Doll has listened to the proposal to revolt on May Day, she says 'ther's my hand' (*More* l. 99); when Jerom has listened to Hoffman's proposals for peace, he says 'Giue me your hand of that' (l. 1277). Both scenes speak of *remedy* (*More* l. 89; *Hoffman* l. 1258) and of *confusion* (*More* l. 91; *Hoffman* l. 1243, which is not readily explicable as a consequence of the subject-matter as the word is a malapropism for *conclusion*). In *More, remedy* and *confusion* are rapidly followed by '*tis excellent* and *No doubt*; *Hoffman* has 'It's most expedient . . .Noe doubt his excellence will like that well' (Q '. . . excellence will life . . .', miscorrected during printing to '. . . kxcellence will lihe . . .') at the end of the insurrection sequence (l. 1329), and elsewhere ''tis excellent' (l. 663). The two phrases in *More* are perhaps common enough, but form part of a wider association of words and ideas (in both contexts '*tis excellent* is an ironic comment).

Scene ii

'And these embraces serue' (l. 239) is close to 'And this one sentence serues' (*Hoffman* l. 2185). The embraces facilitate crime; the sentence extenuates it.

Scene vi

The structural similarities between the part of this scene refurbished by Hand D and the insurrection scene in *Hoffman* are discussed by Gary Taylor (pp. 118–19). He concludes that in *Hoffman* Chettle recalled Shakespeare's addition. But the scene in its original form was probably his own. We do not know how much of it (if any) Shakespeare simply transcribed, nor how closely he followed the pattern of the original. But the last three lines of the episode are in the original text, and, in content though not language, they logically follow from the point where Shakespeare broke off. They also supply a fairly close precis to Hoffman's speech at ll. 1249–64. The stage direction at l. 476, 'they lay by their weapons', uses the same idiom as Duke Ferdinand's instruction that the rebels 'Lay by your vniust armes' (l. 1297). After the plea for mercy, More says, 'No doubt his maiestie will graunt it you'; as we have seen, in *Hoffman* the insurrection episode concludes with Hoffman, who plays an analogous role in quelling the rebellion, saying, 'Noe doubt his excellence will like that well'.

Scene vii

The repeated 'God saue the King', twice each at ll. 710 and 733, is formulaic, but as a reaction to a royal pardon for insurrection it recalls the rebels' 'God saue Duke *Ferdinand*' (l. 1299) and Old and Young Stilts' 'God saue Duke *Ferdinand* and Prince *Otho* (l. 1307). In both plays the first imprecation immediately follows the formal announcement of pardon, and in both is repeated a few lines later. As in scene vi and in *Hoffman*, it is the play's eponymous main character who intercedes for pardon. Line 710, spoken by 'All', has the stage direction 'flinging vp cappes'; earlier in the same scene of *Hoffman* Chettle calls for '*All on Ieroms side*' to '*cast vp their caps and cry a Ierom*' (l. 1187). Two brief passages show further particular similarities:

1 Sir Thomas Moore humbly *vpon his knee*,
    did begge the liues of all, since on his woord
    they did so gently yeeld. The King hath *graunted* it,
    and made him Lord high Chauncellour of England,
    according as he woorthily deserues.
    Since *Lincolnes* life cannot be had againe,
    then for the rest, from my dread *Soueraignes* lippes,
    I heere pronounce free pardon for them all.   (*More* ll. 702–9; emphases added except in l. 707)

                Soueraigne on my knees
    I beg your Highnes *graunt* to there request . . .
        Fer. True soule of honor, substance of my selfe,
    Thy merit wins the mercy . . .
    I pardon all . . .   (*Hoffman* ll. 1290–305; emphases added)

2 Surrey describes the King's mercy:

        which in the armes of milde and meeke compassion
        would rather clip you, as the loouing Nursse
        oft dooth the waywarde Infant . . .   (*More* ll. 77–9)

This may be set against Hoffman's account of Duke Ferdinand:

        And arme your selues with mercy of your Prince
        Who like a gracious shepheard ready stands
        To take his lost sheepe home in gentle hands.   (*Hoffman* ll. 1262–4)

The image is different, but the significance and emotional register are identical. It is decidedly significant to find *arme(s)* used contrastingly.

Hoffman does indeed appear to be the later play. *More* is following historical material, and the consistent ironic dimension in *Hoffman* represents a move to a more complex mode and so suggests an elaboration on an original. (Hoffman, the interposer for peace, is secretly the arch-villain.) Scene vii has links with other parts of *Hoffman* which do not look so premeditated. At l. 584, *More* has 'God for his pittie help these troublous times'; this just about conflates 'God for thy mercy! treason vpon treason' (*Hoffman* l. 1627) and 'Looke to your persons, these are dangerous times' (l. 1652) – lines located significantly closely to each other, but not in the insurrection episode.

Lincoln's death-speech may be little more than conventional platitudes, but has particular similarities with the death-speeches of Lucibell and Lodowick (*Hoffman* ll. 990–1008). More noteworthy is, at l. 666, 'heere I beginne this cuppe of death to thee'. Doll speaks figuratively of death by poisoning, but such a scene is enacted literally in *Hoffman*. At l. 1533 the distinctive use of *begin* (='toast'), which has no earlier citation in the *OED*, is again linked with the poisoning, again with the idea that both the beginner and the person toasted who next drinks from the *cup* will be poisoned: 'Heere cozen, will you begin to my father?'.

In Doll's next speech, she exhorts her companions 'cheerely Lads' (l. 682) which is followed three lines later by a mention of the *strangers*; in *Hoffman*, Mathias says 'Cheerely Prince *Otho*' (l. 773) five lines after a reference to *stranger Knights*. 'Casheere me' (*More* l. 877; *Hoffman* l. 476; also 'Casheere you' in the following line) may be a more significant parallel than it looks: Shakespeare, for example, has *cashier'd* just four times and *cashier* only once, and there without an object.

A striking comparable rhyme that does now show in the rhymed words test should also be mentioned: 'grace / . . . the outward place' (ll. 772–3), which finds an echo in 'grace / . . . the outward face' (*Hoffman* ll. 590–1).

Scene xiii

Four parallels deserve recording:
1 More's stoical speech opening the scene may be compared with lines addressed to, and then spoken by, the duchess Martha;

> sit good Madame, | lowe stooles
> vppon an humble seate, the time so craues,
> rest your good hart on earth, the roofe of graues.
> you see the floore of greatnesse is vneuen,
> the Cricket and high throane alike neere heauen. (*More* ll. 1413–17)

> Spread me a Carpet on the humble earth:
> My hand shall be the pillow to my head,
> This step my bolster, and this place my bed. (*Hoffman* ll. 1715–17)

Tis true, the wise, the foole, the rich, the poore
The fayre, and the deformed fall; their life turnes
Ayre: the King and Captaine are in this alike,
None hath free hold of life, but they are still
When death heauens steward comes, tennents at will.
I lay me downe, and rest in thee my trust, *(Hoffman* ll. 1734–9)

The passage in *More* has a linked rhyme which has already been noted. The closeness of thought and feeling between it and the lines from *Hoffman* are underlined by the vocabulary links: in particular *humble* and *earth* occur within two lines in *More*; the one actually qualifies the other in *Hoffman*.[21] The stage actions, in each case involving the play's most prominent woman, are closely analogous in their visual reinforcement of the poetic imagery. The property of low stools in *More* is exactly equivalent to the step in *Hoffman* for bringing the characters literally close to a symbolically-invested ground. Then the theme of spiritual equality is made manifest in lines of unmistakeable resemblance.

2 those were but painted dayes, only for showe, *(More* l. 1504)

shee's like a painted fire vpon a hill . . .
As all such strumpets are, Angell in shew, *(Hoffman* ll. 825–8)

Both images provide unpredictable variants on a commonplace idea. The repeated words *painted* and *show* find the same position in their respective lines.

3 tis *well,*
the *bell* (*earths* thunder) soone shall *toale* my *knell.*

(More ll. 1570–1; emphases added)

Nor layd the hallowed *earth* vpon thy lips,
Thou wert not houseled, neither did the *bells* ring
Blessed peales, nor *towle* thy funerall *knell,*
Thou wentst to death, as those that sinke to *hell;*

(Hoffman ll. 2030–3; emphases added)

Both passages emphasize that the death in question is premature.

4 Gramercies, freend *(More* l. 1588)
god-a-mercy friend *(Hoffman* l. 759)

Scene xvii

An interesting though not entirely conclusive parallel may indicate that Chettle was involved in the scene's final section: 'There is a thing within me, that will raise' (l. 1966), and 'there is a somewhat cries / Within me noe' (*Hoffman* ll. 1489–90). It is therefore relevant that in his fair copy Munday revised the play's concluding lines: this activity suggests (though not conclusively) that Munday was transcribing another writer's work.

'Hoffman' Vocabulary

A final test may not be quite as reliable as might be desired, as it operates on a smaller statistical basis than would be needed for conclusive results. Nevertheless, the results it gives are suggestive, and the test is therefore briefly reported.

The index to my thesis edition of *Hoffman* provided a convenient list of almost 500 words which may be expected to contain a high proportion of vocabulary distinctive to Chettle.[22] In order to filter the vocabulary, each word was checked against the Shakespeare concordance; those which occurred in Shakespeare over 20 times were eliminated. When these commoner words were filtered out, over half (278) remained. Each of the remaining words occurs in Shakespeare on average little more than once in every four plays.[23] The same limit of 20 determined the extent to which uninflected forms and plurals, inflexions and adverbial suffixes were taken as admissible roots and adjuncts of the word as it appeared in *Hoffman*; so, for example, if a plural in *Hoffman* occurred as a plural 18 times in Shakespeare, only that form was admitted, whereas if singular and plural totalled 18, both could be included. The words were then sought in *More*. Their occurrences are as follows:

Scene	No. of words	Words/100 ll
i	6	5.7
ii	2	1.0
iii–v	0	0
vi	5	5.3
vii	8	4.7
viii	1	0.7
ix	2	0.7
x	3	2.4
xi	1	1.0
xii	0	0
xiii	2	1.0
xiv	1	1.4
xv	2	3.5
xvi	3	2.2
xvii	3	2.3

The result for scene xv is perhaps based on too low a count for it to be significant. Otherwise scenes i, vi , and vii clearly stand out from the others as having a high incidence of *Hoffman* vocabulary. This provides at least a pointer to the authorship of those scenes, though the narrowness of the word sample means that the results may not be entirely trustworthy.

Summary

The relationship between the results from the various tests and investigations outlined above may be established most economically in the following table, where they are ranked according to the quality and quantity of evidence they give. C is

Chettle and M Munday; the lower-case letters indicate where there is a reasonable though not entirely convincing indication of authorship.

Aggregated Indications of Authorship

Scene	1	2	3	4	5	6	7	8	9	10	11	12	13	14	15	16	17
1 Rhymed words			m			C		C	M	C	m	C	C		c	m	c
2 You/ye			m	M		C	C	c		C			C	C	M	C	m
3 Parallels (*Hoffman*)	C	c				C	C	c					C				
4 Asseverations		c				C	c	M			m	C		m			
5 *Hoffman* vocabulary	c					c	c										
6 Partridge's evidence									C			C					
7 Parallels (*KHD*)											c						
8 Errors of transcription											c						
9 Austin's Chettle-favoured words		c															

Tests 1, 3, 4, 5, 7, and 9 are specific to Chettle in that they go beyond establishing crude binary oppositions; tests 1 and 4 are similarly specific to Munday. It is not entirely surprising that Chettle is the more successfully demonstrated.

The general pattern is of impressive consistency between the different kinds of evidence, 'objective' and impressionistic, dense and dispersed, alike. There are obvious exceptions to this assertion. The short scenes yield an indequate amount of information. There are, in addition, contradictory suggestions of authorship for four scenes. Here a pattern emerges: these scenes are four of the last six in the play (scenes xii, xv, xvi, xvii; scene xiii provides a stark contrast). Furthermore, the quantity of evidence for Chettle is less than in almost all earlier pro-Chettle scenes (only scenes ii and xv are comparable). However, the distribution does effect a contrast with the admittedly weakly-marked pro-Munday scenes earlier in the play (scenes iii, iv, ix, xi): if it is true that the aggregated tests give a less adequate profile of Munday than of Chettle, it remains doubtful that the 'mixed' scenes should simply be accounted Munday's – especially as some of the tests which suggest otherwise provide positive pointers to Chettle in those scenes. Similarly, a third hand cannot be ruled out, but a more convincing explanation would be that the scenes are (whatever the processes of composition involved) of mixed authorship.

With the exception of scene ix, the scenes for which there is a heavy accumulation of evidence are Chettle's. One may hesitate to pronounce on scene ii, but to Chettle may be attributed, with little fear of contradiction, scenes i, vi, vii, viii, x, and xiii.

A comparison of tone, structure, and style of scenes xiii and xi leaves a strong if unquantifiable impression that they share a single author, and the rhymes in scene xii testify that Chettle could have written that scene too. It does therefore remain possible that, as Oliphant proposed, Chettle wrote scenes x–xiii in their entirety, though not these scenes alone. If one accepted every possibility that Chettle wrote at least the first draft of a scene, he could be credited with the greater part of the play. The present discussion does not sustain such conclusions; the exact extent of Chettle's contribution may be impossible to establish. That Chettle did contribute to the original text must now be difficult to dispute. A cautious estimate of his role in its composition, grounded on the best of the aggregated conclusions from nine varyingly effective tests, would assign to him six or perhaps seven scenes – at a minimum, over one-third of the original text.

NOTES

1 E.H.C. Oliphant, 'Sir Thomas More', JEGP, 18 (1919), 226–35.

2 These are reasons for treating Oliphant with scepticism, not for dismissing him out of hand. MacD.P. Jackson has observed that despite Oliphant's unscientific approach, 'his pronounce-ments and suggestions are extremely valuable as hypotheses to be tested by the newly developed objective criteria', and that, 'About Middleton Oliphant was, according to my evidence, almost always right' (*Studies in Attribution: Middleton and Shakespeare*, Salzburg Studies in English Literature, 79 (Salzburg, 1979), p. 3). Munday's avoidance of prose, except for specific clown characters, was noted by Carol Chillington, 'Playwrights at Work: Henslowe's, not Shakespeare's, *Book of Sir Thomas More*', ELR, 10 (1980), 439–79, p. 463). Of course clownish characters can and do make up the dialogue of the entire part-scenes or scenes.

3 A.C. Partridge, *Orthography in Shakespeare and Elizabethan Drama: A Study of Colloquial Contractions, Elision, Prosody and Punctuation* (London, 1964), pp. 43–66.

4 'Young Anthony Mundy again', SP, 56 (1959), 150–68.

5 For a full account of Chettle, see Harold Jenkins, *The Life and Work of Henry Chettle* (London, 1934). The case for Chettle's authorship of *Groatsworth* is made by Warren B. Austin, in *A Computer-Aided Technique for Stylistic Discrimination: The Authorship of 'Greene's Groatsworth of Wit'* (Washington, 1969).

6 *Orthography*, p. 45.

7 My work was assisted by an old-spelling concordance of the original text generated from the Oxford University Computing Service tape of *More*.

8 See also Giorgio Melchiori, 'The Contextualization of Source Material: The Play Within the Play in *Sir Thomas More*', in *Le Forme del Teatro*, 3 (1984), 59–94.

9 *Orthography*, pp. 50–2.

10 Conspicuously, the opening soliloquy. Few plays can open with a seven-syllable verse-line.

11 Apart from anomalous figures for the short scenes xii and xv, neither test gives a differential ratio of over two between any two scenes.

12 'The Booke of Sir Thomas Moore Re-examined', SP, 69 (1972), 169–73.

13 See note 5.

14 'Anthony Mundy and *Sir Thomas More*', NQ, 208 (1963), p. 96.

15 Compare *Richard II*, II.iii.30 (Q): 'Because your Lo: was proclaimed traitor'. The contraction was not needed to fit the verse-line to the type-line, so probably reflects copy.

16 Some of these discriminants are listed by David J. Lake, in *The Canon of Thomas Middleton's Plays: Internal Evidence for the Major Problems of Authorship* (Cambridge, 1975), 13 and 4, in tables following p. 252.

17 The evidence presented here is nevertheless too obvious to go unrecorded. I do not mention other investigations which yielded no effective results.

18 In *The Problem of Henry VIII Reopened* (Cambridge, 1949), A.C Partridge used the variation in ye

and *you* as part of his evidence for Fletcher's hand in that play, but R.A. Foakes noted in his new Arden edition (London, 1957) that such variation might be distorted by scribal interference.

19 The 'strong' preferences are based on a minimum differential ratio of 4 (20–80); the 'weak' preferences on a ratio of 2 (33.3–66.7).

20 References are to the Malone Society Reprint of *Hoffman* (Oxford, 1950 (1951)).

21 *Humble earth* may not be a remarkable collocation, but it is not found in Shakespeare, who never describes the earth, clay, ground, etc. as *humble*.

22 'The Tragedy of Hoffman: An Edition' (unpublished Ph.D. thesis, University of Liverpool, 1983).

23 On the basis of a canon equivalent to almost 40 plays (38 plays plus poems), and an average count of about half the permitted maximum count of 20. An obvious criticism of the test would be that the vocabulary is nevertheless thicker on the ground in Shakespeare than in *More*. This observation gives predictable testimony to Shakespeare's breadth of vocabulary, but does not invalidate the test: even if Shakespeare used the vocabulary sample from *Hoffman* more frequently than Chettle himself elsewhere in his work, Chettle's usage may be expected to be significantly higher than Munday's. In fact the incidence in the three marked scenes is considerably higher than in Shakespeare, and remains appreciably higher over the six scenes most likely to be Chettle's on the basis of aggregated tests.

7

Webster or Shakespeare? Style, idiom, vocabulary, and spelling in the additions to *Sir Thomas More*

CHARLES R. FORKER

Carol Chillington's recent essay denying that Shakespeare is Hand D in *The Book of Thomas More* and ascribing the passage instead to Webster has infused new energy into an old controversy that, until her article appeared, had resolved itself into something approaching consensus.[1] G. Blakemore Evans included the fragment in D's handwriting (Addition II in Greg's terminology) together with a soliloquy by More in C's hand (Addition III) in his highly conservative Riverside edition of Shakespeare (Boston: Houghton Mifflin, 1974). This, of course, is the edition to which Spevack's standard concordance is keyed, and the attribution, although not universally accepted, had commanded very general assent. Chillington's essay appears to have changed all this. No less an expert in Shakespearean textual studies than George Walton Williams has described her contribution to the ongoing debate as 'brilliant', 'commanding', and 'by far the most arresting to have come along in many years'.[2] Indeed, some sense of how far-reaching has been the revolutionary impact of her findings may be gauged by the reviewer of a book on Shakespeare's sonnets who takes its author to task for uncritically accepting the old ascription by stating flatly that 'the *Sir Thomas More* fragment . . . is no longer thought to be Shakespeare's'.[3]

Chillington's argument is multidimensional and too complex to be summarized neatly or briefly, but her conclusion that Hand D is none other than John Webster hangs upon several prior contentions. The most important of these are (1) that the manuscript was written and revised in 1601–3 after the Essex rebellion and during a period when Webster was actively collaborating with Munday, Chettle, Heywood, and Dekker, the other authors of the play, (2) that *More* was one of Henslowe's enterprises (probably for Worcester's men) and is specifically referred to in his famous *Diary*, although not by title, and (3) that the typical methods and commercial pressures of such collaborations rule out Shakespeare, who by 1601 had established himself as a major dramatist with significant financial interests in a rival company, the Lord Chamberlain's men. The implication is that Shakespeare would have had neither the time nor the incentive in 1601–2 to involve himself in the theatrical affairs of a competing organization. Since Hand D's part in the play is of more than pedestrian literary quality and since, if not Shakespeare's, it must have been written by a dramatist for whom no identifiable autograph survives, Webster becomes, partly by default, the candidate who best fits the postulated historical conditions.

Chillington's case, although impressive, is less watertight than it might at first appear. Neither the seventeenth-century date nor the link with Henslowe can be demonstrated on the basis of external evidence, however plausible these assumptions may seem in the light of internal pointers.[4] I must confess that as a longtime student of Webster's style and canon I resisted the attribution to the Jacobean tragedian from the beginning – but intuitively and on wholly subjective grounds, for the style seemed to me eminently Shakespearean. It was not until I began studying Hand D closely, using Spevack's indispensable *Complete Concordance* to Shakespeare and the equally valuable concordance to Webster by Corballis and Harding, that I was able to collect evidence that seems to me to justify my initial scepticism.[5] The new Webster concordance has proved especially vital to my investigation because it includes not only the acknowledged non-collaborative works of Webster, as presented in Lucas's four-volume edition, but also the Websterian sections of *Westward Ho* (1604) and *Northward Ho* (1605), definitively edited by Bowers and reliably separated by Murray from Dekker's share in these comedies.[6] The Webster concordance has the further advantage of recording that playwright's language in old spelling. It is therefore now possible to compare the usages of Hand D with similar usages in the total Webster *oeuvre* (except for collaborative works in which Webster's share is doubtful or ambiguous) and to pay especial attention to early works written between 1604 and 1607 – namely, the Induction to Marston's *Malcontent, Westward Ho* (I, III, and IV.i), and *Northward Ho* (I.i, II.ii, III, and v.i.1–262). Unfortunately *Sir Thomas Wyatt* (1602–7), a play that Chillington invites us to compare with the Ill May Day scene of *More*, must be excluded from the test, not only because it is a bad quarto, probably the result of memorial reconstruction, but also because the mutilated state of its text makes the disentangling of Webster's share from Dekker's and from that of other putative or feasible collaborators virtually impossible.

The evidence that follows (presented where appropriate in tabular form) divides into three categories. The first embraces miscellaneous features of style (common idiomatic expressions, subvoluntary or semi-automatic linguistic habits, phrases, figures of speech, and rhetorical devices that might be thought unusual or distinctive). The second and third categories comprise basic vocabulary and individualistic spellings. In order to minimize confusion in the first two categories I cite Evans's modernized text of Adds. II and III from *The Riverside Shakespeare*. For the third category I quote Evans's old-spelling text, checking individual spellings in every case against Greg's as yet unsuperseded Malone Society edition. Although More's soliloquy (Add. III) is written in C's hand rather than D's, I nevertheless include this passage in my data because Chillington assigns it to Webster and because it has traditionally been associated with Shakespeare. The exception, obviously, is the category devoted to spelling, where Hand C's habits become largely irrelevant. I must stress at the outset that these data seem to me weightier as negative than as positive evidence – that is, they tell more heavily *against* Webster' claim than *for* Shakespeare's. It is theoretically possible, of course, that Hand D might be neither Shakespeare nor Webster – might, in truth, be a dramatist otherwise unknown to us. But, given the number of gifted poets writing for the stage during the period we are considering, this hypothesis seems unlikely. The practical effect of eliminating Webster would be to restore Shakespeare to the position of principal claimant.

FEATURES OF STYLE

Sir Thomas More	*Shakespeare*	*Webster*
1 'come to that pass' (II, 4)	Forms of this idiom appear in Shakespeare, e.g., 'brought to such a silly pass' (*Shr.*, v.ii.124); 'brought him to this pass' (*Lr.*, iii.iv.63); 'to no other pass' (*Son. 103*, l. 11)	Webster never uses *pass* (=juncture, predicament)
2 'upon th' hip' (II, 18)	This expression appears three times in Shakespeare: *MV* (i.iii.46, iv.i.334); *Oth.* (ii.i.305)	Webster never uses it
3 'accept of' (II, 19)	This idiom appears in Shakespeare: *Shr.* (ii.i.59, iv.ii.112); *1H4* (iv.iii.112); *1H6* (v.iii.80)	Webster never uses it
4 'how say you . . . ?' (II, 22)	This expression is very common in Shakespeare, e.g., *Tmp.* (ii.i.254); *Wiv.* (i.iv.28); *MM* (ii.iv.58); *Err.* (iv.iv.45); *AYL* (iv.iii.1); *Shr.* (i.i.140–1); *TN* (i.v.82); *WT* (i.ii.54); *H5* (v.ii.130); *1H6* (ii.iii.61, iv.i.70, v.iii.126); *R3* (i.i.96); *Tit.* (ii.ii.16); *Mac.* (iii.iv.68); *Oth.* (ii.i.163)	Webster never uses 'how say you?' He prefers 'say you?' or 'what say you?'
5 'Friends, masters, countrymen –' (II, 27)	Compare 'Friends, Romans, countrymen' *JC* (iii.ii.73); 'friends and countrymen' (*MV*, iii.ii.223); 'my countrymen, my loving friends' (*R2*, i.iv.34); 'brothers, friends and countrymen' (*H5*, iv, Chorus, 34); 'my friends and loving countrymen' (*1H6*, iii.i.137)	Webster associates *friend* and *countryman* only once in the *Ode* prefixed to Harrison's *Arches of Triumph* (1603): 'good Countryman and friend' (l. 19)
6 'Peace, ho, peace' (II, 28)	'Peace, ho' is a common expression in Shakespeare: *JC* (i.ii.1, iii.ii.54, iii.ii.72, iii.ii.234, iii.ii.246); *Rom.* (iv.v.65); *MM* (iv.iii.106); *AYL* (v.iv.125); *Cor.* (v.vi.123). Compare also 'ho, peace' (*MM*, i.iv.6, iii.i.44)	Webster never uses *peace* and *ho* together

Sir Thomas More	*Shakespeare*	*Webster*
7 'Both, both, both, both!' (II, 34)	Compare 'both, both' in *Tmp.* (I.ii.61); *AWW* (v.iii.308); and *Lr.* (IV.ii.81)	Webster never repeats *both* in this way
8 'Are you men of wisdom or what are you?' (II, 35–6)	The employment of 'or what are you?' as a rhetorical question is a Shakespearean usage. Compare 'My masters, are you mad? Or what are you?' (*TN*, II.iii.86) and 'What dost thou? or what art thou, Angelo?' (*MM*, II.ii.172); also 'What art thou that keep'st me out from the house I owe?' (*Err.*, III.i.42); 'Sir, what are you that offer to beat my servant?' (*Shr.*, v.i.64); and 'What art thou that usurp'st this time of night?' (*Ham.*, I.i.46)	Webster uses the question rhetorically or semi-rhetorically only rarely and never precedes it by *or*; compare *Westward Ho* (I.i.101, I.i.106) and *Northward Ho* (v.i.211)
9 'men of wisdom' (II, 35, 37)	Compare 'we of wisdom' (*Ham.*, II.i.61)	No comparable phrase appears in Webster
10 'no, no, no, no, no!' (II, 38)	The five successive repetitions of *no* occur in two Shakespearean plays: *Cor.* (III.i.279) and *Ant.* (III.xi.29). Compare also 'no, no, no, no' (*MV*, I.iii.15; *TN*, II.iii.112; and *Lr.*, v.iii.8). Three repetitions of *no* occur six times: *AWW* (IV.v.1, IV.v.35), *2H4* (II.iv.309), *3H6* (II.v.83), *Cor.* (II.i.120), *Cym.* (II.iv.106). 'Never, never, never, never, never' (*Lr.*, v.iii.309) may also be indicative	Webster tends to avoid multiple repetitions of *no*. The closest parallel is 'no, no, no' in *The Duchess of Malfi* (IV.ii.102)
11 "A keeps a plentiful shrievaltry, and 'a made . . .' (II, 42). See also 'Faith, 'a says true' (II, 141)	Shakespeare commonly uses the contraction '*a* (=he). Spevack lists 178 instances in the *Complete Concordance* from *Wiv.*, *Err.*, *Ado*, *LLL*, *MV*, *Shr.*, *AWW*, *Jn.*, *2H4*, *H5*, *2H6*, *Tro.*, *Cor.*, *Rom.*, *Ham.*, *Ant.*, and *Per.*	Webster uses '*a* (=he) very sparingly. Only three undoubted instances occur in the canon: *The Devil's Law-Case* (II.i.98, II.i.137, II.iii.161). A possible fourth instance is *Appius and Virginia* (v.i.78). With Webster, the form creeps in only after 1616

Sir Thomas More	*Shakespeare*	*Webster*
12 'voice and credit' (II, 51)	The use of *credit* as the second element in a doublet is characteristic of Shakespeare: 'worth and credit' (*MM*, v.i.244); 'name and credit' (*Shr.*, IV.ii.107); 'reputation and credit' (*AWW*, IV.iii.133–4)	Webster never uses *credit* in a doublet
13 'Good masters' (II, 57)	Compare 'good masters' in *WT* (v.ii.174) and *Oth.* (I.iii.77)	Webster never uses the phrase
14 'cry upon' (II, 61)	This is a Shakespearean idiom. Compare 'And cried . . . upon Rosalind' (*AYL*, IV.iii.149); 'He cried upon it' (*Shr.*, Induction, 23); 'Sowter will cry upon't' (*TN*, II.v.123); 'Cry fie upon my grave!' (*WT*, III.ii.54); 'Cried hate upon him' (*2H4*, IV.i.135)	Webster nowhere uses this idiom
15 'the state of men' (II, 67)	Parallel or closely related phrases appear in Shakespeare. Compare 'my single state of man' (*Mac.*, I.iii.140); 'This is the state of man' (*H8*, III.ii.352); 'the state of a man' (*JC*, II.i.67); also 'the kingly state of youth' (*LLL*, IV.iii.289)	No comparable phrase appears in Webster
16 'cannot choose but' (II, 70)	Shakespeare employs this idiom repeatedly: *Tmp.* (I.ii.186), *TGV* (IV.iv.77–78), *Wiv.* (v.iii.17), *MV* (III.i.114–15), *AWW* (I.i.146, I.iii.214–15), *TN* (II.v.174, IV.i.57), *WT* (I.i.24), *1H4* (I.iii.279, v.ii.44), *2H4* (III.ii.207), *R3* (IV.iv.289), *Tro.* (I.ii.135), *Tit.* (IV.iii.75), *Rom.* (I.iii.50, III.v.77), *Tim.* (v.i.177), *Ham.* (IV.v.69), *Oth.* (IV.i.28–9), *Cym.* (I.vi.71–2, II.iii.34), *Ven.* (l. 79), *Son. 64* (ll. 13–14). Compare also 'shall not choose but' (*Shr.*, v.i.11; *Ham.*, IV.vii.65)	Webster avoids it. His single instance is 'could not have chos'd but' in the *Characters* (*A Water-man*, l. 3)
17 'strong hand' (II, 81)	Shakespeare favours this phrase: *Err.* (III.i.98), *Jn.* (II.i.33, IV.ii.82), *Ham.* (I.i.102), *Son. 65* (l. 11). Compare also 'strong right hand' (*3H6*, II.i.152)	Webster never uses it

Sir Thomas More	Shakespeare	Webster
18 'an aged man' (II, 83)	Compare 'The aged man' (*Luc.*, l. 855); also 'aged men' (*Tit.*, III.i.23; *Tim.*, v.i.172)	Webster never uses these phrases
19 'self-same hand, self reasons, and self right' (II, 85)	Shakespeare habitually uses *self* as an adjective (=same). Compare 'self chain' (*Err.*, v.i.10), 'self way' (*MV*, I.i.148), 'self king' (*TN*, I.i.38), 'self mould' (*R2*, I.ii.23), 'self bill' (*H5*, I.i.1), 'self place' (*3H6*, III.i.11), 'self blood' (*Tit.*, IV.ii.123), 'self metal' (*Lr.*, I.i.69), 'self hand' (*Ant.*, v.i.21), 'self exhibition' (*Cym.*, I.vi.122)	Webster never uses *self* (=same)
20 'would shark on you' (II, 86)	The use of *shark* as a verb is highly unusual. It occurs once in Shakespeare: 'Shark'd up a list of lawless resolutes' (*Ham.*, I.i.98)	Webster never uses the verb. The noun *sharke*, used literally, appears in *Appius and Virginia* (III.ii.61)
21 'this' a sound fellow' (II, 89)	Shakespeare uses the contraction *this'* (=this is) fairly often. Compare 'This' a good friar' (*MM*, v.i.131); 'this' my daughter here asleep' (*MND*, IV.i.128); 'Why, this' a heavy chance' (*Shr.*, I.ii.46); 'This' your son-in-law' (*WT*, v.iii.149); 'this' [miching] mallecho, it means mischief' (*Ham.*, III.ii.137); 'This' a good block' (*Lr.*, IV.vi.183); 'This' Antioch then' (*Per.*, I, Chorus, 17)	Webster uses the contraction rarely, if at all, in plays. It occurs once 'This the sum of all . . .') in *Appius and Virginia* (v.ii.143), a scene Lucas attributes to Heywood. The other possible examples (the syntax is ambiguous) appear in the very late *Monuments of Honor* (1624), (ll. 56, 233, 246)
22 ''tis a sin' (II, 93)	Compare ''Tis sin' (*3H6*, v.vi.3), ''tis' no sin' (*1H4*, I.ii.104; *MM*, IV.i.72); ''Twas sin' (*3H6*, v.v.76)	No such expression occurs in Webster
23 'Marry, God forbid' (II, 96)	This and related exclamations are extremely common in Shakespeare. 'Marry, God forbid' occurs in *MV* (II.ii.66), *Shr.* (IV.ii.78), *R2* (IV.i.114), and *Oth.* (II.iii.261). 'God forbid' appears in *Ado* (I.i.217, I.i.219–20), *Shr.* (v.i.146), *R2* (II.i.200), *1H4* (v.ii.35, v.iv.11),	Webster never uses these expressions

Sir Thomas More	Shakespeare	Webster
	2H4 (v.i.44), H5 (1.ii.13), 2H6 (111.ii.23, 1v.iv.10), 3H6 (1.ii.18, 11.i.190, 111.ii.25, 1v.i.21, v.iv.48), H8 (11.ii.114), Tit. (1v.iii.91), Rom. (1.iii.4), and Son. 58 (l. 1). 'The gods forbid' appears in MND (111.ii.276), AWW (111.v.74), Tro. (v.x.3), Cor. (111.i.232, 111.i.288), and Ant. (1v.ii.19, v.ii.213). Compare also 'God in heaven forbid!' (R2, 11.ii.51); 'Marry, heaven forbid!' (Oth., v.i.72); 'Marry, the gods forefend!' (Cym., v.v.287); and 'Marry, God forfend!' (2H6, 111.ii.30)	
24 'Nay, certainly' (11, 97)	We find this locution in AYL (111.iv.20), Ant. (11.vii.34), and Per. (111.ii.78)	Webster never uses it
25 'O desperate as you are' (11, 107)	Shakespeare regularly uses such clauses as as you are or as thou art after an adjective or noun in vocative constructions. Compare 'welcome as you are' (Tit., v.ii.91); 'Celestial as thou art' (LLL, 1v.ii.117; PP, v, 13); 'Damn'd as thou art' (Oth., 1.ii.63); 'invisible as thou art' (Tmp., v.i.97); 'Filth as thou art' (Tmp., 1.ii.346); 'coward as thou art' (R3, 1.iv.279); and 'traitors as ye are' (3H6, v.v.36)	Webster never uses this construction
26 'unreverent knees' (11, 110)	Shakespeare applies unreverent or unreverend to parts of the body: 'unreverend tongue' (TGV, 11.vi.14); 'unreverent shoulders' (R2, 11.i.123)	The adjective does not occur at all in Webster
27 'In, in to your obedience!' (11, 113)	In, used adverbially in absolute expressions (=get you in), occurs frequently in Shakespeare. Compare 'in, or we are spoil'd' (Err., v.i.37); 'Father, in' (MV, 11.ii.156); 'In at the window' (Jn., 1.i.171); 'In to my tent'	This use of in is extremely rare in Webster. It occurs only once: '[In] you Pandar!' (The White Devil, 1v.ii.51). Even here there may be a

CHARLES R. FORKER

Sir Thomas More	*Shakespeare*	*Webster*
	(*R3*, v.iii.46); 'In, in, in, in!' (*Cor.*, iv.v.235); 'In, and prepare' (*Tim.*, v.ii.16); 'Good nuncle, in' (*Lr.*, iii.ii.11–12); 'In, boy, go first' (*Lr.*, iii.iv.26)	shade of doubt, for uncorrected copies of Q1 (1612) read 'No you Pandar?'
28 'put down' (II, 119)	Shakespeare regularly uses *put down* (=abolish, destroy, subdue): *MM* (iii.ii.6, iii.ii.103); *Wiv.* (ii.i.29); *LLL* (iv.i.141); *Ado* (ii.i.283–4); *TN* (i.iii.81, i.iii.83, i.v.84); *Jn.* (ii.i.346); *2H6* (iv.ii.36, iv.iv.40); *3H6* (i.i.200); *R3* (v.iii.255)	Webster entirely avoids the verb to *put down*
29 'To slip him like a hound' (II, 122)	Shakespeare was attracted to metaphors involving greyhounds held by or released from *slips* (=nooses). Compare 'Lucentio slipp'd me like his greyhound' (*Shr.*, v.ii.52); 'Before the game is afoot thou still let'st slip' (*1H4*, i.iii.278); 'like greyhounds in the slips' (*H5*, iii.i.31); 'let slip the dogs of war' (*JC*, iii.i.273); and 'like a fawning greyhound in the leash, / To let him slip at will' (*Cor.*, i.vi.38–9)	Webster nowhere uses *slip* (either as a noun or verb) in connection with dogs
30 'come too short' (II, 124)	'Come short' and 'come too short' are among Shakespeare's favorite idioms. Compare 'come too short' in *Ado* (iii.v.41), *LLL* (v.ii.738), *AWW* (v.iii.176), *H8* (iii.ii.170), *Lr.* (i.i.72, ii.i.88), *Ant.* (i.i.58, ii.v.8), *Son. 83* (l. 7); also 'come short' in *MM* (v.i.220), *R2* (i.iv.47), *Tro.* (i.iii.11), *Ham.* (iv.vii.90)	Webster never uses the idiom
31 'like as if' (II, 135)	Shakespeare uses the double periphrastic conjunction *like as* several times. Compare 'like as there were husbandry in war' (*Tro.*, i.ii.7); 'And like as rigor of tempestuous gusts / Provokes the mightiest hulk' (*1H6*, v.v.5–6);	Webster never uses the conjunction *like as*

Sir Thomas More	Shakespeare	Webster
	'like as it would speak' (*Ham.*, I.ii.217); 'Like as the waves make towards the pibbled shore' (*Son. 60*, l.1); 'Like as to make our appetites more keen' (*Son. 118*, l. 1)	
32 'It is in heaven that I am thus and thus' (III, 1)	The doublet *thus and thus* is characteristic of Shakespeare. Four instances occur: 'Still thus, and thus' (*MM*, III.ii.53); 'Your son did thus and thus' (*2H4*, I.i.76); 'the wisdom of nature can reason it thus and thus' (*Lr.*, I.ii.104–5); 'With tokens thus, and thus' (*Cym.*, v.v.203). Compare also the parallel syntax of ''tis in ourselves that we are thus or thus' (*Oth.*, I.iii.319–20)	Webster never uses the doublet
33 'But, More, the more thou hast . . .' (III, 14)	Wordplay on names is a well-known trait of Shakespearean style. Compare 'It shall be call'd "Bottom's Dream", because it hath no bottom' (*MND*, IV.i.215–16); 'shame on Angelo . . . O, what may man within him hide, / Though angel on the outward side!' (*MM*. III.ii.269–72); 'Old Gaunt indeed, and gaunt in being old' (*R2*, II.i.74); 'Discharge yourself of our company, Pistol' (*2H4*, II..iv.137); 'Mark, Marcus, mark!' (*Tit.*, III.i.143); 'Brutus kill'd me . . . It was a brute part of him to kill so capital a calf' (*Ham.*, III.ii.104–6); 'Whoever hath her wish, thou hast thy *Will*, / And *Will* to boot, and *Will* in overplus' (*Son. 135*, ll. 1–2); The pun on More's name may be somewhat exceptional, however, since Erasmus had made a famous play on More's name – *More < Mora* (=folly) – in the Preface to his *Praise of Folly*	I am aware of no such punning on names in Webster. It may be significant that it is wholly absent from *Westward Ho*, and *Northward Ho*, comedies in which other kinds of *double entendre* are especially prevalent

It will instantly appear that most – perhaps all – of the thirty-three stylistic features listed above are fairly common aspects of Elizabethan idiom and therefore undoubtedly part of the regular linguistic currency of numerous dramatists in the period. Taken individually, they could prove nothing about authorship. Even as a group, striking as the parallels to Shakespeare often are, they constitute the shakiest of bases for the purpose of attribution since other playwrights of the era (including Webster) are known to have imitated Shakespeare. The point is not that these linguistic details identify Shakespeare as Hand D but that they appear to rule out Webster. This would seem to hold true even if we make some allowance for differences of date and subject matter between various works of the dramatists. The two additions to *More* are brief – 147 and 21 lines respectively – and it would strain credibility very far indeed to suppose that in the space of 168 lines Webster was able consciously to imitate twenty-six linguistic habits of Shakespeare or of some other playwright (or playwrights) for which there are no parallels elsewhere in the Webster canon. In any case, a theory of imitation (if we imagine that Webster was copying Shakespeare's style) cannot explain the many verbal parallels to Shakespeare's Jacobean dramas, for of course these postdate *More*. Even the remaining seven features of style in *More* (as illustrated above) are very rare in Webster, and, of these seven, only two can be paralleled in Webster's works that are close in date (1603–5) to the supposed date of the *More* additions.

A few additional linguistic traits of the *More* fragment that point away from Webster and towards Shakespeare may be mentioned here. Webster shows a distinct preference for the contractions *i'th* and *i'th'* (117 times), *o'th* and *o'th'* (42 times), *on't* (40 times), *of't* (15 times), and *'s* (=*his* in such compounds as *on's, in's, for's, by's, up's,* and *upon's*; 54 times). If Webster had written the three pages that Chillington attributes to him, it would be reasonable to expect at least some of these forms to appear. None does.

Two of Hand D's connectives may also be indicative – namely, *among* (line 46) and *whiles* (line 39). Throughout his corpus, Webster prefers *amongst* (20 times) to *among* (11 times), a ratio of almost two to one. Moreover, if we differentiate between relatively early and relatively late works, Webster's bias is even more strongly in favour of *amongst*, for 10 of the 20 occurrences are in *Westward Ho, Northward Ho*, and *The White Devil*, whereas *among* appears only once in these three plays. Shakespeare's preference is definitely for *among* (94 times) over *amongst* (41 times). It is therefore safe to say that the likelihood of Shakespeare's having written *among* is at least twice as great as Webster's having done so. The use of *whiles* in *More*, when we compare the respective habits of Webster and Shakespeare, yields an even more striking imbalance of probabilities. Webster uses *while* and *whilst* a total of 72 times throughout his canon but *whiles* only twice – in *The Devil's Law-Case* (1.i.54) and in the *Characters* (*An Excellent Actor*, l.4). Shakespeare's total count for combined *while* and *whilst* is 461 and for *whiles* 81. The probability of Webster's having written *whiles* in *More* is exceedingly remote. The two Webster occurrences constitute only 2 percent of his total usage in this respect, and even these two instances belong to works written in 1614 or later. Like Webster, Shakespeare also prefers *while* and *whilst* (a total of 461 times) to *whiles* (81 times), but the percentage of *whiles* is much higher (almost 15 percent as compared with 2 percent). With such a short sample of Hand D's usage to go on, we dare not attach too much weight to statistical probabilities, but, such as they are, these probabilities are entirely consistent with evidence of other kinds. Indeed all of the stylistic evidence considered here makes Shakespeare a far likelier author of the *More* additions than Webster.

VOCABULARY

Excluding proper names, the two additions to the *More* manuscript contain 545 different words. Of these, 485 (almost 89 percent of the total) are common to both Shakespeare and Webster. Of the remainder, 50 words (slightly more than 9 percent of the total word count) appear in Shakespeare but not in Webster. Only one word (less than one-fifth of a percent of the total) occurs in Webster but not in Shakespeare. Nine words from the two *More* additions (approximately one and a half percent) occur in neither Shakespeare nor Webster. The breakdown (with line references to the Riverside text after each word) may be presented as follows:

Words in Shakespeare But Not in Webster	*Words in Webster But Not in Shakespeare*	*Words in Neither Shakespeare Nor Webster*
1 abode (II, 133)	1 transportation (II, 76)	1 Harry (in 'Harry groat'; II, 1)
2 accite (III, 16)		2 lyam (=leash; II, 121)
3 adheres (II, 129)		3 mountainish (word doubtful; II, 140)
4 advantage, *vb.* (II, 71)		
5 ampler (II, 101; *ample* occurs in Webster).		4 parsnip (II, 9, 15)
		5 red (in 'red herring'; II, 1)
6 apostle (II, 94)		
7 appropriate, *adj.* (II, 137)		6 shrievaltry (II, 42)
8 Ay (=yes; II, 58)		7 simplest (II, 21; *simple* does occur in both Shakespeare and Webster)
9 babies (II, 75)		
10 brawl (II, 78)		
11 charter'd (II, 138)		
12 clement (II, 123)		8 stone (=weight; II, 3)
13 cloth'd (II, 79)		9 troy (in 'troy weight'; II, 7)
14 detested (II, 134)		
15 dexter (III, 11)		
16 forewarn (II, 94)		
17 gospel (II, 88)		
18 halfpenny (II, 7)		
19 handicrafts (II, 71)		
20 harbor, *n.* (II, 127)		
21 hip (II, 18)		
22 hug (III, 16)		

Words in Shakespeare
But not in Webster

23 hurly (II, 113)
24 inhumanity (II, 140)
25 insolence (II, 81;
     insolencies occurs in
     Webster)
26 installs (II, 105)
27 loaf (II, 7)
28 luggage (II, 75)
29 maxime (III, 19)
30 mediation (II, 145;
     mediate occurs in
     Webster)
31 mutines (II, 115)
32 physick'd, *vb.* (III, 13)
33 plentiful (II, 42;
     plentifully occurs in
     Webster)
34 profanely (III, 2;
     prophanest, adj., occurs
     in Webster)
35 pumpions (II, 16)
36 qualify (II, 119)
37 quell'd (II, 82)
38 rebel, *adj.* (II, 114; *rebel,*
     n., occurs in Webster)
39 rout, *n.* (II, 116)
40 self, *adj.* (II, 85)
41 short (II, 124; Webster
     uses *short* in
     compounds, e.g., *short-*
     liv'd, short-winded)
42 Shrieve (II, 41)
43 silenc'd (II, 78)
44 step, *vb.* (III, 7)
45 stillness (II, 52)
46 Submit (II, 144)
47 topp'd, *vb.* (II, 64)
48 Trash (II, 10)
49 trespass, *n.* (II, 124)
50 unreverent (II, 110)

Of the 485 words common to both Shakespeare and Webster, the writer of the
More additions uses eight in special senses that can be paralleled in Shakespeare but
not in Webster:

1. bottom (=ball of thread; III, 21)
2. meal (=grain; II, 2)
3. merely (=entirely; II, 8)
4. number (=populace, crowd; II, 51)
5. Owed (=possessed; II, 136)
6. pass (=juncture, predicament; II, 4)
7. ports (=seaports; II, 76)
8. sorry (=contemptible, regrettable, wretched; II, 9)

The lopsided ratio of 50 to 1 (or 9 percent to a mere fraction of a percent) suggests that the *More* additions are significantly more congruent with Shakespeare's habits of vocabulary than with Webster's. Of the relatively uncommon words in the two passages, only the single appearance of *transportation*, which Webster uses once in *The Duchess of Malfi* (IV.ii.60) and which Shakespeare never uses, could be construed as pointing towards the authorship of Webster. Even this single instance of a Websterian but non-Shakespearian word is of dubious importance because Shakespeare throughout his canon uses closely related words such as *transport* (7 times), *transportance* (once), *transported* (12 times), *transporting* (twice), and *transports* (once). Since we know that Shakespeare's working vocabulary greatly exceeded that of any of his contemporaries, the large margin of Shakespearian over Websterian words is scarcely surprising, but the evidence from vocabulary does chime resoundingly with that from the idiomatic and linguistic habits of the two dramatists. Even the improbable hypothesis that the author of the additions is neither Shakespeare nor Webster but an unknown dramatist accords better with the analysis of the vocabulary presented above than with the assumption that he is Webster, for the 168 lines contain nine words (as opposed to one) that appear in neither canon.

Two additional Shakespearian indicators are worth mentioning here, although, taken alone, they would hardly weigh more than a hair in the argument. A recognized trait of Shakespearian style is the tendency to use nouns as verbs – a use not particularly characteristic of Webster. At least four instances occur in the *More* additions: *advantage, physick'd, shark*, and *topp'd*. Also the author of Add. II makes the Ill May Day insurgents irrationally associate parsnips and pumpkins as unhealthful vegetables not fit for human consumption:

> Lincoln   . . . our infection . . . partly comes through the eating of parsnips.
> Clown   True, and pumpions together.   (ll. 13–16)

In an earlier speech Hand D originally intended to make Lincoln speak of a 'watrie' parsnip and then, striking out the words 'a watrie,' corrected the phrase to read 'a sorry psnyp' (l. 9). We may wonder whether it is sheer coincidence that in *The Merry Wives of Windsor* Mistress Ford refers to Falstaff as 'this unwholesome humidity, this gross wat'ry pumpion' (III.iii.40–41). Certainly the idea of a watery and unwholesome pumpkin in *The Merry Wives* together with the link between watery unwholesome parsnips and pumpions in *More* suggests a possible Shakespearian image cluster or pattern of association. Also, as Partridge points out,[7] *pumpion* was a rare word in the period, especially in drama. Chillington notices the putative link between the growing of parsnips in dung in the *More* fragment and the ripening of apricots in dung in *The Duchess of Malfi* (pp. 456–457), but, as J.H. Pafford correctly reminds us,[8] Shakespeare always associates dung with that which is base and injurious, never with healthy fertilizing. Since both Shakespeare and Webster refer to dung in pejorative contexts, associating it with disease, whether horticulturally or otherwise, the references in the *More* passage settle nothing about a distinctive pattern of imagery in either dramatist. The vocabulary test, however hesitant we may be to use it as evidence in Shakespeare's favour, would seem to be overwhelmingly negative as evidence for Webster.

SPELLING

Attempts to support a theory of authorship on the basis of distinctive ortho-graphical preferences have always been suspect when applied to printed texts because of the unknown degree to which various compositors might alter or regularize their copy. In order to make a really strong case for either Shakespeare or Webster on such grounds, we would need to be able to match Hand D's supposedly unusual spellings with those from an undoubted Shakespearean or Websterian holograph. For practical purposes neither exists. We have nothing at all in Webster's handwriting and only the words 'By me' from the will and the six authenticated signatures in Shakespeare's. Clearly, any argument *for* Shakespeare or Webster on the basis of orthography must be accounted weak for lack of reliable data. Nevertheless, investigators have been struck by the fact that not a few spellings from the *More* fragment, some of which appear to be idiosyncratic, do escape into Shakespeare's printed texts (the regularizing tendency of compositors notwithstanding) or can be plausibly inferred from the spelling of analogous words or from compositorial misreadings. J. Dover Wilson contributed the pioneer study in this domain years ago,[9] and Evans mentions the most notable idiosyncrasies of spelling in his running commentary to the Riverside edition of Hand D's addition to the *More* manuscript.

I have been able to discover no comparable agreement between the more unusual spellings of the *More* fragment and those of the Webster canon, although, admittedly, the line between 'common' and 'unusual' spellings is not easy to draw.[10] To be sure, we should not expect to find many rare spellings in printed texts, assuming that compositors would ordinarily suppress such irregularities, but the theoretical possibility remains that, in a substantial body of Webster texts extending over some two decades, a peculiar spelling might here and there slip through the compositorial net. A thoroughgoing comparison of spellings in the canons of Shakespeare and Webster must await complete concordances (including stop-press corrections and variants) of the good quartos and the First Folio of Shakespeare as well as of a more modern old-spelling edition of the complete works of Webster. By way of a mere beginning, I list below only selected and perhaps distinctive spellings from Hand D for which parallels or near parallels have been noticed in Shakespeare and for which no corresponding parallels have yet been found in Webster. The evidence here is tenuous and woefully incomplete, but, so far as it goes, it seems once more to direct our eyes away from Webster and back towards Shakespeare. The Shakespeare spellings are taken from Dover Wilson's famous essay but keyed to the Riverside edition.

Sir Thomas More	*Shakespeare*	*Webster*
1 adicion (118)	addicions (*Lr.* [Q1], 1.i.136; *LC*, l. 118)	
2 afoord (133)	affoord (*1H4* [Q1], 111.ii.78; *LLL* [Q1], v.ii.223; *Ado.* [Q1], 1.i.174; *Rom.* [Q2], 111.i.60, 111.iv.8; *AWW* [F], iv.i.48; *Son. 79*, l. 11); affoords (*Rom.* [Q2], v.i.73); affoordeth (*Oth.* [Q1], 1.iii.114)	
3 a levenpence (=eleven pence; 2)	a leuen (*MV* [Q1], 11.ii.162; *Rom.* [Q2], 1.iii.35; *LLL* [Q1], 111.i.171; *Tro.* [Q1], 111.iii.295; compare also *a leauen* in *Ham.* [Q2], 1.ii.251)	
4 ar (=are; 21, 35, 35, 36, 39, 97, 107)	Compare *y'ar, yar* (*Lr.* [Q1], iv.vi.9, iv.vii.48); also *or* (misprint for *ar*, *Ham.* [Q2], 1.iii.74)	
5 argo (=ergo; 5)	argo (*2H6* [F], iv.ii.29); *argall* (*Ham.* [F], v.i.12)	
6 aucthoryty (78, 94)	aucthoritie (*LLL* [Q1], 1.i.87)	
7 banck (39)	bancke (*Ham.* [Q2], 111.ii. dumbshow); bancks (*Luc.*, l. 1442); banckes (*Son. 56*, l. 11)	
8 basterdes (12)	basterd (*Son. 124*, l. 2)	
9 braule (78)	braule (*LLL* [Q1], 111.i.9)	
10 byth (=by the; 58)	by th', by'th, byt'h, bith, bit'h, bi'the, bi'th (*LLL* [Q1], v.ii.61, v.ii.474; *LC*, l. 112; *Lr.* [Q1], 11.iv.8, 11.iv.9; *Rom.* [Q2], 1.v.110; *Oth.* [Q1], 1.iii.401, 11.iii.378, v.ii.355)	by'th (*The Devil's Law-Case*, 111.iii.149)

Sir Thomas More	Shakespeare	Webster
11 Charg (28)	charg (*LLL* [Q1], v.i.83)	charg'd (*Appius and Virginia*, IV.i.293; *The White Devil*, II.i.154)
12 com (124)	com (*Ado* [Q1], II.iii.29; *Ham.* [Q2], v.ii.106; *LLL* [Q1], I.i.59); coms (*Ham.* [Q2], v.i.141; *Ven.*, l. 444)	
13 deule (=devil; 53, 56)	deule (*Rom.* [Q2], II.iv.1, III.i.103; *Ham.* [Q2], III.ii.129; *H5* [F], II.iii.31); deale (misprint for *deule*, *Ham.* [Q2], II.ii.599)	
14 doon (=done; 141)	don (*Lr.* [Q1], v.iii.35); doone (*Ham.* [Q2], III.ii.20, III.ii.162, III.ii.238, IV.i.40, IV.ii.5, v.i.235; *2H4* [Q1], III.ii.48)	
15 elamentes (136)	element (*Ham.* [Q2], IV.vii.180); elamentes (*LLL* [Q1], IV.iii.326)	
16 ffraunc (=France; 127)	Shakespeare sometimes omitted the final *e* in such words as *France, insolence, obedience*, and *office*. Compare *ingredience*, a misprint for *ingredient* (*Oth.* [Q1], II.iii.308); *intelligence*, a misprint for *intelligent* (*Lr.* [Q1], III.vii.11); *pallat*, a misprint for *palace* (*Rom.* [Q2], v.iii.107); *instance*, a misprint for *instant* (*LLL* [Q1], v.ii.807)	
17 gott (68, 80)	gotte (*Lr.* [Q1], v.iii.173)	
18 harber (=harbor; 127)	harber (*Luc.*, l. 768)	
19 hiddious (132)	hiddious (*Ham.* [Q2], II.ii.476)	
20 Iarman (=German; 128)	Iarman (*2H4* [Q1], II.i.145). Compare *Iamanie*, a misprint for *Iarmanie* (*Wiv.* [F],	

Sir Thomas More	Shakespeare	Webster
	iv.v.87); also *Iermane* (*LLL* [Q1], iii.i.190); also *Iarmen* (*Cym.* [F], ii.v.16)	
21 Ingland (73, 129)	Inglish (*Wiv.* [Q1], ii.iii.63)	
22 mas (=mass; 58)	mas (*2H4* [Q1], ii.iv.4, ii.iv.19, v.iii.13)	
23 obay (100, 116, 146)	obay (*Ham.* [Q2], i.ii.120, v.ii.217; *Lr.* [Q1], iii.iv.80, iii.iv.149; *Tro.* [Q1], iv.v.72, v.i.44, v.v.27; *LLL* [Q1], iv.iii.213)	
24 obedienc (94, 113, 114)	See item 16	
25 obedyenc (39)	See item 16	
26 offyc (98; Greg transcribes 'offyce')	See item 16	
27 scilens (50)	Scilens (appears 18 times in *2H4* [Q1], iii.ii, v.iii; the spelling is apparently unique with Shakespeare)[11]	
28 sealf (85, 85, 85, 146)	Compare *seale slaughter*, a misprint for *sealf-slaughter* (*Ham.* [Q2], i.ii.132)	
29 sealues (46)	See item 28	
30 straing (8)	straing (*LC*, l. 303); compare also *straying*, a possible misprint for *straing* (*LLL* [Q1], v.ii.763)	
31 straingers (20, 70, 74, 119, 130, 139)	See item 30	
32 thart (=thou art; 58)	thar't (*Lr.* [Q1], i.iv.22); th'art (*Ham.* [Q2], v.ii.342)	th'art (*Appius and Virginia*, ii.ii.49, ii.iii.167; *The White Devil*, v.vi.241)
33 theise (12, 67, 144)	theise (*H5* [F], iii.ii.114)	
34 thinck (138)	thincke (*Ado* [Q1], i.i.104)	
35 tooth (=to the; 76)	too'th, toth', to'th (*Lr.* [Q1], ii.iv.181, v.iii.246; *Ham.* [Q2], ii.ii.278; *Oth.* [Q1], i.iii.133, v.ii.156)	toth (*The Devil's Law-Case*, iv.ii.171, iv.ii.301, iv.ii.306)

Sir Thomas More	*Shakespeare*	*Webster*
36 weele (=we'll; 31, 33, 38, 142)	weele (*Ham.* [Q2], I.ii.175, I.v.156, II.ii.84, II.ii.429, II.ii.430, II.ii.535, II.ii.540, IV.vii.131, v.i.295; *1H4* [Q1], I.ii.173, I.iii.291, II.i.44, II.ii.79, II.ii.91, III.i.265, IV.ii.3, IV.iii.1, IV.iii.107; *2H4* [Q1], II.iv.276, v.iii.28; *LLL* [Q1], v.ii.219; *MV* [Q1], I.i.68, III.iv.58, IV.ii.2; *Ado* [Q1], I.iii.75, II.iii.42, II.iii.43, III.iii.180, IV.i.297, v.iv.44, v.iv.120; *MND* [Q1], II.ii.37, III.ii.412, IV.i.185, v.i.46, *Rom.* [Q2], I.i.1, I.i.3, I.iv.4, I.iv.10, I.iv.41, II.iv.140, III.iv.27, IV.ii.37, IV.v.145; *Tit.* [Q1], I.i.410, I.i.494, IV.i.122, v.i.13; *Tro.* [Q1], I.iii.381, II.iii.134, II.iii.140, II.iii.183, III.i.60, III.ii.45, III.iii.50, IV.i.50, IV.i.79, IV.v.147, v.iii.92; *Lr.* [Q1], I.iv.181, II.ii.127, II.iv.67, III.vi.84; *TNK* [Q1], II.ii.149, II.iii.55, v.ii.108, v.iv.127)	wee'l (*Appius and Virginia*, II.ii.163, II.iii.155, III.ii.182, IV.ii.42); wee'le (*Appius and Virginia*, II.ii.93, II.ii.164, II.ii.165, III.ii.155; *The White Devil*, II.i.76, III.ii.306); wee'll (*The Duchess of Malfi*, III.ii.12)
37 wer (=were; 63, 95, 137)	wer (*Rom.* [Q2], II.ii.11, II.v.16); wer't (*Lr.* [Q1], IV.ii.63; *Oth.* [Q1], II.iii.343)	wert (*A Monumental Column*, l. 279; *The Duchess of Malfi*, IV.i.110, IV.ii.138; *The Devil's Law-Case*, III.iii.84, IV.ii.157; *Appius and Virginia*, I.iv.66; *Northward Ho*, III.i.4); wer't (*The White Devil*, II.i.4)
38 ymagin (74)	ymaginary (*Tro.* [Q1], III.ii.19)	

CONCLUSION

If Webster were indeed the author of Adds. II and III from *Sir Thomas More*, it would be reasonable to expect some degree of correlation between the idiomatic features of these passages and those parts of Webster's corpus from which we can confidently exclude collaborators. At least in thirty-three instances (a high number for these comparatively brief texts) this is clearly not the case. Moreover, *most* (though perhaps not quite all) of the stylistic evidence adduced is of a kind that it would be difficult to attribute to conscious imitation on the part of Webster, even admitting that Shakespeare's verbal and dramatic influence on his younger contemporary was pervasive. The evidence from vocabulary, although somewhat less conclusive, agrees with the idiomatic and stylistic evidence. The orthographical data presented here are too selective and incomplete to inspire much confidence and, in any case, are undermined by the necessity to rely exclusively on printed texts of Webster's works, many of them at some chronological remove from the dating limits of the *More* fragment. Our present knowledge of Webster's spelling preferences is insufficient, and more reliable information will be difficult, perhaps impossible, to acquire. Nevertheless, what little we do have to go on again seems to militate against his authorship of the *More* additions.

If Webster was not the author (as I believe to be the case), Shakespeare once more becomes the leading contender. Problems, of course, remain. The different size of the two canons and of the two vocabularies makes it impossible to assess Shakespeare's and Webster's habits with equal assurance. Spevack gives the total number of lines in Shakespeare's corpus (combining prose and verse) as 118, 406; the corresponding figure for Webster, based on the works and parts of works concorded by Corballis and Harding, is 15,843 – 13 per cent of the Shakespearean total. Shakespeare's vocabulary (as recorded by Spevack) runs to 29,006 different words. No comparatively precise figure for Webster exists, but we can approximate his vocabulary by extrapolating from the Corballis–Harding concordance – that is, by computing the average number of entries per page from a representative sample, then adjusting the number downward to compensate for variant spellings of the same word and for the high proportion of pages (those with one or no entries) that list the 43 commonest words in the language (*the, and, I, to, of, a*, and the like). On this basis, Webster's vocabulary is 13,727 words – a little less than half the size of Shakespeare's.[12] Elsewhere in this volume Gary Taylor offers an account of how an established Lord Chamberlain's man such as Shakespeare might have become involved with a text composed mainly by dramatists who seem in 1601–3 to have been principally associated with the writing of plays for Henslowe. Certainly there is nothing inherently impossible about his having done so; and, as internal evidence of various kinds continues to accumulate, the working hypothesis that Hand D is indeed Shakespeare becomes ever more difficult to dismiss.

NOTES

1 Carol A. Chillington, 'Playwrights at Work: Henslowe's, not Shakespeare's, *Book of Sir Thomas More*', *ELR*, 10 (1980), 439–79.
2 Williams, 'Textual Studies' in 'The Year's Contributions to Shakespearian Study', *ShS*, 35 (1982), 190.

3 Katherine Duncan-Jones, Review of Hallett Smith's *The Tension of the Lyre: Poetry in Shakespeare's Sonnets.* (San Marino, California, 1981), *NQ*, ns 29 (December 1982), 538.

4 Independently of Chillington, and without attempting to deny Shakespearean authorship, some scholars have argued for a date of 1600 or later. See D.J. Lake, 'The Date of the *Sir Thomas More* Additions by Dekker and Shakespeare', *NQ*, ns 24 (April 1977), 114–16; also MacD. P. Jackson, 'Linguistic Evidence for the Date of Shakespeare's Addition to *Sir Thomas More*', *NQ*, ns 25 (April 1978), 154–6. It is a pleasure to be able to acknowledge the important assistance of MacD. P. Jackson, who privately suggested to me a number of ideas for this study.

5 Marvin Spevack, *A Complete and Systematic Concordance to the Works of Shakespeare*, 9 vols. (Hildesheim, 1968–80); Richard Corballis and J.M. Harding, *A Concordance to the Works of John Webster*, 12 vols. (Salzburg, 1978–81).

6 F.L. Lucas, ed., *The Complete Works of John Webster* (London, 1927); Fredson Bowers, ed., *The Dramatic Works of Thomas Dekker*, II (Cambridge: Cambridge University Press, 1955); Peter B. Murray, 'The Collaboration of Dekker and Webster in *Northward Ho* and *Westward Ho*', *PBSA*, 56 (1962), 482–6, and *A Study of John Webster* (The Hague, 1969), 25–9, 264.

7 A.C. Partridge, *Orthography in Shakespeare and Elizabethan Drama* (Lincoln, 1964), p. 62.

8 Pafford, 'The Play of *Sir Thomas More*', *NQ*, ns 28 (April 1981), 145.

9 Wilson, 'Bibliographical Links between the Three Pages and the Good Quartos', in *Shakespeare's Hand*, pp. 113–41.

10 Partridge (*Orthography in Shakespeare*, pp. 57–63) shows that several of Hand D's spellings cited by Wilson as abnormal can be found in the works of authors other than Shakespeare. I am indebted to Gary Taylor, who provided me with valuable assistance in the location of some spellings given in Wilson's essay only by category.

11 [But see Metz above – *Ed.*]

12 The Corballis–Harding Webster concordance gives no line totals or word frequencies. My figure for the total number of lines in Webster (verse and prose combined) is derived from the editions on which Corballis and Harding based their work. My estimate of the size of Webster's vocabulary in relation to Shakespeare's is founded on the following computation. The Corballis–Harding old-spelling concordance contains 1,950 pages that list every variant spelling as a separate lexical item, whereas the Spevack Shakespeare concordance, being in modern spelling, eliminates most such variants. In Shakespeare's vocabulary 43 common words, which it is impossible to avoid, constitute 40 percent of the total number of words in the entire corpus. If we assume that Webster's use of these common words would be roughly proportionate to Shakespeare's – a not unreasonable assumption – we can estimate the size of Webster's vocabulary by taking a random sample of 50 pages from the concordance (about 2.5 percent of the total number of pages) that do not contain any of the 43 words commonest to Shakespeare's usage. The average number of entries per page in this sample is 13.6. By multiplying the 1,950 pages by 13.6, we get a total of 26,520 estimated entries in the entire concordance. If we then reduce this number by 40 percent (=10,608) to compensate for the high percentage of common words on pages with anomalously few or zero entries, we get 15,912. The average number of words per page with more than a single spelling is 2 (or approximately 14 percent of the total). If we now reduce 15,912 by 14 percent (=13,684) to allow for variant spellings of the same word and then add back 43 (the common words excluded in the process of averaging), we get a total vocabulary of 13,727.

8

Sir Thomas More and the Shakespeare canon:
two approaches

JOHN W. VELZ

I

A new collection of essays on problems in *Sir Thomas More* ought to re-examine the canonical approach that R.W. Chambers took to the authorship question in Addition IIc sixty years ago.[1] It may be that we should extend his plausible conclusions.[2] One recognizes the era in Chambers's conservative stance; understated conclusions were appropriate when disintegration was crescent.[3] Chambers was more diffident than we might be about evidence drawn from *Henry VI, Part II*,[4] though he was bold enough to make use of *Troilus and Cressida*, a play commonly rejected from the canon in his time. By 1931, when Chambers answered the critics of his original essay,[5] he was using *2H6* more confidently: the cast of mind one associates with Frederick G. Fleay, E.H.C. Oliphant, and John MacKinnon Robertson was already beginning to fade from fashion. Nevertheless, Chambers still made no use of *Titus Andronicus*, a play that can be mined, as will appear, in important support of his analysis.

A less guarded response to the canonical question is possible now. From the seminal 1923 volume a scholarly consensus has evolved that the 148 lines in Hand D are Shakespeare's work,[6] and one can go over Chambers's ground again in a stance rather more demonstrative and suggestive than polemical. One can say now, for instance, what Chambers would have been very reluctant to say in 1923: that Shakespeare may have been recruited to revise the scene in which the Ill May Day Riot is quelled precisely because he had succeeded with similar scenes in Act IV of *2H6*.[7]

Another shift in scholarly perspective was imminent when Chambers first wrote on *More*, and it was reflected in his masterful second essay in 1931. Influenced by the early work of Caroline Spurgeon (and perhaps by the early work of G. Wilson Knight as well), Chambers's rationale in the second essay gave prominence to pattern in Shakespeare's thought.[8] Concatenation and configuration were now determinants in defining authorial characteristics, and this was a great advance over the naked parallel passage method Chambers had relied on in 1923. As Chambers came to recognize, pattern tells us more about an author's thought than single elements can, and pattern is therefore a better tool for authorship investigation. My extension of Chambers, intended to be indicative rather than definitive, will focus on two patterns, one in *2H6* which escaped Chambers's notice and another, an association of moral ideas, which Chambers discusses, but which has a broader basis in the Shakespeare canon than Chambers observed and which can be interpreted more fully than he realized.

The 1931 essay finds significance in the concatenation of seven elements in the *More* fragment in light of the concatenation of the same seven elements in Act IV of *2H6* (pp. 258–9). The ringleader of a rebellion enters haranguing his followers; a half-penny loaf is the focus of 'false economics' (p. 262) early in both scenes; logic-chopping (underscored by the use of *argo*, a nonce word, for *ergo*) is prominent; popular grievances are enumerated; the emotions induced by the enumeration lead to absurd, paranoid logic in which harmless things (literacy in *2H6*, parsnips in *More*) are blamed for the ills of the poor; genial absurdity in the crowd is strangely combined with brutality; the mutability of the crowd is commented on.[9] This is persuasive evidence.

An instructive pattern that appears in the *More* fragment and in the Jack Cade scenes of *2H6* can be added to Chambers's evidence. In both sequences the author seeks a dramatic climax by having the rebels appealed to in vain by a succession of authorities until the last of them finally succeeds in pacifying the crowd. Sir Humphrey Stafford and his brother William, who first confront the rabble in IV.ii of *2H6* and are later killed, are followed by Lord Say (also killed by the rebels) and by Buckingham before Clifford finally succeeds in dispersing the mob. In *More* Add. IIc the Sergeant is followed by the Lord Mayor, Surrey, and Shrewsbury, all to no effect, before Sheriff More obtains a hearing and wins the crowd to compliance. This analogy between the two plays is obscured by the fact that Shakespeare lingers over this dramatic strategy in *2H6*, spreading the pattern of rejection through seven scenes (nearly 400 lines) while in *More* he condenses it into a whirling forty lines which convey the crowd's energy admirably but mute the intended climax. We may conclude that Shakespeare miscalculated in trying to force the broad pattern of his earlier use of the structural *gradatio* into a narrow compass.

Shakespeare tried for the same climactic effect more successfully in *Julius Caesar*, modifying the device of *gradatio* more astutely. There he has the first confrontation with an unruly mob succeed; Brutus wins the hostile Plebeians to his will (as he does not in Plutarch).[10] Antony's successful confrontation with the Plebeians seems greater to us because he must woo them by directly undoing the achievement which Brutus has earned moments before. The crowd, at the same time, is made to seem greatly more fickle than in Plutarch, where they never really change their collective mind. The mutability of the Plebeians in *JC* is not paralleled by shifting allegiances of the commoners in Add. IIc, though the Ill May Day mob gives realistic evidence of indecisiveness. The dynamics of *JC* III.ii originated in IV.viii of *2H6*, where Clifford and Cade alternate in addressing the crowd of Cade's men, each winning temporary commitment from '*All*' in nearly ritually univocal exclamations: 'God save the King! God save the King!' (19); 'We'll follow Cade, we'll follow Cade!' (33); 'A Clifford! a Clifford! we'll follow the King and Clifford' (53–4). Even the contrast between Cade's temporarily victorious prose and Clifford's ultimately victorious verse anticipates the Brutus/Antony configuration in III.ii of *JC*.[11]

If we assume that Shakespeare's contribution to *More* antedates *Julius Caesar* – I regard the question as still an open one, though I am inclined toward that scenario – then we may regard *JC* III.ii as the beneficiary of a less successful attempt in *More* to re-use a device first employed in *2H6*. Whether or not Add. IIc came first, it is apparent that there is an intimate relation between the form of address to the Plebeians employed by Brutus and Antony and the tricolon of address Surrey uses in his abortive effort to get the Ill May Day rioters' attention:

Surrey	frendes masters Countrymen	(149)
Brutus	Romans, countrymen, and lovers	(III.ii.13)
Antony	Friends, Romans, countrymen	(III.ii.73).[12]

Countrymen is a preferred form of address in political contexts in Shakespeare, an implicit appeal to patriotism; it appears in this way twelve times in *JC* alone and another thirteen times in other plays. Three instances are worthy of notice in the present investigation: a tricolon in the fourth-act prologue of *Henry V*, where Henry is said to call his soldiers 'brothers, friends, and countrymen' (34); the passage in *2H6* IV.viii where Clifford addresses Cade's followers; and Lord Say's unsuccessful address to the same rebels shortly before (IV.vii.114).

Lent significance by the pattern common to *2H6* and *More* are a number of individual elements in both plays that alone would be inconsequential. The mercy of the King to repentant rebels is stressed in both rebellions, and by the first representative of authority to speak in each *gradatio*. Sir Humphrey Stafford first addresses Cade's followers with insults but promptly shifts tone to offer amnesty:

> Rebellious hinds, the filth and scum of Kent,
> Mark'd for the gallows, lay your weapons down,
> Home to your cottages, forsake this groom:
> The King is merciful, if you revolt.   (IV.ii.122–5)

The Sergeant's first words to Lincoln's followers are of amnesty, but with a hostile innuendo in them that Lincoln is prompt to perceive:

> *Seriant* what say you to the mercy of the king do you refuse yt
> *Lin* you woold haue vs vppon thipp woold you
>   no marry do we not, we accept of the kings
>   mercy but wee will showe no mercy vppo*n* the straingers   (Add. II, 139–42)

The illogic in this reply will remind us of Cade's replies to Stafford, especially the xenophobic *non sequitur* in which Cade labels Lord Say a traitor because he can speak French, an enemy's language (IV.ii.166–7). The crowd's enmity toward the French is built into the Original Text of *More*; we must accordingly put the Francophobe analogy down to coincidence, unless we wish to believe that it might have been one of a number of elements that drew Shakespeare's attention to the Cade scenes as a potential model for Add. IIc. The two interlocutors, Sir Humphrey Stafford and the Sergeant, respond similarly to the xenophobic fallacies:

Staf.   O gross and miserable ignorance!   (168)
Seriaunt You ar the simplest things that eu*er* stood in such a question   (143)

Chambers juxtaposed (1923, p. 164; 1931, p. 258) two other distortions of logic: Cade's boast that the rebel army is 'in order when we are most out of order' (iv.ii.189–90) and More's lines (later partly cancelled by Hand C): 'to kneele to be forgyven / [is saifer warrs, then euer you can make] / [whose discipline is ryot]' (iic, 234–6).

More's deliberative oration builds to a climactic *comparatio* of the special kind in which the hostile listener is asked to imagine himself in the position of the one he has been abusing. In lines 122–40, More constructs a hypothetical scenario in which the King banishes the rebels who thus find themselves in exile on the Continent persecuted as foreigners just like the foreign exiles they themselves are now persecuting. The argument by inverse analogy ('do as we may be doon by' is the moral definition the rioters give it at iic 264) is one that Isabella makes good use of in ii.ii of *Measure for Measure*, her first confrontation with Angelo. She puts Angelo in Claudio's place and Claudio in Angelo's, exactly as More does with the rioters and foreigners:

> If he had been as you, and you as he,
> You would have slipp'd like him, but he like you,
> Would not have been so stern.   (ii.ii.64–6)

Isabella will come back to this *comparatio* exactly, at the climax of her disputation:

> Go to your bosom,
> Knock there, and ask your heart what it doth know
> That's like my brother's fault. If it confess
> A natural guiltiness such as is his,
> Let it not sound a thought upon your tongue
> Against my brother's life.[13]

In the meantime she makes the ultimate *comparatio* for a Christian, the logic of the Lord's Prayer:

> How would you be
> If He, which is the top of judgment, should
> But judge you as you are? O, think on that,
> And mercy then will breathe within your lips,
> Like man new made.   (75–9)

Once again we may find a precedent in the Jack Cade scenes, this time at the moment of Lord Say's death in *2H6* iv.vii. It is clear that in the early 1590s Shakespeare knew the dramatic value of Isabella's rhetoric and More's.[14] Cade has ordered Lord Say beheaded, and the condemned man makes the ultimate plea:

> Ah, countrymen! if when you make your pray'rs,
> God should be so obdurate as yourselves,
> How would it fare with your departed souls?
> And therefore yet relent, and save my life.   (112–17)

This is a draft for Isabella's persuasive rhetoric, complete with the dramatic impact of having the hearer turn a deaf ear to the ultimate argument for mercy. More's rhetoric wins consent – the dramatic peripety is prescribed as comedic – but it is recognizably the same rhetoric. There is even a hint of a cosmic dimension when the Ill May Day crowd respond by quoting The Golden Rule: '. . . letts vs do as we may be doon by' (264).[15]

It seems evident from what has been said about *gradatio* and *comparatio* in *Sir Thomas More* that rhetoric judiciously weighed can and should bear a part in authorship investigations as a partner to imagery, diction, allusions, and thought. Chambers perceived something of this in his arguments from 'sequences of thought' in 1931. One might do more than he or I have done, and not do all.

Extending to other contexts in the Shakespeare canon the small number of parallels Chambers typically offers to an idea or a sequence in *More* is a useful exercise. It will emphasize the firmness with which a metaphor or pattern was rooted in Shakespeare's consciousness and in some cases it may offer us a hint about the provenance of the metaphor or the pattern and about what the ultimate significance was for Shakespeare. The case of flood and related images is exemplary.

Chambers cites images of flood from four speeches in the canon in which rebellion is the subject; without much analysis he juxtaposes them with More's impatient exclamation about the unruly crowd:

> whiles they ar ore the banck of their obedyenc
> thus will they bere downe all things   (IIC 162–3)

> Each thing [meets]
> In mere oppugnancy: the bounded waters
> Should lift their bosoms higher than the shores.
> And make a sop of all this solid globe;   (*Troilus and Cressida* I.iii.110–13)

> The ocean, overpeering of his list,
> Eats not the flats with more impiteous haste
> Than young Laertes, in a riotous head,
> O'erbears your officers.   (*Hamlet* IV.v.100–3)

>   Will you hence
> Before the tag return, whose rage doth rend
> Like interrupted waters, and o'erbear
> What they are us'd to bear?   (*Coriolanus* III.i.246–9)

> Like an unseasonable stormy day,
> Which makes the silver rivers drown their shores,
> As if the world were all dissolv'd to tears,
> So high above his limits swells the rage
> Of Bullingbrook, covering your fearful land
> With hard bright steel, and hearts harder than steel.   (*Richard II* III.ii.106–11)

The verbal, situational, and conceptual analogies between the *More* passage and the other four are compelling.[16]

Further analogues can be cited from *Julius Caesar*, a play that in other ways is specially close to *More*, as the pages above have implied.[17] We might half expect *JC*, dominated as it is in its first half by unruly crowds, to embody the metaphor, and the metaphor is there, not once only, as in *More*, but several times. One of the most striking instances directly connects flood to rebellion, as in *More*: Antony alludes in his funeral oration to his capacity to stir the Plebeians 'To such a sudden flood of mutiny' (III.ii.211).[18] The image of a river over its banks also occurs in *Caesar*, as in Add. IIc and in the *R2* and *Cor.* passages. In the first scene of the play, Flavius exhorts the Plebeians to weep into the Tiber for their disloyalty to Pompey's memory 'till the lowest stream / Do kiss the most exalted shores of all' (59–60). Here is a fanciful variation on the metaphor flood = mutiny that probably draws also on the conceit about a river flooded by tears in *R2*. Shakespeare was evidently intent on the metaphor of the Tiber's rising water in *JC*, as he reverts to it almost immediately, in I.ii, when Cassius vividly describes the swimming match he once had with Caesar in 'The troubled Tiber chafing with her shores, . . . this angry flood' (I.ii.100–9). Other allusions to water threateningly out of control, out of bounds, appear in Casca's recollection of storms he has seen (I.iii.6–8) and in Cassius' excited comparison of the coming turmoil of battle to a sea tempest (V.i.67–8).[19]

Caroline Spurgeon, like R.W. Chambers, observed the rising-water images in Shakespeare – she counted 26 images of a river in flood in the canon – and traced this imagery to Shakespeare's childhood on the banks of the Avon, which often spreads impressively over its floodplain.[20] Her comparative analysis shows that Shakespeare was more interested in rivers, especially rivers in flood, than his fellow dramatists were; and it seems obvious that the Avon must have shaped this obsession. But there is more to floods and watery turbulence in Shakespeare than rivers, as the storms at sea in *Julius Caesar* make clear.[21] Shakespeare's vision also comprehends inundation on a scale that dwarfs the Avon and its banks. He alludes to floods so vast as to 'make a sop of all this solid globe' (*Tro.* I.iii.113) so vast as to 'have drench'd our steeples, [drown'd] the cocks' (*Lr.* III.ii.3). The flood that suffering Titus Andronicus pictures leaves him solitary, surrounded by the encroaching sea, waiting for apocalypse:

> For now I stand as one upon a rock,
> Environ'd with a wilderness of sea,
> Who marks the waxing tide grow wave by wave,
> Expecting ever when some envious surge
> Will in his brinish bowels swallow him.   (*Tit.* III.i.93–7)

Global flood is Shakespeare's ultimate vision of chaos, what the mushroom cloud has become for many since 1945.

The hyperbolic flood image half way through the action of *Titus Andronicus* is supported by other, lesser, flood images in the context.

One hour's storm will drown the fragrant meads,
What will whole months of tears thy father's eyes?   (Marcus to Lavinia, II.iv.54–5)

My grief was at the height before thou cam'st,
And now like Nilus it disdaineth bounds.   (Titus to Lavinia, III.i.70–1)

The cheeks of the mourners in the family

. . . are stain'd like meadows yet not dry,
With miry slime left on them by a flood   (III.i.125–6)[22]

Finally comes a mad confusion of the image, as chaotic as what it describes:

If there were reason for these miseries,
Then into limits could I bind my woes:
When heaven doth weep, doth not the earth o'erflow?
If the winds rage, doth not the sea wax mad,
Threat'ning the welkin with his big-swoll'n face?
And wilt thou have a reason for this coil?
I am the sea; hark how her sighs doth [blow]!
She is the weeping welkin, I the earth:
Then must my sea be moved with her sighs;
Then must my earth with her continual tears
Become a deluge, overflow'd and drown'd . . .
(Titus to Marcus about himself and Lavinia, III.i.219–29)

These images in *Titus Andronicus*, spectacular as they are, lack the political dimension one finds in *More* Add. IIc, unless one stresses the collapsing social order in the play.[23] There is no rioting mob here. Yet the floods in *Titus* are worth our attention, because they indicate where Shakespeare got the flood=mutiny, flood=chaos, metaphor which appears in *More* Add. IIc and in so many other places in the canon.

Titus Andronicus draws on Book I of Ovid's *Metamorphoses* for its moral design: Robert Miola has shown that 'the Rome which the play presents is a horrifying embodiment of the bestial chaos and universal impiety of the iron age'.[24] *Titus* is accordingly most immediate of all Shakespeare's plays to what I take to be the source of Shakespeare's imagery of cosmic flood. The Lycaon and the Deucalion/Pyrrha stories from Book I of the *Metamorphoses* underlie the flood imagery in *Titus*; it was Lycaon's offences, especially cannibalism and impiety, that decided Jupiter to drown the world. Cannibalism and impiety are prominent in *Titus*.[25] A third evil of the Iron Age which appals Jupiter (and Ovid) is also vivid in the play: familicide. Just before Astraea, the goddess of Justice, abandoned the earth in revulsion:

non hospes ab hospite tutus,
non socer a genero, fratrum quoque gratia rara est;
imminet exitio vir coniugis, illa mariti,
lurida terribiles miscent aconita novercae,
filius ante diem patrios inquirit in annos:
victa iacet pietas . . .   (*Meta.* I, 144–9)[26]

Guest was not safe from host, nor father-in-law from son-in-law; even among brothers 'twas rare to find affection. The husband longed for the death of his wife, she of her husband; murderous stepmothers brewed deadly poisons, and sons inquired into their fathers' years before the time. Piety lay vanquished. . . .

Immediately came the impious rebellion of the Giants, and the morally hideous offspring that the Earth brought forth from the Giants' spilled blood (I, 151–62). Jupiter, investigating the horrors on earth he had heard of, was offered by Lycaon, King of Arcadia, a cannibalistic meal (a murdered hostage, as in *Titus*). The first of the metamorphoses in the poem is the punishment Jupiter exacted: Lycaon became physically what in a moral sense he already was – a wolf.[27] In utter disgust Jupiter decided 'to destroy the human race beneath the waves' (260–1).

The description of the flood that follows is wonderfully vivid. After he has seen to the winds, clouds and rain, Jupiter gets Neptune to command that the rivers bear their part in the inundation:

> ' . . . aperite domos ac mole remota
> fluminibus vestris totas inmittite habenas!'
> iusserat; hi redeunt ac fontibus ora relaxant
> et defrenato volvuntur in aequora cursu.
> . . . . .
> exspatiata ruunt per apertos flumina campos
> cumque satis arbusta simul pecudesque virosque
> tectaque cumque suis rapiunt penetralia sacris.
> si qua domus mansit potuitque resistere tanto
> indeiecta malo, culmen tamen altior huius
> unda tegit, pressaeque latent sub gurgite turres.
> iamque mare et tellus nullum discrimen habebant:
> omnia pontus erat, derant quoque litora ponto.   (I, 279–82, 285–92)

' . . . Open wide your doors, away with all restraining dykes, and give full rein to all your river steeds.' So he commands, and the rivers return, uncurb their fountains' mouths, and in unbridled course go racing to the sea . . . The rivers overleap all bounds and flood the open plains. And not alone orchards, crops and herds, men and dwellings, and shrines as well and their sacred contents do they sweep away. If any house has stood firm, and has been able to resist that huge misfortune undestroyed still do the overtopping waves cover its roof, and its towers lie hid beneath the flood. And now the sea and land have no distinction. All is sea, and a sea without a shore.

One sees the moral meaning for Ovid in the fact that among the first things the gods do to bring the orderly world out of chaos earlier in the poem is to establish limits for rivers:

> fluminaque obliquis cinxit declivia ripis. . . .   (I, 39)

and [he] hemmed down-flowing rivers within their shelving banks . . .

Nearly every detail in Titania's description of the consequences to the world of her quarrel with Oberon (*A Midsummer Night's Dream* II.i.88–97) comes from *Meta.* I, 262–73.[28] The piling of Mount Pelion on Mount Ossa that the rebellious giants undertook to reach heaven (I, 151–5) is alluded to in *Hamlet* (v.i.251–4, 283). Gonzalo recollects Ovid's description of the Golden Age in his account of his imagined commonwealth (*Tempest* II.i.144–65). Shakespeare quotes the climactic phrase from Ovid's description of the Iron Age in *Titus Andronicus* IV.iii.4: '*Terras Astraea reliquit*'. Shakespeare's favourite phrase from Ovid is in line 7 of Book I: '*rudis indigestaque moles*', 'a rough, unordered mass of things', the world before order was imposed on chaos.[29] Book I of the *Metamorphoses* was very important to Shakespeare.

The whole syndrome – cannibalism, familicide, impiety, and flood – is in *Titus Andronicus*. It is also in the passage from Ulysses's 'degree' speech that Chambers quotes as a parallel to the concatenation in the *More* fragment:

> Take but degree away, untune that string,
> And hark what discord follows. Each thing [meets]
> In mere oppugnancy: the bounded waters
> Should lift their bosoms higher than the shores,
> And make a sop of all this solid globe;
> Strength should be lord of imbecility,
> And the rude son should strike his father dead;
> Force should be right, or rather, right and wrong
> (Between whose endless jar justice resides)
> Should lose their names, and so should justice too!
> Then everything include itself in power,
> Power into will, will into appetite,
> And appetite, an universal wolf
> (So doubly seconded with will and power),
> Must make perforce an universal prey,
> And last eat up himself.   (*Tro.* I.iii.109–24)

Ulysses evokes the Ovidian pattern so precisely that one is tempted to find Lycaon in the predatory wolf of universal appetite.

The entire syndrome also appears in *King Lear* in a pattern Chambers did not cite. As Lear is casting off all 'paternal care', all 'propinquity and property of blood' to Cordelia, Shakespeare makes him protest in terms Ovid would have thought of as impious:

> The barbarous Scythian,
> Or he that makes his generation messes
> To gorge his appetite, shall to my bosom
> Be as well neighbor'd, pitied, and reliev'd,
> As thou my sometime daughter.   (I.i.113–20)

Here in a context of family malice are the familicide and the cannibalism of Ovid, combined as in *Titus*.[30] The infanticide and the preying voraciously on one's own kind will emind us of Addition IIc, where

> by this patterne
> not on of you shoold lyve an aged man
> for other ruffians as their fancies wrought
> with sealf same hand sealf reasons and sealf right
> woold shark on you and men lyke ravenous fishes
> woold feed on on another[.][31]

Lear is punishing Cordelia for what he regards as rebellion. The heavens open afterward in a horrifying storm which the King orders to drown the world and which is described in hyperboles and personifications worthy of Ovid's description of the terrible storm Jupiter's wrath evokes against Lycaon and his kind:

> madidis Notus evolat alis,
> terribilem picea tectus caligine vultum;
> barba gravis nimbis, canis fluit unda capillis;
> fronte sedent nebulae, rorant pennaeque sinusque.
> utque manu lata pendentia nubila pressit,
> fit fragor: hinc densi funduntur ab aethere nimbi (1, 254–9)

Forth flies the South-wind with dripping wings, his awful face shourded in pitchy darkness. His beard is heavy with rain; water flows in streams down his hoary locks; dark clouds rest upon his brow; while his wings and garments drip with dew. And, when he presses the low-hanging clouds with his broad hands, a crashing sound goes forth; and next the dense clouds pour forth their rain.

In Lear's hyperbolic image of weathercocks drowning on the submerged steeples of churches (III.ii.3), Shakespeare is evidently remembering Ovid's lines quoted above (p. 178) in which shrines and their sacred contents are swept away and what houses survive the flood are submerged, even the towers (287–90).[32]

Above all, the nightmare world of family relationships in *Lear* precisely reflects the morally appalling Iron Age world which Ovid portrays in the memorable lines quoted above (1, 145–9). Of Ovid's catalogue of family evils, only the wicked stepmother brewing poisons is absent from *King Lear*. Cornwall is an Ovidian son-in-law; the hostility of Edmund towards Edgar is glossed in the same line – (the motif in *Lear* comes to culmination in two cases of fratricide in Act v); Goneril precisely fills the role of the wife who longs for her husband's death; Albany restrains himself with difficulty from tearing his wife limb from limb and Edmund's forged letter portrays Edgar as a son of the Iron Age, enquiring into his father's years before the time. What makes *King Lear* seem vast to us is the cosmic consequences of these familial evils. That is just what made Ovid's first Book seem vast to Shakespeare.

More IIc is a much lesser thing, but it comes recognizably out of the same Ovidian matrix. Ovid's ingredients are present there as they are present in *Titus Andronicus*, in *Troilus and Cressida*, in *King Lear*: predatory cannibalism, familicide, rebellion as impiousness, and water out of limit.

II

As Shakespeare can be said to have mined his own contribution to *More*, he may be thought to have exploited the 'non-Shakespearian' bulk of the play as well. Shakespeare has sometimes been said to have had only a superficial knowledge of the play he was contributing to, because he leaves some speeches unassigned in Addition IIc and includes apprentices who are not in other insurrection scenes added to the Original Text, but makes no use of the Clown who is prominent in those scenes. Scott McMillin's study of the play elsewhere in this volume proposes that Hand D's 'three pages' were contributed early in the process, before the Clown was devised, and before the Apprentices were edited out of the play. It may be that Shakespeare knew the Original Text well enough, and two or three probable echoes of it in Shakespeare plays written between 1595 and 1601 may be cited as evidence.

More's generous response to his wife's expectation of inadequacy in the players' preprandial entertainment recalls Theseus' generous response to Hippolyta's contempt for the mechanicals' postprandial playlet: 'if Arte faile, weele inche it out with looue' (†999); 'The kinder we, to give them thanks for nothing' (*MND* v.i.89).[33] In both scenes the matter is elaborated, and genial Theseus ('I will hear that play; / For never any thing can be amiss, / When simpleness and duty tender it' 81–3) might well be thought an ektype of genial More ('wife, hope the best, I am sure theyle doo their best, / they that would better, comes not at their feaste' †992–3); analogies extend even to discussion in both scenes of seating the ladies (†977–88; v.i.83). If, with Anne Barton, we regard *Love's Labour's Lost* as a companion piece to *Dream* at about the same date, *c.* 1595,[34] we might choose to regard the 'o'er parted' performers of the pageant of the Worthies as traceable ultimately to *More*, though there is no Theseus/More figure in this play to offset the scornful onstage audience. As late as *Hamlet* Shakespeare was looking backward – so far back as *The Spanish Tragedy* – for models for his plays-within; there is no reason to doubt that he might draw on *More* for *MND* and *LLL*.

The likelihood is increased when we recognize, as L.L. Schücking did early in this century, that there is a close analogy between Hamlet's reaction to his achievement in the production of *The Murder of Gonzago* and the player's incongruous notion of More as one of the King's troupe after the latter's success as an impromptu actor in *The Marriage of Wit and Wisdom*.[35] Hamlet's mock boast after the successful performance that he merits 'a fellowship in a cry of players', a whole share, not a half (III.ii.275–80) might have been inspired by the player's enthusiastic exclamation: 'would not my Lord make a rare player? Oh, he would vpholde a companie beyond all hoe' (†1150–1). The motif recurs in Add. IV of *More*, where Randall, who is about to impersonate More (quite inadequately) says he will 'deserve a share for playing of yor Lo. well' (l. 21); if Shakespeare was influenced by Add. IV, we would have to acknowledge that he consulted the play some time after he made his own contribution to it, as his addition, IIc, may very possibly predate all others – if we accept the McMillin scenario.[36]

The impersonation of More may be at the core of another connection to the Shakespeare canon, this one to a play so early that we must surely think *More* the debtor, if any relationship actually exists. The attempt to deceive Erasmus with a pretended More in the person of Randall is reminiscent of the attempt to deceive Joan la Poucelle with Reignier posing as the Dauphin in *The First Part of Henry VI*, I.ii. In each case someone's famous and extraordinary powers are being put to the test in what amounts to a practical joke, and in each case the probationer passes the test easily. The stronger exemplar, dramaturgically, may be the earlier one. In *1H6* Reignier is not so contemptible a substitute as Randall is, and moreover the matter is not dwelt on as it is in *More*. In ten lines it is all over – Joan instantly identifies Reignier 'though never seen before' (67). On the other hand, the scene in *More* seemed worth borrowing to the author of *The True Chronicle Historie of the whole life and death of Thomas Lord Cromwell* (1602); Schücking has pointed out the unmistakable analogy between the servant Randall as More and the servant Hodge as Bedford in *Cromwell*.[37] In any case, the Randall scene in *More* has a background beyond *1H6*; in part at least it is a survivor of the probably apocryphal anecdote in which Erasmus and More identified one another at a banquet – 'Aut tu es Morus aut nullus'; 'Aut tu es Erasmus aut diabolus' – though the two men had never been face to face before.[38]

Mistress More's allegorical dream of drowning with her husband in the Thames after the current had separated them from the King's barge (†1290–1308) is interestingly like Clarence's prophetic dream of drowning in the English Channel at his brother Richard's hands (*R3* i.iv.9–63). The role of the Tower of London in both dreams and the political circumstances in each case enhance the probability that one of these dreams was father to the other.[39] The question of date makes a decision about indebtedness very difficult here; if the Original Text of *More* is dated late 1592–3, it is approximately coincident in time with *R3*, if one adheres to the chronology of the canon proposed by E.K. Chambers.[40] In favour of Clarence's dream as source are the notable eclecticism of *More* and the great popularity of Shakespeare's early plays in their time. In favour of Mistress More's dream as source is the fact that Clarence's dream is more elaborate, and contains some elements (the sensations of a drowning person, for instance) that one supposes would naturally have been borrowed if *R3* were the source of infection. It might be relevant as well that Mistress More's dream has counterparts in her daughter's allegorical dream that More fell from the rood-loft of Chelsey Church while at prayer (1320–5) and an unnarrated dream by Roper that 'meet[s] in one conclusion' with the other two, 'ffatall, I feare' (†1326–7).

There is a more impressive cluster of probable echoes of *More* in *Henry VIII*, and this should not surprise us, though so far as I am aware, no one except Richard Flatter has attempted to relate the two plays to one another.[41] Shakespeare,[42] whose creative imagination habitually conflated analogous sources, would surely have been struck, even at two decades' remove, by the analogy between the fall of Wolsey he was portraying at the mid-point of *H8* and the fall of More, another of Henry VIII's ill-fated Lords Chancellor; More is actually mentioned as successor to Wolsey at iii.ii.393–4 of *H8*. The likelihood that the analogy would occur to Shakespeare is enhanced by the fact that there were four plays on the reign of Henry VIII, all written between *More* and *H8*.[43] About two of these, *The Life of Cardinal Wolsey*, and *The Rising of Cardinal Wolsey*, written respectively June–August 1601 and August–November 1601, nothing is known other than that Chettle apparently

wrote *The Life* for Henslowe and revised it for him in the spring of 1602, and that
Chettle collaborated with Munday, Drayton, and Smith for Henslowe in *The
Rising*.[44] Shakespeare seems clearly to have known the other two plays, *Thomas Lord
Cromwell* (1602), alluded to above as indebted to *More* for a scene, and Samuel
Rowley's *When You See Me, You Know Me* (1605). Geoffrey Bullough thought *When
You See Me* a 'positive influence' on *H8* as a whole, especially on the use of
pageantry,[45] while Joseph Candido has argued that the character of Henry in
Shakespeare's play owes something to the conception of Henry in *When You See
Me*.[46]

Of the four intervening plays, *Thomas Lord Cromwell* is perhaps the firmest link
between *More* and *H8*. Beyond its imitation of the Randall scene, *Cromwell* probably
is indebted to the earlier play for the hero's quip on the scaffold that execution is
medicinal; the rising/falling action is another, less definitive, analogy.[47] The
personal rectitude of Thomas Cromwell, so unrelated to the condemnation he
undergoes, may remind us of the similar moral paradox in Thomas More's fall in the
earlier play. Both men are refreshingly generous of spirit, and we feel that the world
has been diminished with their deaths. At the same time, *Cromwell* resembles *H8*.
The portrayal of Gardiner's conspiracy against Cromwell, including suborned
witnesses to a fictitious threat against King Henry's life, anticipates Wolsey's
conspiracy against Buckingham, again including perjury and an alleged dagger
turned towards the King. Shakespeare must have known the play well – acted in it –
as it was (according to the 1602 title page) in the Lord Chamberlain's men's
repertory, and Gardiner's gnomic comment on the three Thomases who served
Henry must surely have caught his attention:

> Theres *Thomas Wolsay*, hees alreadie gone,
> And *Thomas Moore*, he followed after him:
> Another *Thomas* yet there doth remaine,
> That is farre worsse then either of those twaine.[48]

Cromwell and *When You See Me* were both reprinted in 1613, no doubt as a result of
topical interest in *H8*, which was in performance by 29 June of that year, the day the
Globe burned, and which may have been written for performance in February, in
conjunction with Princess Elizabeth's wedding to Frederick the Elector Palatine.
Someone besides Shakespeare evidently saw a relationship between *H8* and other
plays about the reign of King Henry.

Henry VIII is an eclectic play, reaching back into Tudor drama for some of its
elements, as Alexander Leggatt suggested in a provocative paper read at the
Twenty-first International Shakespeare Conference, Stratford-upon-Avon,
August 1984; one may readily find analogues to moments in *H8* in plays as diverse as
2H6, *The Arraignment of Paris*, *Kynge Johan*, and *Richard III*. In this retrospective
eclecticism *H8* is typical of Shakespeare's other last plays. Three decades ago J.M.
Nosworthy illustrated the 'integrity' of the Shakespeare canon from *Cymbeline*,
which contains in the scene in Imogen's bedchamber allusions to concepts and

literary works that dominated Shakespeare's thinking in his early plays and poems.[49] One could certainly write an analogous essay on *Pericles*, and could probably write one on each of the other last plays. *H8* is overtly retrospective. Buckingham reminds us on his way to the scaffold of his father's analogous execution: *H8* II.i is simply a revision of v.i of *R3*, where the elder Buckingham is led off to the block, and Shakespeare calls our attention to his reuse of the scene. One need not look very closely at *H8* to detect *de casibus* structure in its first half, an episodic sequence of falls traceable ultimately to the *speculum principis* genre by way of *R3*.[50] Other Tudor conventions in *H8* are *contemptus mundi* (in Wolsey's fall, III.ii) and the *ars moriendi* (in Katherine's last moments, IV.ii).[51] The late-Tudor *JC* contributed the images of the flood of politics and the sea of history which occur in *H8*.[52] Because *More* is an episodic chronicle play,[53] its genre and design presented no obstacle to Shakespeare's creative imagination; he had used this design in the *H6* plays and *R3*, and was employing a modification of it in *H8*. The inherent probability that Shakespeare knew the whole of *More* well enough to draw on it many years later is, I believe, strong; for all we know he planned at one time to act in it. What Shakespeare seems to have remembered from *More* twenty years later was theme, character, and situation; wording, not surprisingly, had largely evaporated.

Xenophobia, which dominates the early scenes of *More*, which has its analogue in the Jack Cade scenes of *2H6*, and which Shakespeare had Thomas More refute in 'the three pages', is a substantial element in *H8*, no doubt because Shakespeare was intent on building our Protestant sense that meddlers from Rome in English political and religious life are an evil.[54] It is not just peculation and signing diplomatic correspondence 'Ego et Rex meus' (III.ii.314) that destroy Wolsey, but also and especially treasonous collusion with the Vatican about the divorce and remarriage plans of King Henry (III.ii.30–9). So we find in *H8* suspicion of foreigners that begins in the first scene, where the opulence of the Field of the Cloth of Gold is spoken of as an expensive and merely temporary disguise of the hostility between France and England. In I.iii choric characters – who abound in *H8* and are used for just the purposes they are used for in *More* – discuss approvingly the measures taken by the English Court to stamp out imported French manners and fashion, from tennis to tall stockings. The pretensions of the French in *H8* are analogous to the presumption of the 'Lombards' (a euphemism for *Frenchmen*) in *More*, for example in the high-handedness of the expropriation of the pair of doves.[55] There is nothing a foreigner does in *H8* to compare to the debauching of citizens' wives by arrogant Lombards in *More*, but the strongly anti-French sentiments of the choric characters in *H8* I.iii will remind us of the patriotic chauvinism of the Ill May Day rioters. Sir Thomas Lovell reports that Englishmen

> must either
> (For so run the conditions) leave those remnants
> Of fool and feather that they got in France,
> . . . . .
> And understand again like honest men,
> Or pack to their old playfellows. . . .

And the old curmudgeon, Lord Sands, is relieved that now

> An honest country lord, as I am, beaten
> A long time out of play, may bring his plain-song
> And have an hour of hearing. . . .   (I.iii.23–46)

Later in the play even the foreign Queen Katherine insists that the Pope's emissaries address her in plain English, not Latin (III.i.42–50).[56] Perhaps her speech is intended as a side-glance at the abandonment in later years of the Vulgate in English Common Prayer. Having made his Protestant/English point, Shakespeare abandons the xenophobia of the first part of the play with the fall of Wolsey, just as the authors of *More* abandon it with the end of the Ill May Day episodes.

A second theme of *H8* that is foreshadowed in *More* is the difference between ceremony and substantive merit. The motif is articulated in *More* where Randall's disguise as More fails to deceive Erasmus, who easily detects the absence of true merit beneath a veneer of ceremony (*750–1 and Addition IV, 19–20). More moralizes the episode:

> thus you see
> my loving learned frends how far respecte
> waites often on the Cerimonious traine
> of bace Illiterat welth whilst men of schooles
> shrowded in povertie are cownted fooles   (Add. IV, 140–4)

The ceremony/merit contrast can be seen as a dominant motif in *H8*. Making a thematic virtue of theatrical convention, Shakespeare fills the play with pageantry (a masque, a coronation, a celestial vision, four trials, and a christening) and then suggests that the wise king is the one who reveres true worth, undeceived by 'thrice-gorgeous ceremony' which is, finally, an 'idol' (*H5* IV.i.266, 240).[57] Not until King Henry can see the idolatry beneath Wolsey's contrived ceremonies[58] and look away from them towards moral substance and true religion of the kind he finds in unpretentious Cranmer late in the play will he truly 'know himself' (*H8* II.ii.22).[59] We might interpret *H8* as Henry's progress from ostentation (the Field of the Cloth of Gold) to true kingship (the rescue of the meritorious Cranmer) and observe that Queen Katherine rejects the panoply of her rigged trial, setting us a standard of royal dignity that Henry will attain only later.[60]

Two corollaries to this theme of ideal sovereignty in *H8* are to be found also in *More, contemptus curiae* and the discrimination and rewarding of good servants. Moral rejection of the Court by those who are out of power is a common motif, especially in pastoral literature; one thinks of *AYL* II.i.1–20 *et passim*. Shakespeare had made use of it in a historical context in the 'molehill' speech of Henry VI (*3H6* II.v.21–54), and he did not need *More* to show him how to have Wolsey contemn the arena of ambition in which he has just failed (III.ii.365–85 and so forth). But *More* does voice sentiments when Henry has deprived him of office that are analogous to Wolsey's sentiments when Henry has found him out:

> O happy banishment from worldly pride
> when soules by priuate life are sanctifide   (*More*, Add. I, 30–1)

Vain pomp and glory of this world, I hate ye!
I feel my heart new open'd   (Wolsey, III.ii.365-6)

The concepts are elaborated *in extenso* in both plays: More and Roper moralize about the evils of worldly power so frankly in the Original Text that one of More's long speeches reads like sedition and was marked for deletion; the milder sentiments of Add. 1 were substituted. In *H8* Wolsey's *contemptus curiae* in soliloquy and monologue to Cromwell extends for more than 100 lines (340-459), ending with a Morean sentiment in shocking contrast to all we have heard from the tough-minded Wolsey when he was in power: 'Farewell / The hopes of court! my hopes in heaven do dwell'.[61]

The discrimination of good servants from bad is inherent in the design of *H8*, unifying the play, as Harold Brooks has pointed out.[62] Certainly there are servants, good and bad, everywhere one turns in *H8*, from the perfidious retainers of Buckingham who betray him to his death to the faithful Griffith and Patience, Queen Katherine's Gentleman Usher and Waiting Woman, whom we see with her in her last hours. We recall that Anne Bullen is Katherine's Maid of Honour, a servant who will end by assuming her mistress' role. Such elements in the play offer support for the all-important distinction between the two Archbishops, Wolsey who would be his master's master and Cranmer the loyal servant of his King. It is therefore most ironic that Cranmer should be degraded to the status of 'a lousy footboy' (v.ii.174) by the malice of the Privy Council, who make him wait ''Mong boys, grooms, and lackeys' (v.ii.18) outside their Chamber door; Shakespeare is so intent on this penetrating irony that he employs the image of basest servitude for Cranmer in two other places in the scene (24-5, 32). Henry first began to take on stature at the end of Act II when he said aside:

My learn'd and well-beloved servant, Cranmer,
Prithee return; with thy approach, I know,
My comfort comes along.   (II.iv.239-41)

And here in Act v he validates his good judgement by rescuing Cranmer from the enmity of his peers.

What is a major element in *H8* in this case is a minor one in *More*, but it is noteworthy that More is merciless to the false servant who appropriates to his own use a part of the gold intended for the players (Add. vi); here we may think of Wolsey's peculation (III.ii.107-10, for example).[63] More's response is as vigorous as Henry's in the later play; he orders someone to pull the cheating servant's livery over his ears. His treatment of 'a well affected Seruaunte' (†1701) is just as demonstrative: in Addition 1 he indicates that his 'cheefest care' is for those faithful servants who will lose by having followed his sinking star; the passage is prominent (48-71). At a later point in the Original Text, the choric prologue to More's execution is a heartfelt if inarticulate lament by his household servants (†1676-1727). Gough, his secretary, announces that by way of legacy

On euery man,
he franckly hath bestowne twentie Nobles
the best and wurst together, all alike,

and Catesby the steward, disburses the bequest, telling the servants to 'Take it, as it is meante, a kinde remembraunce, / of a farre kinder Lord' (†1716–21). We may think here of Queen Katherine's last request of Henry as she dies:

. . . my men (they are the poorest,
But poverty could never draw 'em from me),
That they may have their wages duly paid 'em.
And something over to remember me by.   (IV.ii.148–51)

The passage has a source in Holinshed, but Shakespeare seems to have been as struck by the moral significance of this parting concern for the welfare of former servants as the *More* authors were; he anticipates it in the fallen Wolsey's concern for Cromwell, who has loyally followed his fortunes and now must seek another way to rise (III.ii.412–21), and as the scene ends Wolsey sees himself as a misguided servant who has just been denied the protection that the perfect master gives to his good servants:

O Cromwell, Cromwell,
Had I but serv'd my God with half the zeal
I serv'd my king, He would not in mine age
Have left me naked to mine enemies.   (454–7)[64]

Much of what has been said of theme here embraces character as well, since the major themes of both plays are matters of personal and public morality. But there is one thing more to be said of character in *More* and *H8*. Thomas More is portrayed in the earlier play as a witty eccentric who is quick to take part in a morality play impromptu, to spring a morally edifying practical joke on a self-righteous accuser, and to jail a man whimsically for being whimsically hirsute. More is the sort of man to announce his resignation of his office to his family in circumlocution. There are moments in the play when we are tempted to say with Lady Alice More, 'Lord that your Honor nere will leaue these Iests, / In faith, it ill becomes yee' (†1350–1); but under the appearance of a fey imagination there is a deep seriousness in the ironies More contrives.

Henry VIII is not so cheerfully and unpretentiously frolicsome as More, but the moral irony in the traps he constructs for Wolsey in III.ii and for the Privy Council in v.ii have the More touch about them nevertheless. King Henry, holding in his hand the inventory of Wolsey's expropriation of public funds, suggests that the Cardinal's absent-mindedness at the moment is a result of meditation on 'heavenly stuff . . . the inventory / Of . . . best graces' (III.ii.137–8); the puns are worthy of More. Then Henry, with almost painful irony, lures Wolsey into professing 'That for your Highness' good I ever labor'd / More than mine own' (190–1). After 65 lines of such moral irony the King hands Wolsey the evidence of his worldly malfeasance; the moment is devastating. More's *tu quoque* exposure of Suresby's pompous finger-pointing in the scene where he gets Lifter to 'lift' Suresby's purse has less serious consequences than either Wolsey's fall or the exposure of the Privy Council's attempts to destroy Cranmer. But it might be said that the same sort of mentality produced the three traps. A fourth instance of this mentality can be found in the trap Henry V baits for the traitors Cambridge, Scroop, and Grey in II.ii of *H5*; he lures them into urging rigour for a relatively innocuous man who has railed in his cups against the King and then uses their moral urgings to condemn them to the rigour of the block for their analogous but more grievous attempt on the King's life. This wit, like Henry VIII's, has a dark side More's wit entirely escapes, but in other respects the More of the old manuscript play may be taken as a more genial adumbration of two Shakespeare kings: the moral is the same in all four traps – 'Judge not, lest ye be judged'.[65]

In some measure, the limited and localized analogies of situation between the two plays are as interesting as the analogies of theme and character. There are four notable instances. *More* begins with the outrageous high-handedness of foreigners that has been mentioned before. Caveler justifies his seizure to his own use of the doves just purchased by Williamson on the ground that common carpenters should yield the delicacies of life to the bourgeoisie. In the same scene another arrogant Lombard tries to carry off Williamson's wife, Doll, by force. The incidents are intended to epitomize other arrogancies and to explain what follows. Something similar happens in II.ii of *H8*, where the Lord Chamberlain receives a letter from his man in the North explaining that the horses he had gathered at the Lord Chamberlain's request had been forcibly taken from him by 'a man of my Lord Cardinal's' on the ground that 'his master would be serv'd before a subject, if not before the King'. As in *More* the unjust abuse of rank is intended to epitomize moral character; the Chamberlain comments ominously and profoundly on the Cardinal's arrogance: 'He will have all, I think' (II.ii.1–11).[66]

Buckingham's speeches on his way to execution in II.i may remind us of John Lincoln's last words on the scaffold – though the conventions of gallows rhetoric might account for the analogy.

> The law I bear no malice for my death;
> 'T has done, upon the premises, but justice;
> But those that sought it I could wish more Christians.
> Be what they will, I heartily forgive 'em;   (Buckingham, II.i.62–5)

> I paciently submit me to the lawe.
> But God forgiue them that were cause of it.
> and as a Christian, truely from my hart:
> I likewise craue they would forgiue me too.   (Lincoln, *627–30)

One close situational parallel between *More* and *H8* is quite peculiar. There is no hint in Holinshed for the part of *H8* I.ii where Queen Katherine intercedes for the commoners who are rebelling against the oppressive tax that Wolsey has imposed in the King's name.[67] If Shakespeare found inspiration in *More* for this rich means of characterizing the Queen, he would have had to find it not in the play itself, but in one of the sources of the play, 'The Story of Ill May-Day . . . and how Queen Catherine begged the lives of Two Thousand London Apprentices' printed in [Richard Johnson's] *A Crowne Garland of Goulden Roses* (1612).[68] This old ballad provided several details for the Ill May Day scenes, but Queen Catherine's successful intercession is transferred in the play to Thomas More. Shakespeare, it may be, knew not only *More* but its sources as well.

The last of the situational parallels between the plays is the crowd scenes which introduce the public events with which the two plays end. The press in the street and on the bridge outside the Tower of London where More is to be incarcerated, and eventually executed, are commoners there to 'burie him in teares', 'the best freend that the poore ere had' (†1615, 1648). The mob of commoners in *H8* v.iii are in a different mood, jovial, exultant, energetic to the point of belligerence as they struggle for a view of the newly christened Princess. The difference in mood is less than the similarity in technique. The crowd is used in each play to convey a unified national mood: 'I neuer heard a man since I was borne, / so generally bewailde of euery one' (†1616–17); 'We may as well push against Powle's as stir 'em' (v.iii.16). And the principals appear only after that mood has been established for us. We see the crowds from the point of view of a Porter/Warder and his assistant(s), who marvel and complain at the size of their problem in keeping order and making room for the passage of the famous principals.[69] When these principals enter in procession in each play there is a sudden tonal contrast to what has preceded. More quibbles jovially with the Porter about which garment he must surrender as he enters the Tower[70] while the crowd grieves for his fate. The genial and jocular obscenity with which the crowd at the christening has been characterized for us ('a fry of fornication', 'he or she, cuckold or cuckold-maker')[71] yields to joyful solemnity at the christening itself.

There are other mobs in both plays: the Ill May Day scenes in *More* and the coronation in *H8* iv.i respectively support the two crowd scenes discussed above. More rises to prominence because of his success with an unruly mob; his exit from public life is made through a lamenting mob that a good director would dot with the Williamson couple, George Betts, Sherwin the goldsmith, and other commoners we saw at the outset.[72] The support the christening scene gets from the narrated coronation scene is more direct: the general rejoicing when Anne is ceremonially legitimized as Henry's Queen is a fit – perhaps a necessary – prologue to the general rejoicing when her daughter Elizabeth takes her place in England's royal lineage. The vivid and earthy description of the crowd in Westminster Abbey in iv.i is a close analogue to the description of the crowd in the Court precincts in v.iii. It may be more than mere coincidence that May Day crowds are alluded to in v.iii.15 of *H8* and that women struggling for position in the crowd are central both to the description of the coronation and to the portrayal of More's entry into the Tower of London.[73]

We should not make more of the analogies between *More* and *H8* than conservative interpretation allows. Some instances here might be attributed to commonplace or coincidence. In some others the relationship between *H8* and *More* is clouded by Shakespeare's earlier exploitation of analogues in other dramatists. But on balance and cumulatively there would seem to be ample evidence to urge our looking at *More* and *H8* together. If we adopt such a comparative stance, differences will become as significant as similarities. One difference has important aesthetic implications.

Henry VIII is systematically designed on a principle of tonal alternation that is different from the nearly single rise and fall of the action in *More*. Acts IV and V of the later play take us from joyful narration of the coronation of Anne Bullen to sombre narration of Wolsey's death and the deep solemnity of the last moments of Katherine, Henry's other Queen; and from there we go forward by way of the happy issue of a most difficult childbed to the attempt to betray Thomas Cranmer and finally to the joy and optimism of the christening of the Princess Elizabeth. This alternation between the tragic or ominous and the comedic is deeply embedded in the play. Even the coronation of Anne, with which this two-act sequence begins, looks back to the fall of Buckingham in Act I and Act II:

> *1. Gent.* Y' are well met once again.
> *2. Gent.*   So are you.
> *1. Gent.* You come to take your stand here, and behold
> The Lady Anne pass from her coronation?
> *2. Gent.* 'Tis all my business. At our last encounter,
> The Duke of Buckingham came from his trial.
> *1. Gent.* 'Tis very true; but that time offer'd sorrow,
> This, general joy.   (IV.i.1–7)

There is nothing in *More* to rival this masterful coherence-through-contrast. If *H8* was a collaboration, it was an even closer collaboration than the close collaboration that produced the unity of *More*.

NOTES

1 'The Expression of Ideas – Particularly Political Ideas – In the Three Pages, and in Shakespeare', *Shakespeare's Hand*, pp. 142–87.

2 An intelligent beginning in this direction was made in 1973 by Karl P. Wentersdorf; see 'Linkages of Thought and Imagery in Shakespeare and *More*', *MLQ*, 34 (1973), 384–405. Wentersdorf extended greatly the number of analogues in the Shakespeare canon to a configuration of elements in 'the three pages' in *More*. This configuration will be discussed here from a somewhat different point of view and with different canonical evidence than Wentersdorf's; the interested reader of Part I of this chapter should also consult Wentersdorf.

3 Pollard emphasized the conservatism and the defensive posture of the contributors, aware that anti-Stratfordians would certainly challenge the arguments of the research team (see *Shakespeare's Hand*, p. [v]).

4 *Shakespeare's Hand*, p. 144.

5 R.W. Chambers, 'Some Sequences of Thought in Shakespeare and in the 147 Lines of "Sir Thomas More"', *MLR*, 26 (1931), 251–80. Chambers brought up his leading points once again in *Man's Unconquerable Mind* (London, 1939), pp. 204–49. He lectured on the play from this perspective in 1937 and discussed other aspects of the play in his biography of Thomas More (1935) and in *TLS*, 3 June 1939, p. 327.

6 An exception, Carol A. Chillington's argument that Add. IIc is the work of John Webster, is countered (convincingly, I feel) by Charles Forker elsewhere in this volume. The pendulum of scholarly taste has swung so far retrograde to disintegration that it has recently been seriously proposed that Shakespeare's characteristic stylistic traits are discernible in the whole of *More*; see Thomas Merriam, 'The Authorship of *Sir Thomas More*', *ALLC Bulletin*, 10 (1982), 1–7. This view appears as vulnerable as Chillington's. Without prejudice, I set aside for the purposes of this chapter Add. III (in Hand C), the soliloquy of More that has sometimes been attributed to Shakespeare.

7 See Melchiori above, pp. 84, 94, and p. 110, *cf.* Taylor, p. 120.

8 Caroline F.E. Spurgeon, 'Imagery in the *Sir Thomas More* Fragment', *RES*, 6 (1930), 257–70. To an extent not generally recognized, Chambers' *MLR* essay anticipates the critical perspective of Edward A. Armstrong's *The Shakespearian Imagination* (London, 1946) – association of ideas in Shakespeare. To a lesser extent Chambers is also a precursor of Wolfgang C lemen in *Shakespeare's Bilder* (Bonn, 1936; trans. 1951) – dramatic function of imagery.

9 Quotation from the Shakespeare canon is from the Riverside edition by G.B. Evans, *et al.* (Boston, 1974).

10 The orations are both mentioned in 'The Life of Marcus Brutus', but they are not juxtaposed, as in Shakespeare, nor is Brutus said to have won the crowd: 'When Brutus began to speake, they gave him quiet audience: howbeit immediately after, they shewed that they were not all contented with the murther' (Geoffrey Bullough, ed., *Narrative and Dramatic Sources of Shakespeare*, V (London, 1964), p. 103; Bullough points out the contrast with *JC* III.ii.48–54). *Cf.* 'The Life of Julius Caesar', *ibid.*, p. 87: 'The next morning, Brutus and his confederates came into the market place to speake unto the people, who gave them such audience, that it seemed they neither greatly reproved, nor allowed the fact: for by their great silence they showed, that they were sory for Caesar's death, and also that they did reverence Brutus.' Antonius' oration is not mentioned in this Life; conversely, in 'The Life of Marcus Antonius', Brutus' oration is not mentioned.

11 Cade, of course, is given a commoner's prose and Clifford an aristocrat's verse. In *JC* Brutus' prose results from Shakespeare's mistaken inference from Plutarch's 'Life of Brutus' that Brutus' oratorical style was like his Laconic epistolary style; Antony's verse, vivid by contrast, is intended to represent the Asiatic oratorical style that Plutarch attributes to Antonius (See *SStud*, 15 (1982), pp. 55–6 and notes).

12 Surrey's colleague, Shrewsbury, adds his voice, 'my maisters Countrymen' (151), and later More echoes it, 'good masters' (180). Chambers (1923, p. 164; 1931, p. 262) prints the whole effort to gain the attention of the crowd in Surrey's and Shrewsbury's cases side-by-side with the attempt in Brutus's and in Antony's, but without analysis. The similarities in crowd responses are as remarkable as those in forms of address.

13 II.ii.136–41. We may compare Escalus' use of the same *comparatio* in his plea to Angelo for Claudio's life in the immediately preceding scene (II.i.8–16). Sister Miriam Joseph, C.S.C. emphasizes that Isabella's speech is a climax, the last of eight arguments she has used on Angelo. See *Shakespeare's Use of the Arts of Language* (New York, 1947), pp. 232–3.

14 Shakespeare would probably have studied *comparatio* in grammar school under the heading *similitudo* in Johannes Susenbrotus' *Epitome Troporum ac Schematum et Grammaticorum et Rhetoricorum* (Zurich, 1541). For the rhetorical curriculum, see T.W. Baldwin, *William Shakspere's Small Latine & Lesse Greeke* (Urbana, 1944), II, Chs. 31–7, Susenbrotus Ch. 35.

15 L.L. Schücking regarded this unanimous response in Golden Rule terms as the product of 'a more sentimental mind than Shakespeare's'. See 'Shakespeare and *Sir Thomas More*', *RES*, 1 (1925), 40–59 (at 47). The sentimental mind was Heywood's, he believed.

16 The first three of these analogues were brought forward in the 1923 essay, the fourth in the 1931 redaction.

17 Schücking was first to observe the parallels to *JC* III.ii in Add. IIc; he pointed out one or two echoes that Chambers did not assimilate. (Schücking believed that *More* as a whole derived from

JC, Ham., and other plays; he dated it originally 1604–5, later moved the date back to just after *Ham.*) See 'Das Datum des Pseudo-Shakespeareschen *Sir Thomas Moore*', *Englische Studien*, 46 (1913), 228–51 (pp. 233–5 for *JC* parallels). Cf. his 1925 essay in note 15 above.

18 *Mutiny* and its cognates appear 44 times in the canon (including *mutynes* at Addition IIc, 238, and *mutiny* four times in Antony's oration). Wentersdorf (p. 397) also notes this analogy between *JC* and *More*.

19 There are also tide metaphors in *JC* which are less evidently relevant to *More*. Discussion of waves, tides, and flood in *JC* from a quite different perspective can be found in 'Undular Structure in *Julius Caesar*', *MLR*, 66 (1971), 21–30. A third perspective is Frederick Kiefer's in *Fortune and Elizabethan Tragedy* (San Marino, 1983), pp. 244–52.

20 *Shakespeare's Imagery and What It Tells Us* (Cambridge, 1935; rpt. Boston, 1958), pp. 91–9.

21 The Shakespeare canon is, as it were, replete with storms, especially storms at sea, as G. Wilson Knight first noticed. See *The Shakespearian Tempest* (Oxford, 1932; rpt. London, 1953), *passim*.

22 Spurgeon observes Shakespeare's interest in the appearance of receding waters (cf. *Jn.* v.iv.53–6); *ibid.*, p. 93.

23 That Shakespeare intended a symbolic political equivalence between the personal fates of the Andronici and the fate of Rome itself is suggested by Lavinia's name (in Virgil Lavinia is *mater patriae* – if she is violated in *Titus*, Rome is, likewise) and by the image of the multilated body politic that Marcus Andronicus uses at v.iii.70–2.

24 Robert S. Miola, '*Titus Andronicus* and the Mythos of Shakespeare's Rome', *SStud*, 14 (1981), 85–98 (at 94).

25 The cannibalism of v.iii has usually been traced to Seneca's *Thyestes* or (more plausibly) to the Tereus/Philomela/Procne story in *Meta.* VI; it seems likely that Shakespeare conflated the Lycaon and Philomela stories. Andronicus is 'surnamed Pius / For many good and great deserts to Rome' (1.i.23–4), but impiousness dominates the action, beginning with the 'cruel irreligious piety' (1.i.130) of the sacrifice of Alarbus and continuing through the play. See also Miola.

26 Quotations and translations of the *Metamorphoses* are from the Loeb Edition, by Frank Justus Miller (Cambridge, Mass., 1916); 3rd edn. revised by G.P. Goold (Cambridge, Mass., 1977).

27 I, 214–39. *Lycaon* derives from the Greek *LUKOS, wolf.*

28 Harold Brooks gives parallels from Golding's Ovid in the commentary of the Arden Edition of *MND* (1979).

29 Shakespeare paraphrases the line at *2H6* v.i.157, *3H6* v.vi.51, *R3* 1.i.16, *Jn.* v.vii.26, and *Son.* 114.5.

30 Karl P. Wentersdorf has added another element to the pattern: savage cruelty ('such barbarous temper' and 'your momtanish [=Mahometanish] inhumanyty', II.c, 254, 263) [Blayney reads 'mountanish', *Ed.*]; cf. *Lr.* IV.ii.41–50 and passages in 8 other Shakespearian plays. 'Linkages of Thought' pp. 400–5. Ovid's version of barbarism in Book I is bestiality of Lycaon's sort.

31 Lines 205–10. Shakespeare insisted on cannibalism in *King Lear*; 'the pelican daughters' allusion (III.iv.75) implies feasting on family as in 1.i.117–18. Gloucester's fear that Goneril might 'In his anointed flesh [rash] boarish fangs' (III.vii.57–8) implies it also. Albany's fear that 'It will come, / Humanity must perforce prey on itself, / Like monsters of the deep' (IV.ii.48–50) is the only cannibalism passage Chambers cites from *Lear*. The best study of cannibalism in Shakespeare is Francois Laroque's essay in *Cahiers Elisabéthains*, No. 19 (Avril 1981), 27–37; but it does not deal with the Ovidian roots of the motif one finds in *More, Titus, Lear* and other Shakespearian *loca*.

32 Ovid is not cited in commentary on this line in the editions I have consulted. William R. Elton's study of the intellectual backgrounds of the play as a whole in *King Lear and the Gods* (San Marino, 1966) does not treat the materials of *Meta.* I.

33 Charles R. Forker and Joseph Candido allude to More's reply to his wife as 'a Theseus-like enjoinder' in 'Wit, Wisdom, and Theatricality in *The Book of Sir Thomas More*', *SStud*, 13 (1980), 85–104 (at 87).

34 *Riverside Shakespeare* Introduction to *LLL*, pp. 174–8 (at 174–5).

35 'Das Datum', pp. 236–9. Schücking adduces several other parallels (not all as compelling as this one); among the better ones are the greeting of the players in both plays and the hero's role as intepreter of the play-within in both cases. Schücking's analysis leads him to the conclusion that *More* echoes *Ham.* in these instances.

36 See elsewhere in this volume (pp. 60, 71). Jean-Marie Maguin has kindly pointed out to me that another apparent analogue to *More* in a Shakespearian play from the period 1595–1601 is a proverb to be found in Tilley's *Dictionary*. Doll Williamson's fearless observation on the scaffold, 'I doo owe God a death, and I must pay him' (*670), might otherwise be thought an inverse analogue of Falstaff's cowardice in the moments before Shrewsbury: '*Prince.* Why, thou owest God a death. [*Exit*]./*Fal.* 'Tis not due yet, I would be loath to pay him before his day.' (*1H4* v.i.126–8).

37 'Das Datum', pp. 242–3.

38 A garbled version of More's Latin appears in the margin of Add. IV; in his edition of *More* (1844), Alexander Dyce cited Cresacre More's *Life and Death of Sir Thomas Moore* (1630), the earliest printed version, which is much too late to have been a source for *More*, but the story may have been well known in tradition.

39 There are, of course, other sources in classical and Elizabethan literature for the details of Clarence's dream. See the two major studies of the eclectic backgrounds: Wolfgang Clemen, *Clarences Traum und Ermordung*. Sitzungsberichte der Bayerischen Akademie der Wissenschaften: Philosophisch-historische Klasse 1955, v, 3–46; Harold F. Brooks, '"Richard III": Antecedents of Clarence's Dream', *ShS*, 32 (1979), 145–50. Neither points to *More*.

40 *William Shakespeare: A Study of Facts and Problems* (Oxford, 1930), I, 270.

41 In 1960 Flatter staged a composite of all of *More* and the one-third of *H8* he regarded as Shakespeare's work (Karlsruhe, West Germany). The reviewers thought the result amorphous; see *Shakespeare-Jahrbuch*, 97 (1961), 215; *ShS*, 15 (1961), 134.

42 *H8* is being regarded here as R.A. Foakes regards it in the Arden Edition, as entirely Shakespeare's work. The evidence to be offered here would tend to support the theory of single authorship, as putative debts to *More* appear in all parts of the play.

43 I wish to thank Professor Scott McMillin for the suggestion that led to my investigation of the four plays.

44 E.K. Chambers, *The Elizabethan Stage* (Oxford, 1923), III, 266. A play about Wolsey was on the public stage in London in July 1602, as a contemporary allusion printed by Chambers indicates.

45 *Narrative and Dramatic Sources of Shakespeare* IV (London; New York 1962), 442.

46 'Fashioning Henry VIII: What Shakespeare Saw in *When You See Me, You Know Me*', *Cahiers Elisabéthains*, No. 23 (Avril 1983), 47–59.

47 These two parallels, and the Randall/Hodge parallel, are pointed out by John Munro in *The London Shakespeare* (London, 1957/8), IV, 1260.

48 Sig. F1^v, lines [2–5]. Quotation is from the facsimile of the British Library copy by John S. Farmer in the Tudor Facsimile Texts (1911, rpt. New York, 1970). If, as seems likely, Shakespeare borrowed the conception of the conspiracy against Buckingham from *Cromwell*, he was doing no more than collecting an old debt, for *Cromwell* imitates *Julius Caesar* III.i in the scene where Bedford attempts to warn Cromwell by means of a letter that there is a conspiracy against him. Cromwell, like Caesar in the presence of Artemidorus, puts off reading the warning and goes forward to his death. The author of *Cromwell* also alludes to the death of Hector as staged in Act v of *Troilus and Cressida* (see sig. C3^v, lines [20–5]); the allusion is discussed in *NQ*, n.s. 33 (1986), 358–60.

49 'The Integrity of Shakespeare: Illustrated from *Cymbeline*', *ShS*, 8 (1955), 52–6.

50 Frank Kermode, 'What is Shakespeare's *Henry VIII* About?' *Durham University Journal*, n.s. 9 (1948), 48–55.

51 Herschel Baker points out in the *Riverside Shakespeare* (p. 976) that Edmond Malone found sufficient Tudor flavour in *H8* to posit that it was first written in the 1590s; he notes that E.K. Chambers tentatively identified this hypothetical early draft as the lost *Buckingham* recorded in Henslowe's *Diary*, 1593.

52 See 'Episodic Structure in Four Tudor Plays: A Virtue of Necessity', *Comparative Drama*, 6 (1972), 87–102 (99 esp.).

53 This is not to say, however, that it is therefore necessarily naif. Two articles that point out respectively the thematic and the dramaturgical excellences of the play are Charles R. Forker and Joseph Candido (note 33 above), and Scott McMillin, '*The Book of Sir Thomas More*: A Theatrical View', *MP*, 68 (1970), 10–24.

54 R.A. Foakes points out in the Arden Edition (pp. xxviii–xxx) that a Protestant stance would be *de rigueur* for a play put on to honour the staunchly Protestant Elector Frederick.

55 The pretentious are implicit in the argument of Caveler, the expropriator: 'Beefe and brewes may serue . . . a coorse Carpenter' like Williamson (22), but doves are a delicacy reserved for a foreigner's refined palate. *Doves* may be explicated from *The Merchant of Venice* II.ii, where Old Gobbo thinks a dish of doves a fittingly ostentatious gift for his son's master (100–9, 135–6).

56 There is an odd precedent for saintly Katherine in Webster's corrupt Vittoria, who rejects the prosecuting attorney's Latin at her arraignment for adultery, *The White Devil* III.ii.13–20; *WD* was staged and published in 1612.

57 As these phrases from *H5* suggest, Shakespeare had himself made important use of the contrast between ceremony and substantive kingship; one finds the theme prominent in *R2* and *H5*.

58 Wolsey is associated throughout the first half of the play with pomp and false appearance; he has arranged the Field of the Cloth of Gold, and he hosts the masque at which Henry meets Anne Bullen; he orchestrates the trials of Buckingham and Katherine.

59 Edward I. Berry's defence of pageantry in the play comes to conclusions different from my own; see '*Henry VIII* and the Dynamics of Spectacle', *ShS*, 12 (1979), 229–46.

60 We may compare the contrast between a noble Queen and her as yet inadequate King-husband in the rigged trial of Hermione in III.ii of *WT*, written two or three years earlier.

61 The complete reversal of Wolsey's character has a precedent in Buckingham's sudden alteration from spleen to charity earlier in the play. More, by contrast, has been modest and unpretentious throughout and is not morally changed by his fall from power.

62 See Foakes's Arden Edition, note p. xlviii.

63 An analogue to the *More* passage is to be found in I.i of Chapman's *Bussy D'Ambois*, where Maffé, Monsieur's steward, attempts to defraud Bussy by giving him only 100 of the 1000 crowns Monsieur has told him to disburse. Maffé is caught in the act by the shrewd Bussy as the servingman is caught by the shrewd players in *More*. The episode in *Bussy* is not founded on historical circumstance.

64 There is a hint for Wolsey's anagnorisis in Holinshed (see *Riverside* commentary). The moral roots of Wolsey's speech, and of the servant motif in both plays, are traceable to Luke 16:13 and Matthew 6:24 – 'No servant can serve two masters; for either he will hate the one, and love the other; or else he will hold to the one, and despise the other. Ye cannot serve God and mammon'.

65 We might add Duke Vincentio of *Measure for Measure* to the group of ironists. Certainly the Scriptural motto applies to Angelo, and the Duke/Friar contrives a trap for Angelo that places him precisely in Claudio's legal position.

66 Shakespeare was interested in such abuses, which no doubt were common enough in Tudor and Stuart life. Falstaff thinks that on Hal's accession he has the right to 'take any man's horses' (*2H4* v.iii.135–7), and Hotspur resents bitterly the high-handedness of the perfumed popinjay from Court who has demanded his prisoners in the King's name (*1H4* I.iii.29–69).

67 See *Riverside* commentary.

68 The ballad is reprinted in Alexander Dyce's edition of the play, (1840), pp. xix–xxiii.

69 There is another analogue, in the Beaumont and Fletcher *Maid's Tragedy* (1610–11), to some details of the Porter's attempt to control the crowd in *H8* v.iii. Diagoras' situation in I.ii and his response (breaking heads in the crowd) are obviously imitated in *H8*. The larger values of the scene are closer to *More* than to *MT*.

70 The custom of conferring an upper garment on the Porter when entering the Tower is alluded to (also jokingly, but this time bawdily) by Flamineo in Webster's *The White Devil* (v.iv.40–5), though he transfers the custom to the Castle St Angelo in Rome. At least from Richard II's time the Porter of the Tower of London was entitled to 'have of ev'y p'son co'maunded by the king to the said Tower, his uppermost garment, or ells agree wth him for yt'. *Anno regni Regis Ricardi 2d^l quarto* Lansdown MSS. No. 155 fol. 54, as rpt. in John Bayley, *The History and Antiquities of the Tower of London*, 2 vols. (London, 1821–5), Part II, 'Appendix', II, xcviii.

71 v.iii.35–6, 25. The bawdy in v.iii sorts well with frankness about sexuality elsewhere in the play. *Cf.* the flagrant sexual quips of the Old Lady in her conversation with Anne Bullen (II.iii) and a large number of carnal allusions, witty or serious, in the comments of other choric characters (*e.g.*, in I.iii, IV.i.). There are analogous bawdy allusions from choric characters in *More* 331–62, though bawdy is not prominent in *More* as it is in *H8*.

72 Scott McMillin, 'A Theatrical View' (see note 53 above) has suggested that the same scaffold used for the platform from which More quells the riot early in the play should serve for his execution at the end.

73 In the vivid description of the offstage coronation, pregnant women using their bulk as battering rams 'would shake the press / And make 'em reel before 'em' (IV.i.76–9); an old woman, determined to see More before the end, holds her place in the throng outside the Tower of London at the risk of being 'trod to death annon' (†1617–48).

A table of sources and close analogues for the text of *The Book of Sir Thomas More*

COMPILED BY
GIORGIO MELCHIORI AND VITTORIO GABRIELI

The present table is based on Vittorio Gabrieli's paper '*Sir Thomas More*: Sources, Characters, Ideas', *Moreana* XXIII, 90 (1986), 17–43, taking into account also the following papers by G. Melchiori: 'Hand D in "Sir Thomas More": an Essay in Misinterpretation', *Shakespeare Survey*, 38 (1985), 101–14; 'The Contextualization of Source Materials: The Play within the Play in "Sir Thomas More"', *Le forme del teatro*, III (Roma, 1984), 59–84; 'The Book of Sir Thomas More: A Chronology of Revision', *Shakespeare Quarterly*, 37 (1986), 291–308; 'The Master of the Revels and the Date of the Additions to *Sir Thomas More*', in *Shakespeare: Text, Language, Criticism. Essays in Honour of Marvin Spevack*, ed. B. Fabian and K. Tetzeli v. Rosador *The Book of Hildesheim* (1987), 164–79.

It appears that the primary sources are mostly different from those suggested by Marie Schütt, 'Die Quellen des "Book of Sir Thomas More"', *Englische Studien*, 68 (1933), 209–26: Holinshed rather than Hall, Harpsfield and Stapleton rather than Roper and Ro. Ba. All sources were available also to the authors of the Additions before 1593.

Sc.i (1–103) Whole scene based on Holinshed (1587). III.840–3. Details:
- 10–36: Williamson and the doves, de Bard and the citizen's wife = Hol.III.840 (cf. Hall, *Union*, 1550 ed., lix^v–lx).
- 37–54: de Bard's boast – Caveler's name = Hol.III.841 (cf. Hall lx^v).
- 63: 'two brethren (*Betses* by name)' – Sherwin's name = Hol.III.843 (cf. Hall lxii^v). For Sherwin see also A. Munday, *The Englishe Romaine Lyfe* (1582), 57–65.
- 69–91: Dr Standish, Dr Beale and the bill of complaint = Hol.III.840–1 (cf. Hall lx–lx^v). Bill reproduced *verbatim* from Hol.; in Hall additional words and different punctuation.

Spellings: *STM* – Lincolne, Sherwin, Standish, Spittle.
  Hol. – Lincolne, Shirwin, Standish, spittle.
  Hall – Lyncoln, Shyrwyn, Standiche, Spyttell.

Sc.ii (104–312) More, the Justice and the thief. Translates and amplifies an anecdote first found in Stapleton, *Tres Thomæ* (1588), 263–5. The version in Ro. Ba's ms *Life of More* (*c.* 1599) mistranslates the Latin original.

Sc.iii (313–409) Several passages based on Hol.:
- 331–44: Ambassador's interference = Hol.III.840.
- 346–52: de Bard's boast = Hol.III.841.
- 366–71: the carpenter and the Frenchman = Hol.III.840.

395–9: Dr Beale's responsibility = marginal note in Hol.iii.841 (not in Hall); name: sir Roger Cholmeley = Hol.iii.842 (in Hall, lxii: syr *Richard* Cholmeley).

Sci.iv (410–52)   Based on Hol.iii.842 for ll. 418–35 (St Martin's episode), and 841 for ll. 438–40 (Mayor, More, and Privy Council meeting).
   Spellings: *STM* – Sᵗ Martins, Mewtas, Piccarde, green gate, kennelles.
         Hol. – saint Martins, Mewtas, Picard, Greene gate, kennell.
         Hall – saynct Martynes, Mutuas, Pycardy, Grenegate, canel.

Sc.v (453–72)   Cancelled fragment on prentices' attack on alderman.
   Suggested by Hol.iii.841–2 (from Hall lxiᵛ). Alderman's name not in surviving fragment, but in Add. iib in hand C, as 'Iohn Munday' (Hol. = Iohn Mundie; Hall = Ihon Mondy). Apart from Cheapside, the place names in fragment don't figure in Hol. or Hall, but in Dekker's plays. In the rest of *STM* all place names used are in Hol.

Sc.va   Guildhall scene. Lost in the original, but closely echoed in Add. iib, in hand C, ll. 66–120. Based on Hol.iii.841–2 (cf. Hall lxi–lxii). In detail:
   67–75: attack on Munday = Hol.iii.841–2 (cf. Hall lxiᵛ).
   76–92: prison breaking = Hol.iii.842 (Counters); in Hall lxiᵛ 'counteryes'.
   96–101: arrival of Surrey etc = Hol.iii.842 (cf. Hall lxii).

Sc.vi   The original version of the first part of the scene is lost, but can be partially reconstructed from Addition iic in Hand D (see G. Melchiori, *Shakespeare Survey*, 38 (1985) 101–14. Based on Hol. iii.841–2: the Sergeant-at-arms' name, mentioned in *STM* at †1530 and †1560, is Downes in Hol. and *STM*, but 'dounes' in Hall, lxiᵛ.
The extant second part, *473–565, is put together from hints and passages in Hol. and Harpsfield:
   *481–95: rebels sent to prison = Hol.iii.841 (orders to aldermen), and 842 ('some to Newgate, and some to the Counters'); cf. Hall lxi & lxii respectively.
   *516–22: provisions to guard city = Hol.iii.841 (cf. Hall lxi).
   *533–7: More in Privy Council = Hol.iii.841 (cf. Hall lxiᵛ).
   *538–44: More's acceptance = Harps., 27:15 ff. (from Roper).
   *548 ff: More's loyalty to City = Harps., 22:11–21 (not in Roper).
   *555–60: Croft's message = Hol.iii.843 (arraignment) and 844 (king in Westminster).

Sc.vii   (*566–734) Lincoln's execution and general pardon. Based mostly on Hol.iii.843.
   *566–84: Standard in chepe = Hol.iii.843 (cf. Hall lxiiᵛ).
   *588–92z: keeping servants in = Hol.iii.841 (cf. Hall lxiᵛ).
   *619–36: Lincoln's speech = expanded from Hol.iii.843 (cf. Hall lxiiᵛ).
   *690: pardon = Hol.843 (cf. Hall lxiiᵛ).
   *702–32: Surrey's speech = fuses together Hol.iii.843 (respite; asking pardon on knees; cf. Hall lxiiᵛ); 844 (pardon at Westminster; cf. Hall lxiii–lxiiiᵛ); and 844 (on mercy, not in Hall).
   *710 and *733: God save the king = Hol.iii.843 (cf. Hall lxiiᵛ).

Sc.viiia (*735–96)   Cancelled fragment on More's trick played on Erasmus at their first meeting. Originating in anecdote on More's meeting with unnamed scholar, reported by Harps. 239:1–14 (not in Roper); transformed through oral tradition, it is first related in different form in Cresacre More's *Life* (1630).

Sc.viiib (†797–877)   Cancelled second part of long-haired ruffian scene.
   Fuses together two consecutive episodes in the life of Cromwell in Foxe, *Acts and Monuments* (1583 ed.), ii.1188. From its reworking as Addition iv it appears that the lost

original reported place names found in Foxe; Morris's name is found in marginal note
added to 1583 ed. of Foxe, II.1185 (Rafe Morice), but see also Munday, *Englishe
Romaine Lyfe*, 55–66.

Sc.ix (†879–1157)   Entertainment offered to Mayor. Idea of More as actor from Harps.
   10:26–11:12 (cf. Roper 5:1–14).

Interlude based on Merbury, *Marriage of Wit and Wisdom*, but borrows from *Lusty Iuventus*
and *The Disobedient Child*, and Vice's name from *Trial of Treasure*. Missing beard
connected with anecdote on More's execution in Hall ccxxvi^v, Foxe II.1069,
Hol.III.938, as well as Stapleton, 267–8 and 342, and Harps. 204 (not in Roper). See G.
Melchiori, *Forme del teatro*, III.59–94.

Sc.x (†1158–1281)   Privy Council meeting.
   †1186–1232: attitude towards German emperor = Hol.III.821.
   †1238–44: Rochester's refusal = Harps.167:3–13.
   †1245–51: Rochester remanded = Harps.168:8–11.
   †1257–61: More confined at home = Harps.168:2–4.

Sc.xi (†1282–1379)   Scene in Chelsea garden.
   †1290–1308: Lady More's dream = cf. *R3*.I.iv.1–63.
   †1321–5: Chelsea Church = Harps.64:15–65:14 (from Roper).
   †1334ff: More's merriment = Harps.160:19–161:16 (from Roper).
   †1347–9: 'that's gon' = Harps.66:16–23 (from Roper).
   †1350: jests = Harps.96:24–5 (from Roper).

Sc.xii (†1380–1410)   Rochester in the Tower.
   Only possible but unlikely source ms *Rastell Fragments* now in Appendix I to EETS ed. of
   Harps. Rochester's speeches at †1382–7 and †1394–1400 modelled on More's in prison
   in Harps.171–3.

Sc.xiii (†1411–1602)   More's speech to family and arrest.
   †1411–17: near heaven = Harps.96:15–18 (from Roper).
   †1418–21: to daughters = Harps.19:18–21.
   †1437ff: impatience with wife = Harps.94:27–95:7 (from More's *Works*).
   †1471–1516: speech to family = based on references in Harps. to More's care for
   dependants.
   †1517ff: arrest etc. = reminiscent both of Hol. (Downes) and Harps. Spirit of resignation = Harps.172:14–173:11 (from More's *Works*).
   †1572ff: wife's pleading and equivocation = Stapleton, 304–5 (*Octava tentatio per
   uxorem./Tentator ridiculus.*).

Sc.xiv (†1603–74)   More taken to the Tower.
   †1617–48: poor old woman anecdote = reported in all historical and biographical
   sources except Roper. This version closer to Hol.III.793–4 than Harps.203:17–28 or
   Stapleton 341.
   †1647–8: friend of the poor = Harps.56:19 (from Erasmus, not Roper).
   †1649–56: gentleman porter = in all sources; closer to Harps. 170:8–14 than Hol.III.793
   or Stapleton 267.
   †1662ff: More's monologue = Harps. 95:23–97:6.

Sc.xv (†1675–1727)   servants commenting on trial. Suggested by frequent mention in
   Harps. of More's good housekeeping.
   †1707: 'to liue among the Saintes' = Harps.214ff.
   †1713–19: provisions for servants = Harps.146–7.

Sc.xvi (†1728–1860)   More in the Tower.

†1730–47: execution announced=Harps.201:9–202:26; cf. Harps.172:14–173:11 (on conscience, from *Works*, not Roper).

†1748–59: urinal anecdote=Harps.175 for 'stone', rest from oral tradition followed by Harington (1596) and Ro. Ba. (*c.*1599).

†1750: still merry More=Harps.173:4–11.

†1765–93: poorest Chancellor=Harps.109:22–110:15 (not in Roper), and for 'one hundred pounds' Harps.145:19–146:9.

†1778–86: helping poor and lame=Stapleton, 92.

†1796–1860: last reunion with family=Harps.171:22–173:3 and 198:9–199:6.

†1812–28: equivocation on change of mind=Stapleton, 304–7, quoted by Harington (1596) and translated by Ro.Ba. (*c.*1599).

Sc.xvii (†1861–1986)   More's execution.

†1873–90: dialogue with Lieutenant=Harps., conflating 171:20 (wanton), with 173:1–3 (not in Roper), 12–26 (from Roper), 197:23–198:8 and 202:20–6.

†1900–9: talk with Sheriffs=Harps.13:1–14:10 (from Roper)

†1916–19: weak stairs=anecdote in all historians and biographers, twice in Stapleton (267, 341); closer to Hol. iii.938 than Harps.204:1–5.

†1926–7: sweet gallery=Harps.33:16–18 (More talking to Wolsey of the gallery of York house).

†1931: giving to hangman=Harps.203:12–14.

†1932–4: stage player=Harps.38:3–7 (different context).

†1942: hangman asks forgiveness=Hol.iii.938; also Stapleton, not in Harps. or Roper.

†1949–52: short neck=anecdote in all historians and biographers, (in Stapleton 267–8 and 342, Harps.204:12–14, Hol.iii.938); recalled in Sc.ix above.

†1954–5: cutting beard=adapting Hol.iii.938.

†1984: errour=Harps.184:27–9.

Addition I (1–71)   in Hand A: alternative to ll. †1470–516 of original.

No recourse to new sources. 65–8 echo †1723–5 of original.

Addition IIa (1–65)   in Hand B: re-writing of Sc.iv (410–52) with addition of Clown's part.

No new source. Close analogues:

6 and 26=T. Heywood, *The Four Prentices of London* (*c.*1593), 205, 216, 455.

64=*Jack Straw* (before 1593), 758–63.

Addition IIb (66–120)   in Hand C: Guildhall scene:

re-writing of lost scene in original; see notes to Sc.va above.

Addition IIc (123–270)   in Hand D: More's intervention in riot, replacing lost first part of Sc.vi (see notes to it). New analogues:

123–83=Shakespeare, *2H6*, iv.ii.28–63 and iv.vii.5off.

127–38: English diet=Harrison in Hol.i.165–7.

197–9: deportation=More, *Utopia* (trans. Robinson 1551) sig C7v.

Topical allusions:

185–210=reply to rhyme on Dutch cemetery wall, 5 May 1593.

250–64=echoes Henry Finch's speeches in Commons, 21 and 23 March 1593.

Addition III (1–22)   in Hand C: More's monologue.

Possibly suggested by Harps.54:10–15 (from Roper) on More, when Chancellor, paying daily homage to his father.

Addition IV (1–211)   in Hand C: fusing together Erasmus and long-haired ruffian episodes
  (Scs. viiia and viiib, see above).

  No new recourse to sources. Marginal note at 150–1 refers to unused anecdote reported
    through oral tradition, see note to Sc.viiia above.

  157: reference to Erasmus's *Moriæ Encomium* (probably in original).
Topical allusion:

  209–10: Brownists as short-haired.

Addition IV (212–42)   In Hand E: improves original †862–77.
  Topical allusion:

  215: scouring Moorditch.

Addition V (1–26)   in Hand C: Messenger's and More's speeches.
  New unhistorical invention, no source.

Addition VI (1–67)   in Hand B: anecdote of unfaithful servant.
  New unhistorical invention, no source.

ABBREVIATED BIBLIOGRAPHICAL REFERENCES

STM = *The Book of Sir Thomas More*, edited by W.W. Greg. MSR, Oxford, 1911. All
line references and scene and Addition numbering are from this edition.

Foxe = *The Ecclesiasticall Historie, conteining the Acts and Monuments of Martyrs . . .
Newly recognised and enlarged by the Authour Iohn Foxe*. London, 1583.

Hall = *The Vnion of the two noble and illustre famelies . . .* London, 1550.

Hol. = *The . . . Chronicles . . . First Compiled by Raphael Holinshed . . . Now newly
recognised, augmented, and continued . . . to the yeare 1586*. London, 1587.

Stapleton = *Tres Thomæ . . .* [part three] *D. Thomæ Mori Angliæ quondam
Cancellarij Vita. Authore Thomas Stapletono . . .* Dvaci, 1588.

Harps. = *The life and death of Sr Thomas Moore, knight . . . written in the tyme of Queene
Marie by Nicholas Harpsfield, L.D.,* ed. Elsie Vaughan Hitchcock, EETS, Oxford,
1932. (page: line references).

Roper = William Roper, *The Life of Sir Thomas More*, ed. Elsie Vaughan Hitchcock.
EETS, Oxford, 1935. (page: line refs.).

Ro. Ba. = Ro:Ba:, *The Lyfe of Syr Thomas More . . .* ed. Elsie Vaughan Hitchcock and
P.E. Hallett. EETS, Oxford, 1950.

OTHER WORKS MENTIONED

Anthony Munday, *The Englishe Romaine Lyfe*. London, 1582.

Sir John Harington, *A New Discourse of a Stale Subject, called Metamorphosis of A Jax*
[London, 1596], ed. Elizabeth Story Donno. London, 1962.

Cresacre More, *The Life and Death of Sir Thomas Moore* [Paris, 1630]; facsimile.
Menston, 1971.

The Workes of Sir Thomas More, London, 1557; facsimile. Menston, 1978.

Francis Merbury, *The Marriage between Wit and Wisdom* [*c*. 1577], ed. by Trevor N.S.
Lennan. MSR, Oxford, 1971 for 1966.

Lusty Juventus [*c*. 1565], ed. J.M. Nosworthy. MSR, Oxford, 1971.

The Disobedient Child [c. 1564], in *The Dramatic Writings of Richard Wever and Thomas Ingelend*, ed. J.S. Farmer. London, 1905.

The Interlude of the Trial of Treasure, reprinted from the black-letter edition by Thomas Purfoote, 1567. Edited by J.O. Halliwell. London, 1850.

The Life and Death of Jack Straw [pub. 1594], ed. by Kenneth Muir and F.P. Wilson. MSR, Oxford, 1957.

Thomas Heywood, *The Four Prentices of London* [c. 1593, pub. 1615], ed. Mary Ann Weber Gasior. New York, 1980.

Index